SENTENCE DIGS

SENTENCE DIGS

Teaching the Reading and Writing Connection Through Syntax and Semantics

AIMEE BUCKNER HAISTEN

Foreword by Jeff Anderson

Routledge
Taylor & Francis Group
NEW YORK AND LONDON

A Stenhouse Book

Designed cover image: Getty Images

First published 2026
by Routledge
605 Third Avenue, New York, NY 10158

and by Routledge
4 Park Square, Milton Park, Abingdon, Oxon, OX14 4RN

Routledge is an imprint of the Taylor & Francis Group, an informa business

© 2026 Aimee Buckner Haisten

The right of Aimee Buckner Haisten to be identified as author of this work has been asserted in accordance with sections 77 and 78 of the Copyright, Designs and Patents Act 1988.

All rights reserved. The purchase of this copyright material confers the right on the purchasing institution to photocopy pages which bear the copyright line at the bottom of the page. No other parts of this book may be reprinted or reproduced or utilised in any form or by any electronic, mechanical, or other means, now known or hereafter invented, including photocopying and recording, or in any information storage or retrieval system, without permission in writing from the publishers.

Trademark notice: Product or corporate names may be trademarks or registered trademarks, and are used only for identification and explanation without intent to infringe.

ISBN: 9781032841861 (pbk)
ISBN: 9781003529521 (ebk)

DOI: 10.4324/9781003529521

Typeset in Odile Book
by KnowledgeWorks Global Ltd.

For Brenda Power and Kimberly Lipe
Mentors matter ~
you have been mine.

CONTENTS

Foreword by Jeff Anderson xi

Acknowledgements xiii

INTRODUCTION **Sentence Digs: Expanding the Power of Mentor Sentences** 1

SECTION 1 **Digging into Reading Comprehension** 13

    CHAPTER 1 **Reading: Word Meanings** 15

        Sentence Dig R1.1: Multiple Meaning Words 19

        Sentence Dig R1.2: Connotation 23

        Sentence Dig R1.3: Definition Within the Sentence 27

        Sentence Dig R1.4: Context Clues 32

    CHAPTER 2 **Reading: Important Details** 39

        Sentence Dig R2.1: Participle Phrases: Adding Movement and Details 42

        Sentence Dig R2.2: Relative Pronouns: Developing Character 47

        Sentence Dig R2.3: Coordinating Conjunctions: Starting an Introductory Phrase 51

        Sentence Dig R2.4: Complex Sentences: Establishing Cause and Effect Detail 55

    CHAPTER 3 **Reading: Figurative Language** 63

        Sentence Dig R3.1: Literal vs Nonliteral Phrases 66

        Sentence Dig R3.2: Simile 71

        Sentence Dig R3.3: Metaphor 75

        Sentence Dig R3.4: Repetition for Emphasis 78

        Sentence Dig R3.5: Simile 82

SECTION 2 **Digging into the Craft of Writing** 87

    CHAPTER 4 **Writing: Word Choice** 89

        Sentence Dig W4.1: Clauses and Phrases: Writing Small 91

        Sentence Dig W4.2: Verb Choice: Character Reaction 96

Sentence Dig W4.3: Verb Choice: Creating Mental Images 100

Sentence Dig W4.4: The Just-Right Conjunction: Developing Character 105

CHAPTER 5 Writing: Important Details 113

Sentence Dig W5.1: Prepositional Phrases: Developing Character 116

Sentence Dig W5.2: Appositive Phrase: Theme 122

Sentence Dig W5.3: Compound Predicate: Theme 127

Sentence Dig W5.4: Complex Sentence: Main Idea 133

CHAPTER 6 Writing: Crafting Language 141

Sentence Dig W6.1: Simile: Building Tension 144

Sentence Dig W6.2: Alliteration 149

Sentence Dig W6.3: Onomatopoeia: Supporting Details 152

Sentence Dig W6.4: Repeating Subjects and Verbs: Building Tension 156

SECTION 3 Digging into Content Area Learning 161

CHAPTER 7 Content Areas: Vocabulary 163

Sentence Dig CA7.1: Definition Within a Sentence 165

Sentence Dig CA7.2: Definition at the End of a Sentence 170

Sentence Dig CA7.3: Using Synonyms 174

Sentence Dig CA7.4: Definition by Example 178

CHAPTER 8 Content Areas: Important Details 183

Sentence Dig CA8.1: Using a Semicolon: Metaphors 186

Sentence Dig CA8.2: Appositive Phrase: Naming Key Characteristics 192

Sentence Dig CA8.3: Appositive Phrase: Renaming the Subject 197

Sentence Dig CA8.4: Using Numbers: Duration, Distance, Amount, and Ratios 202

Sentence Dig CA8.5: Participle Phrases: Modifying a Noun by Describing Actions 207

CHAPTER 9	**Content Areas: Sentence Structure** 211
	Sentence Dig CA9.1: Cause and Effect 214
	Sentence Dig CA9.2: Compare and Contrast 219
	Sentence Dig CA9.3: Cause and Effect 222
	Sentence Dig CA9.4: Sequential Order 226

Conclusion 231

Appendix A: Showcase Sentences at a Glance 233

Appendix B: Questions to Ask During Planning 239

Appendix C: Blank Sentence Digs Planning Template 241

Appendix D: Annotated Sentence Digs Planning Template 245

Professional Bibliography 249

Children's Literature Bibliography 251

Index 253

FOREWORD

If you've ever had the pleasure of meeting Aimee Buckner Haisten in person, reading her work, or hearing her present, then you already know how much fun she is and how her curiosity and wonder drive everything she does.

And this book is no different.

In *Sentence Digs*, Aimee echoes that same contagious energy, that same inquisitive nature, while establishing a practical, use-tomorrow framework to help teachers take advantage of the power behind the reading and writing connection. With scaffolded conversations, intentional questions, and just-right pacing, Aimee guides you through an easily replicated structure for digging into the syntax and meaning found in the authentic sentences across your favorite trade books - both fiction and nonfiction - while focusing on grammatical structures and meaning-driven pieces of text.

Aimee has a knack for making heavy work seem effortless. This playful, conversational method of studying beautiful, effective sentences - taking them apart, putting them back together, and then applying what we've learned from them - shows a way teachers can mine the all-important reciprocal relationship between reading and writing that, so often, feels elusive in today's classrooms.

You're in good hands here. As Aimee unearths all the background you need to get started, she shares clear directions for making sentence digs your new go-to method for building rich, text-focused conversations that will bolster your reading and writing communities. With thirty-eight demonstration lessons, well-chosen examples, useful background information, clear explanations, and an appendix filled with suggestions and templates for crafting your own sentence digs, you'll be up and running in no time.

In this treasure of a book, Aimee demonstrates how even the busiest teacher can integrate authentic links between reading and writing in ways that support young learners and nudge them to new levels of text understanding, writing craft, and content knowledge.

From a realistic classroom perspective, student-centered commitment, and guiding, gentle voice, Aimee reveals a truly engaging framework that you - and your students - will want to return to over and over again.

I know you're going to love this book!

So, pull up your sleeves and dig in!

by Jeff Anderson

ACKNOWLEDGEMENTS

There are so many people to thank when putting together a project of this size. I'd like to thank Stenhouse Publishers and all the people behind the scenes of this book. This includes Melanie Moy and the entire production team. Thank you to the Stenhouse authors Jeff Anderson and Whitney La Rocca, who read the proposal and encouraged me to move forward. I especially would like to thank Terry Thompson, my editor at Stenhouse Publishers. Thank you for making that out-of-the-blue phone call in February of 2023 to see if I had any projects in mind. Thank you for seeing the potential and need for this work. And thank you for all of your support, guidance, and humor along the way. Without you, this would not have happened.

A book is rarely written within a year. There is much learning, practicing, and exploring in the years before the idea develops. Thank you to the teachers who planned and tried this type of work in a variety of ways and gave me feedback for how it was working in their classrooms. There were many of you, including Rebecca Ogle, Lindsey Klein, and Danielle Combs. Thank you to Lydia Conway for keeping me around, and Elizabeth Thompson who understood the potential of this work from the very beginning. A special thanks to Angela Schafer and Talia Ryan who not only worked alongside me through this but also pushed my thinking as they continually shared student work and feedback.

When you teach in the relative privacy of your classroom, you don't have to think about artwork and graphic design or whether you chose the just-right font for an anchor chart. Fortunately, I was able to lean on Michelle Gerrells, who helped me to see that there are many beautiful ways to annotate a sentence, and Catherine Donovan, who turned my vague ideas for a cover into a reality. Thank you.

If we're lucky, we don't do this work alone. I feel fortunate to be a part of a literacy team of dedicated professionals. As a part of this group, we have had to ask hard questions, push our thinking beyond our comfort zones, and support each other's professional growth. I truly appreciate your collaboration, professionalism, and continued commitment to serve students and teachers.

How do you thank the friends who not only fuel your mind but also feed your soul? Thank you for being there to pick me up when I needed it and to push me forward when I was stuck: Aimee Litt, Janel Robinson, Wendy Shaw, and Julie Warner. There are no words to tell you how much your friendship and support mean to me.

Finally, thank you to my family. Mom, thank you for being patient. You were patient when I thought I didn't have enough time in my career to continue growing. You were patient when I didn't think I had more books to write. You were patient when I had to turn down mother-daughter outings to work on this project. Your patience and love have held me up in ways I hadn't expected nor deserved. Michael, Sydney, and Samantha, without you, I am nothing. You are my whole heart. And finally, a heart full of gratitude goes out to Rick, my husband. You think I wrote this because you're retiring. The truth is - after all these years - I still want to impress you. Thank you for your encouragement and for picking up all the pieces. I am a better person because of you.

INTRODUCTION
Sentence Digs: Expanding the Power of Mentor Sentences

I was recently in a third-grade classroom where we were knee-deep within a sentence dig. Our tasks were not only to identify figurative language but also to describe the main character Lonnie Johnson by studying a mentor sentence from the book *WHOOSH! Lonnie Johnson's SUPER-SOAKING Stream of Inventions* by Chris Barton and illustrated by Don Tate (2016). We were grappling with pronoun references, subordinating conjunctions, word choice, and interesting punctuation. We were acting out parts, making connections back to the story, and practicing how we could do the same kind of work in our own writing.

In the midst of all this activity, a child blurted out, "I don't understand why we have to do this."

This was a sink or swim moment. Even though I had researched this kind of work and thought this lesson was going well, if my students didn't understand the purpose, I had a lot of rethinking to do. So I asked the class, "What are you learning? Why is this work important?"

Luckily, hands shot up with a sense of urgency.

"This sentence helps us understand Lonnie is a great thinker. He can come up with ideas and collaborate with other people OR he can think of ideas by himself!"

"I was confused about how ideas flow. I just didn't get it. Now I see how the author is describing how the ideas just come to him quickly one after another."

"AND he invented the super soaker water gun… you know… it uses water… it flows."

"I didn't know what those dashes were all about. The word FINALLY in the middle of the sentence was confusing. We figured out that FINALLY is reminding us that Lonnie never had a place all to himself to work on his inventions. Now he does."

A mentor sentence isn't just about being a lovely sentence. It's more than something to ooh and ahh over. A mentor sentence should be a powerhouse of language study. One that will not only inspire our writers to write well but also one that will reveal big ideas around the topics and texts students are reading about and studying.

Teachers often lament that there isn't enough grammar study in their curriculum or the grammar study within their instructional materials isn't transferring to students' writing. Oftentimes, despite yearning for a better option, we find ourselves teaching grammar out of context - with worksheets or editing processes around sentences and topics that do not matter to the children.

In *The Writing Revolution* (2017, 14-15), Hochman and Wexler establish several principles for teaching writing; here are the first five:

1. Students need explicit instruction in writing.
2. Sentences are the building blocks of all writing.
3. When embedded in the content of the curriculum, writing instruction is a powerful teaching tool.
4. The content of the curriculum drives the rigor of the writing activities.
5. Grammar is best taught in the context of student writing.

These principles frame the focus of sentence inquiry as a way to help students move from abstract grammar rules to direct, authentic applications in their writing. And, although *The Writing Revolution* focuses on teaching writing composition - from sentences to paragraphs to essays - the authors do not forget nor minimize the importance of grammar instruction taught in context.

In *Patterns of Power* (2017), Jeff Anderson and Whitney La Rocca also capitalize on sentence-level instruction, using their invitational approach to teaching grammar within the context of student writing. They use a mentor sentence, a beautiful, well-written sentence, not for diagramming but to "invite students into the possible, into what they *can* do rather than what they *shouldn't* do" (14). In this way, they remove the common practice of giving students a sentence riddled with errors to, instead, marvel and investigate a strong sentence from a published piece of children's literature. They invite students to name what the author is doing and nudge them to try something similar as they work on their own writing. In this way, Anderson and La Rocca lead teachers away from diagramming and editing random sentences to analyzing well-written sentences that are worthy of emulation.

Both *The Writing Revolution* and *Patterns of Power* focus on writing but they lean on the inherent reciprocity of reading and writing to support their work. And, in this book, we'll leverage these same connections through sentence inquiry - inviting students to zero in on the sentence level, which is embedded in rigorous content to enhance a multitude of our instructional goals - moving beyond writing to include reading and content area instruction.

With that, let's explore the opportunities mentor sentences can offer for reading instruction.

One connection that immediately comes to mind is syntax and semantics, which we can see emphasized in the different literacy ropes that provide a foundational understanding of Science of Reading research: Scarborough's Reading Rope and Sedita's Writing Rope (see Figures I.1 and I.2).

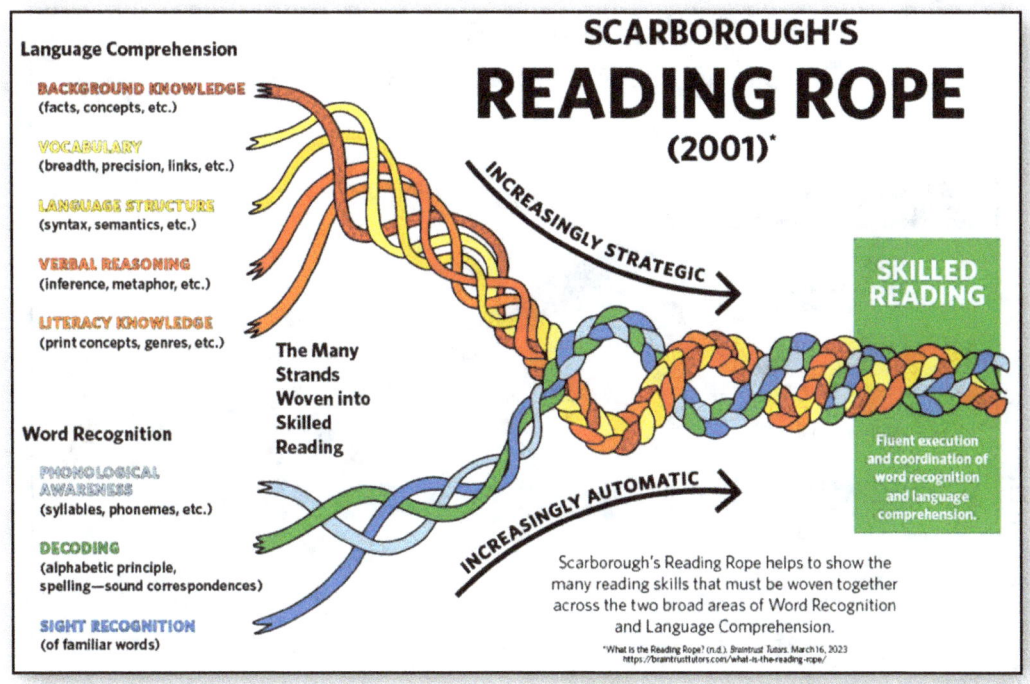

FIGURE I.1
Scarborough's (2011) Reading Rope

Scarborough's (2011) Reading Rope illustrates the multiple strands of proficient reading. Notice, in the upper rope for (oral) language comprehension, Scarborough includes language structures and particularly names syntax and semantics. Syntax focuses on the arrangement of words and phrases to create well-formed sentences in a language. And semantics focuses on the meaning of a word, phrase, or sentence – how words and their arrangement bring meaning to the sentence and text. Readers need to have strong syntactic awareness to realize how the order of the words, the flow of the sentence, brings meaning to the text. This not only helps with comprehension but it will also support the three parts of fluency – accuracy, prosody, and pace.

Alternatively, Sedita's (2023) Writing Rope illustrates multiple strands necessary for proficient writing. Looking closely, you'll see that one of the strands is syntax: grammar and syntactic awareness, sentence elaboration, and punctuation. We use syntax to create meaning with a single word, within a sentence, and across the text. As writers, we write to express our ideas and rely on the reader to bring meaning and understanding to what we have written.

In most classrooms, reading and writing are taught separately in the schedule. They may be separated by topic or content. Many of us do this in an effort to squeeze our vast amount of state/district standards into our days. Or we're trying to adjust the writing assignments to prepare for the state test. These are valid reasons; however, an unintended

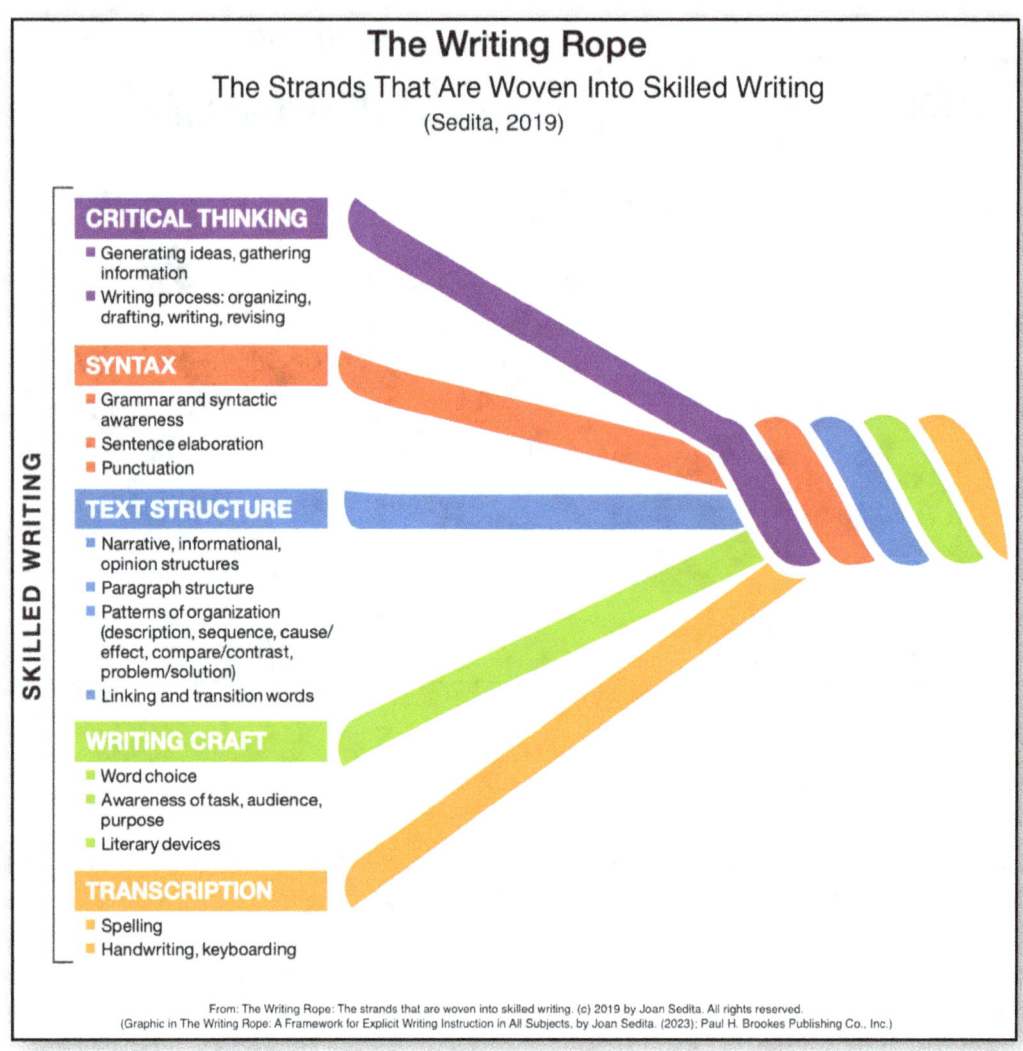

FIGURE I.2
Sedita's (2023) Writing Rope

consequence has been that we do not take advantage of the reciprocity of reading and writing. We can change this.

When we think of the reciprocity of reading and writing, we would do well to take a deep look at syntax and semantics. How are authors structuring their sentences to bring meaning to the text and to the reader? How do readers figure that out and construct a mental image of the text that makes sense to them? And how do readers take that information to articulate their complex ideas and thinking around rich topics by writing stronger sentences and building rich paragraphs and texts? Sentences - mentor sentences - are language powerhouses which we can leverage to teach readers to comprehend both explicit and implicit meanings of a text and to teach writers to write sentences that can articulate their complex thoughts.

TEACHING SYNTAX AND SEMANTICS IN CONTEXT

When I think of teaching syntax and semantics in context, my mind automatically goes to teaching them in the context of student writing. What this means is we model for students how to form various kinds of sentences and use grammar structures in our writing, so they can immediately practice it in their own writing. This is difficult for a lot of teachers - they're concerned it isn't explicit enough. I hear teachers say that they worry kids won't get enough repetitive practice. They are also worried that teaching grammar in context won't show up well on the state test. Thus, many teachers continue to teach grammar - and essentially syntax - in isolation.

Alternatively, it's easier to teach readers in context because it's impossible not to do so. You need a text - word, sentence, story, article - to read, and the context is generally baked into the text. Yet, in an effort to comprehend the whole text, we often teach in broad strokes - character development, event order, setting, theme. Certainly, there is nothing wrong with that - we should do that. However, there is value in digging into a few key sentences that are written with such complexity that analyzing them breaks open meaning for the reader. And if we have these rich sentences in the texts we read and show students how they offer access to complex ideas, these sentence structures - the syntax - authentically become tools the reader can, in turn, use in their own writing. In other words, understanding syntax and semantics of sentences that carry rich meaning will not only support reading comprehension, it will also model for and support students in writing those kinds of sentences. There is gold in this reciprocity.

In this book, we'll explore a basic sentence dig routine stemming from Charles and Lily Fillmore's work (2013) you can use immediately in your classroom to capitalize on this reciprocity. Through this practical and engaging routine, we'll explore ways to explicitly teach syntax in the context of a sentence or two from a text the students are reading which will strengthen their reading comprehension. Next, we'll flip that instruction to also build up students' sentence power within their writing. Then, we'll ride this current of reciprocity all the way into the content areas where reading and writing act as a tool to process, learn, and remember key information.

WHAT IS THE SENTENCE DIG ROUTINE?

Take Apart - Put Together - Apply. That's it. That's the routine. Take Apart - Put Together - Apply. The content will drive the rigor, so we can rely on a simple routine to guide our work. We'll start with a powerful text, one that a teacher is either reading aloud to the class or one in which every student has access. Then, while visions of standards and teaching objectives dance in our heads, we read to recognize any sentences that may be difficult for our students to understand. We're looking for places where comprehension may break down. Using that sentence and all its complexity, we will take it apart, using language structures as our guide. Then, we'll put it back together to understand the semantics of the sentence, how it all works together. Finally students will have the opportunity to apply this new knowledge to their writing about reading, writing projects, or content area learning. Below is a sample plan in the making. We'll go into this more shortly, but for now notice how one sentence holds meaning for the reader and for the writer. Consider how digging into a sentence like this will support readers' comprehension and create opportunities for students to write similarly structured sentences.

Excerpt from *Whoosh! Lonnie Johnson's SUPER-SOAKING Stream of Inventions*
By Chris Barton and Don Tate (2016)

Ideas for other problems to solve just kept on flowing.
They flowed whether Lonnie was working with hundreds of people at NASA or up late tinkering with his own inventions in – finally! – his own workshop.

Sentence

They flowed whether Lonnie was working with hundreds of people at NASA or up late tinkering with his own inventions in – finally! – his own workshop.

Planning questions:

Why did you choose this sentence? What's complex about it?
The pronoun *they* refers back to the prior sentence – problems. The next pronoun *he* refers to Lonnie. The use of multiple pronouns in a sentence can be confusing.

The verb *flowed* is used in a novel way. Flow is a continuous stream of something – typically a liquid or a gas. In this case the author is referring to ideas.

The word *whether* is a subordinate conjunction offering two different times the ideas are flowing – the overall meaning to infer is the ideas were always flowing.
The use of prepositional phrases show the reader where he thinks of his ideas.
The dashes create an interruption for the word FINALLY.

How does understanding this sentence help the reader? How does it connect back to the text?
This sentence continues to build the readers' understanding of Lonnie's work ethic and personality. He was always thinking of new ideas. This summarizes the text so far, as the story tells us about times Lonnie worked on ideas at home and at work (NASA). This sets up how he will work through the ups and downs of the super soaker.

What can writers learn from this sentence?
Clear pronoun antecedent
Word choice – verbs (flow… connects ideas to water which connects to Lonnie's big invention).
Word choice – subordinate conjunction *whether* which indicates two possibilities. What if the author had used *when*. Big difference.
The sentence structure is a complex sentence.

The Sentence Dig Lesson Structure

Now, let's take a closer look at those three main parts: Take Apart - Put Together - Apply.

TAKE APART

Once you choose a sentence for a sentence dig, you'll need to chunk it - divide it into meaningful parts based on what the focus of the instruction will be. I like to put these chunks on sentence strips, so I can move them around on the whiteboard (with magnets).

Show students the whole sentence at the beginning of the lesson. Then, move each chunk to help them focus on the work you're doing bit by bit. As you do this, annotate what the class is thinking on (or around) the sentence chunks. You'll likely find that using sticky notes or drawing/writing directly on the sentence strip work well. This helps to stamp the learning and provides a visual reference of your collective thinking when you are finished.

It will be tempting to teach this as a teacher-directed, whole-group lesson. But many teachers have found that it is important to create opportunities for all students to participate. This means making time throughout the lesson for students to participate in protocols like turn and talk with a partner or talk with a small group. It's easy to let this work run long, but balance your timing with what's essential to prepare learners for a successful experience in the Put Together and Apply parts of this routine that follow.

PUT TOGETHER

After you finish talking about the chunks, mix them up and explore ways to put the sentence back together again. First, work to put it back the way the author had it. Then, ask revision style questions that allow students opportunities to rearrange the sentence, add to the sentence, and delete parts of the sentence. You might even look for ways to break the sentence up into more sentences. This is a playful part of the routine that strengthens students' comprehension as you continuously check - does this change the meaning of the sentence? How does it affect the story element or text characteristic if we make this change?

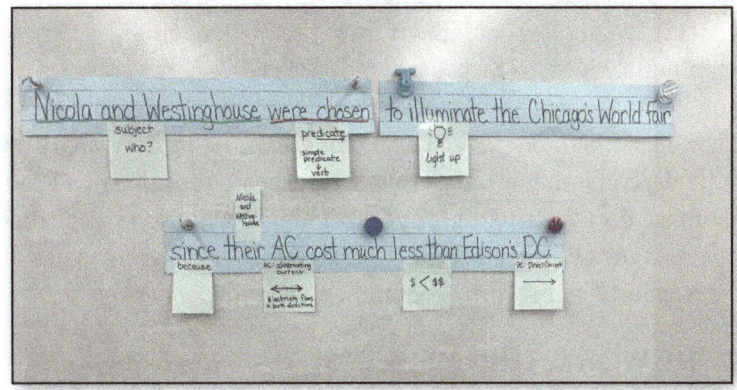

FIGURE I.3

Annotated sentence dig with sketches to support comprehension

Some teachers find it helpful for student pairs or small groups to have similar chunks of the sentences to move around at their desks. This isn't always necessary, but for sentences that might have many possible combinations and/or can be broken down from one long sentence into shorter ones, you'll likely find it helpful for students to have something at their fingertips.

APPLY

Typically, this part of the routine reveals a sentence frame for students to try to write with a similar sentence structure. When planning for this part, I am thinking about all the students in my class, and like you, I know not everyone needs the same kind of support to imitate the sentence structure studied. You'll find that I offer a heavily scaffolded sentence frame and a lighter scaffolded one. Those are for you to consider through the lens of your students. Some of your students may not need a sentence frame at all. I encourage you to use as little of a scaffold as possible but as much as needed. The point is to give students an opportunity to start using more advanced sentence structures when writing. You may find that this application time can also lead to additional sentence-combining work across the week to give more practice and fortify the sentence dig focus.

The timing for sentence digs can take as little as ten minutes or as long as twenty minutes. Sentence digs can also be broken up across days to fit your schedule. The key to your timing will be in knowing your students. What do they need? How much time do we need to talk about each chunk? Are there chunks we can move through quickly, leaving more time to zero in on just one or two? Do we need to spend a lot of time on more than one chunk?

I've provided some sample lessons in the chapters that follow. Because the sentence digs explored in this section are primarily focused on supporting reading comprehension, it will be important for you to read the referenced text to your class before trying the lessons as written. You'll also want to reconsider the questions in the lessons as you adjust them to best meet the needs of their students. The lessons are included to provide an example of how a sentence dig might unfold. If you're just getting started, you might consider using these digs as they're presented - to get the nuance of the routine - and then, as you're ready, write your own sentence dig lessons drawn from the books you are reading and the texts your learning community loves. The possibilities are endless.

Typically, you'll want to make time for one whole group sentence dig each week or twice a month. This can be done in one day or you can break the routine apart over the course of several days. It depends on your class, your time, and your pacing. Then you can fold in additional sentence digs for small groups of students who may need this routine more often. Ideally, the routine will become a go-to strategy students grow to use on their own or with a partner to support their reading comprehension independently.

EXTENDING THE WORK: THINK SHEETS

When we use the sentence dig routine in our classrooms, we're training our students to be strategic readers. We're teaching them to find sentences that create dissonance in our thinking while reading and then to break that sentence up to work through not only its meaning but its impact on the text. The work doesn't stop at the lesson. We need to create practice opportunities for students so that this learning - at the sentence level - impacts their thinking as readers and writers across full texts.

Think sheets are one way to do this. These one page scaffolds offer opportunities for students to continue thinking about the sentence work at hand beyond the current lesson. It's a way for them to collaborate, practice, and extend their thinking. As you work through this book, you'll notice that many sample lessons include Think Sheets, which I encourage you to use both directly with your students but also as a springboard for sentence digs you'll create on your own.

We can use Think Sheets as opportunities to solidify student learning, so they can apply it more effectively to their reading and writing. There is no one right way to create a Think Sheet, because it largely depends on your students' needs. Likewise, you may want to differentiate your Think Sheets for different students. Or there may be weeks where you don't need a Think Sheet at all.

As you craft lessons beyond the collection in this book, you might consider some of these strategies when creating Think Sheets to extend the work around your own sentence digs:

- Sketching the sentence
- Using a timeline with the sentence
- Substituting words (synonyms, antonyms, conjunctions, meanings, etc.)
- Sentence extension work
- Sentence combining work
- Sentence reduction work
- Writing about reading
- Using sentence frames

It will be important for students to have the opportunity to talk with a partner or small group about the work *before* they do the work or as they do the work. It might be tempting to use a Think Sheet as a worksheet... a solo venture to get a grade or as morning work. I strongly encourage you, rather, to use these to spark students' thinking and learning. This spark will happen through conversations. We've all heard the phrase "the one doing the talking is the one doing the learning." Students need time to analyze, synthesize, and reflect in order to take what they learned in the lesson and make it their own. In many instances, you'll find that Think Sheets support this goal perfectly.

WHO IS THIS BOOK FOR?

Considering the national push for placing complex texts in front of every child, students in today's classrooms are encountering increasingly unfamiliar syntactic structures. In addition, as we lean into reciprocity and look at our students' writing and sentence structure, we can't help but wonder if they are writing with sufficient complexity. According to Scott and Balthazar, by kindergarten we should hear students speaking in complex sentences and using some of all three types of dependent clauses. They go on to say that "as children progress through elementary school, average sentence length (in words) roughly corresponds to chronological age to age ten, or about fourth grade. Also around this time, a child's writing should begin to contain sentences with distinctly written syntactic structures" (2013, 24). Are your students consistently speaking and writing with this kind of complexity?

Certainly, the learners in our classrooms need to be exposed to rich complex sentence structures in order to develop their oral language and written sentence structure. However, since the conversational language used by most children isn't typically composed of complicated syntactic structures, we need to intentionally expose readers and writers to these structures, explicitly teaching them how they work and how to use them to comprehend and communicate more effectively.

And this is where the sentence dig routine comes in. I spent several years coaching at a school where this routine was a game changer. We initially started it on days the gifted students were out of the classroom for their separate instruction. This allowed teachers to use the routine with a smaller class size for kids who *needed* it. This was so effective that within a month, teachers in third, fourth, and fifth grades adjusted their schedules to make sure their gifted students were there for the instruction as well. One teacher argued, "My gifted kids need this too! They do things in their writing intuitively, but not intentionally. They struggle to revise because they don't know how to intentionally strengthen their sentences." She added, "Plus in reading, they read so fast, that sometimes they miss important details tucked into these longer sentences. They just need to be there for the sentence dig."

Likely this is ringing familiar. Students at any level of need or capability, whether reading or writing, can benefit from practices that raise their levels of awareness around the power of syntax and sense. You may find you'll use the sentence dig routine to center a whole group discussion in reading, writing, social studies, or even science. You may find your multilingual learners and struggling readers and writers need more of this work, and decide to provide that in small groups or as part of their supplementary support. In time, you'll find that, as you make this Take Apart - Put Together - Apply routine an integral part of your learning community, students will start to do this level of analysis on their own - finding sentences they want to break down, discussing the sentences in small groups or with a partner - and intentionally practicing using different grammatical structures as a form of writing play to create stronger and stronger sentences.

The reason this sentence dig routine works for so many students is the content drives the rigor. The sentence structure drives the rigor. The text they're reading, the topic they're writing about all drive the rigor. So, although a quick sentence like - *They flowed whether Lonnie was working with hundreds of people at NASA or up late tinkering with his own inventions in - FINALLY! - his own workshop -* may *seem* easy to understand, it's actually quite complex. Students typically have to pause and think about the prior sentence in the text to realize that *they* isn't referring to other people. *They* refers to Lonnie's ideas. And as students deconstruct this sentence, they realize that this is really talking about Lonnie's work ethic - he thinks of ideas whether he is collaborating with others or working alone. And don't get me started on that interrupter - FINALLY - and its impact on the reader. And though some of our readers might pick up on these things intuitively, writing a sentence like that within the flow of their own writing takes some know-how.

WHAT TO EXPECT IN THIS BOOK

This book is meant to provide you with a foundation to identify sentences brimming with language structures - syntax and semantics - along with a practical use-tomorrow routine to explicitly teach them in ways that support reading comprehension as well as oral and written expression. The book is divided into three parts. Section 1 will focus on using the sentence dig routine to support reading comprehension with specific looks at vocabulary, important details, and figurative language. Then in Section 2, we'll look at sentences through the lens of writing, digging deeper into the crafts of word choice, adding details, and creating strong structures. Finally, Section 3 will apply the sentence dig routine to the content areas as we unpack vocabulary, important details, and text structure.

A FINAL NOTE

The unavoidable fact is that our school days are long but our teaching time is short. There is never enough time, so we find ourselves having to prioritize instruction. At a conference recently, a teacher asked me - how important is this work... *really*? I had to stop and think for a moment because to me if the same thread appears in both the reading and writing ropes, it must be important. But I knew what she was really asking - *With all the other things I have to do, where does this fall in and what elevates it to a higher priority than anything else on my plate?* This is no small question. As you begin this work with your own students, I trust that you'll quickly find that building students' syntactic awareness through sentence digs to be one of those little BIG things. It's like flossing your teeth - a simple, short act that yields big results for your health. The work we'll explore together in the pages that follow, though relatively simple, is a routine that, in short time, will yield big results because it supports so much of the heavy lifting students do every day in every subject.

So let's dig in!

SECTION 1
Digging into Reading Comprehension

> Reading should not be presented to children as a chore, a duty.
> It should be offered as a gift.
> - *Kate DiCamillo*

I'm guilty. Perhaps you are too. I'm guilty of giving my students two basic strategies when they lose comprehension. In the past, I'd tell them, "If you are reading and realize you don't understand what you just read, stop and go back to where you did understand the text. Then, reread slowly, connecting the new information to what you already know." For many of my students, this became another task for them to do - making reading more of a chore than a labor of love. Or if I was reading the text aloud and a student raised their hand to say they didn't understand or were confused about what a particular part meant, I might reread the sentence more slowly and intentionally, or I ask them "what part did you not understand?" They'd shrug and we'd keep reading, thinking comprehension would somehow click together in a moment. I'm embarrassed even writing this! I hate that I didn't know then what I know now.

Yes, there are times when we lose comprehension because we read too fast or let our mind wander. Rereading and being intentional about adding to our mental image is certainly helpful in many instances. And yes, there are times that we're moving through a text we can't quite piece together and if we keep reading, things fall into place. But, there are times we lose comprehension not because we can't read or understand the words, but because the complexity of the sentence has exposed gaps in our understanding. If we just keep going or try rereading slower, we haven't really addressed the problem. Missing out on one sentence in a text or passage might be okay but not understanding several sentences can derail any reader's understanding.

In this section of the book, our sentence digs will focus on supporting readers who've lost the meaning of what they're reading and need more intentional strategies to help them get back on track. I've chosen to focus on vocabulary, key details, and figurative language that often reveal deep insights as students grapple with the complexities layered throughout a collection of sentences. Each sentence dig has an instructional focus, but like any language loving teacher, I can find ways to wring a sentence to help students explore any number of unexpected complexities. With that, many of the sentences studied in the following lessons include an extended focus with a Think Sheet. These extensions typically address a literary element or a cohesive device students might find interesting. These are optional, and as you consider them, keep your learners in mind. It's important not to overburden our students with too many instructional points, but you'll want to find a balance that offers just enough space to experience an "ah-ha" moment of understanding that fills the gap between acknowledging what the text says and understanding what the author is trying to say.

When you go to plan your own sentence digs using the books you're reading with students, you'll want to consider the same pivotal questions we've discussed earlier. Which sentence in the text is worthy of study and why? What do your students need to understand about this sentence? How will you layer your discussion to lead students to new and profound understanding about the syntax and semantics but also about the text itself? What extension opportunities does the text offer and are your learners ready for them?

Though the lessons in this section are organized around three big categories - vocabulary, key details, and figurative language - you might also consider extending your conversations to help students explore additional cohesive devices like:

- Pronoun references
- Word and phrase substitution
- Ellipsis
- Appositives
- Conjunctions (coordinating and subordinating)

The critical point to remember about sentence digs and the lessons that follow is that you know your students best. You know what they need based on your state's standards, your data, and most importantly your relationship with each reader in the room. Here, you'll apply that expertise and understanding to support them at a sentence level.

CHAPTER 1
Word Meanings

> For me, reading has always been not only a quest for pleasure and enlightenment but also a word-hunting expedition, a lexical safari.
> - *Charles Harrington Elster*

There is nothing better than waking up in the morning to the smell of freshly baked monkey bread. Unlike typical bread, you don't slice it and it's not in cute little muffin tins. The true joy of this cinnamon deliciousness is that it looks almost like a gooey cake and you use your fingers to pull the bread apart - bit by bit - bite by bite. Many friends have looked at this process with a bit of disgust - until they dig in... and then they know.

I want my students to have this same realization about sentence-level work. When we encounter a complex text, it's important to have a way to unravel each sentence - take it apart and digest it in bite-size pieces.

In this section, we'll explore sentence digs that support reading, which enable students to literally use their hands to take sentences apart and take in bite-sized pieces to build a strong understanding not only of the sentence itself but of the overall text at hand. When comprehension begins to break down, reading-based sentence digs help us look at the word or sentence level to start rebuilding. Interventions for word-level decoding work found on Scarborough's lower rope of reading instruction and for vocabulary development found on the upper rope are critical (Scarborough 2011). However, we can extend this further by discussing specifically how those words and vocabulary work together in a sentence and how that sentence works with other sentences, offering greater opportunities to tap into additional areas such as syntax and semantics.

I love words. I love learning new words. I love looking up synonyms and antonyms. I love practicing saying tricky words quickly like *reciprocity* and *cinnamon*. I love the easy access to an online dictionary while reading ebooks - just tap the word and voilà the definition appears. And what language arts teacher doesn't have dreams of vocabulary instruction blooming with Latin roots, word lists, and the Frayer model? However, when we read a text, simply knowing words and definitions isn't the only way readers glean meaning from the text.

Once the writer starts putting words next to each other - semantics takes over. The way words are put together brings meaning to the text. When we tell students to figure out the meaning based on context clues, what we're saying is - pay attention to the semantics. We're asking kids to infer the meaning based on usage. Sometimes we get lucky and the actual definition is in the text. Many times, students have to have the gist of the story in mind while they derive the meaning of unknown words. Juggling a mental picture of the text in order to make sense of new words or a novel arrangement of words takes practice.

Jayden, a first grader, was happy to show off his reading of the text *Creepy Carrots* by Aaron Reynolds and illustrated by Peter Brown (2014). He paused after reading, "His dad thumped into his bedroom and threw on the light."

"What does that mean… *threw* on the light?" Jayden asked.

"What do you think it means?" I responded.

"Well, I thought it meant he threw the light - like across the room - because Jasper is afraid and freaking out about the carrots. Maybe the dad threw the light to scare the carrots. But if you look at the picture… (Jayden points to the lamp on the nightstand in the illustration), the light is on the table. If the dad threw the light, it would be on the floor."

"I see what you mean." I say. "That's tricky but let's think about what's happening in the story."

"Jasper is scared. He screams for his dad. His dad comes running in and throws the light. It doesn't make sense with the picture. The pictures and words are supposed to match!"

"What would make sense if the dad is running into the dark room and wants to see what's going on?" I ask.

"He should *turn on* the light!" Jayden exclaims with a tinge of frustration.

"You got it! When we say… *he threw on the light*, it means he turned on the light really fast. It's like when I tell my son to throw on a jacket before he leaves the house. I mean to put on a jacket quickly before he leaves."

"Ohhhhh!" Jayden replied, smiling and nodding his head. "That makes more sense!"

Like Jayden, many students read words and have a definition in mind for that word. However, when an author uses a word in an unusual way, or in a way with which the reader is unfamiliar, it causes confusion. Unlike Jayden, many students read through unknown vocabulary without much thought. Yet, when words crop up that conflict with or don't add to the reader's mental picture, it will cause confusion. Sometimes we just need a clarifying definition and everything falls into place. Other times, we need to look at how the words are fitting together within the sentence to create meaning. Helping students unravel the semantics of sentences will shed light on the word's individual meaning(s) and its meaning within the sentence.

I realize that we teach students vocabulary with explicit routines for learning key words throughout the week. We also provide some instruction incidentally as we go through the text. Sentence digs are not meant to replace this type of robust vocabulary instruction. Rather, this is a routine that students can learn to use on their own to crack open words when used in complex texts. The fact of the matter is that we cannot possibly explicitly teach every single word and all of its meanings that children will encounter. In her book, *The Reading Comprehension Blueprint*, Hennessy suggests, among other things, "providing rich and varied language experiences" and "fostering word consciousness" (Hennessy 2021, 62). She argues that "Children need a continuum of direct and indirect learning opportunities, given the sheer number of new words they potentially encounter each year" (Hennessy 2021, 62). Sentence digs can be used for this. This involves a bit more than incidental instruction, where you'd just give a quick synonym or example and move on. But it's not quite a full blown, explicit vocabulary routine either. Rather, we'll develop students' word consciousness by helping them learn to identify words that make them raise an eyebrow in wonder, driving them to dig into the sentence to reveal the word's meaning and its contribution to the literary elements at play. For example, you might employ sentence dig routines to help students pay attention to common words that may have unusual connotations. Here is an excerpt from the book *Restart* (Korman 2017, 111) where Chase and two of his friends are having a friendly game of catch.

> I'm not on the team yet, but no one said I couldn't play a friendly game of catch as we make our way to community service.
> The "friendly" part is just for us.
>
> (Korman 2017, 111)

Most of us - and many of our students - would say the word friendly here means that it's not a competitive game - no one gets hurt. It's friendly - nice. This sentence, when pulled out of context, gives us the sense that the boys are just having fun. However, if students are reading sentence by sentence without connecting the sentences together, they'll miss big chunks of meaning.

Now look at the excerpt below - and think how all of the sentences go together to give the reader information about these characters.

> Bear snatches the pass out of the air, hugs the ball close to his body, and executes a lightning spin move around a lady pushing a baby carriage on the sidewalk.
> "Watch it!" she barks as the startled baby begins to scream.
> "Sorry!" I shout over my shoulder, and we continue along Portland Street, tossing the ball between the three of us.
> I'm not back on the team yet, but no one said I couldn't play a friendly game of catch as we make our way to community service.
> The "friendly" part is just for us. It doesn't include our fellow pedestrians, who run for their lives when they see us coming.
>
> (Korman 2017, 111)

The author doesn't come out and say these kids are inconsiderate and a menace to people walking down the street. He simply indicates the word "friendly" with quotes - letting the reader know something isn't as it seems. Korman then follows it up with a humdinger of a sentence, that - if the reader is paying attention - will signify these kids are trouble.

This is the kind of vocabulary work we can bring attention to with a well-timed sentence dig. In leading an investigation around the sentences *The "friendly" part is just for us. It doesn't include our fellow pedestrians, who run for their lives when they see us coming*, and then placing the sentences back into the context of the story, we can help students not only determine the intended meaning of words while also understanding more about the characters, but also develop internal muscle memory for sorting through similar confusions when they encounter them on their own.

PREPARING SENTENCE DIG DISCUSSIONS

Across the rest of this chapter we'll explore the lesson structure for a sentence dig focused on reading, along with some tips to keep your work focused, before rounding things out with a set of example lessons to get you started. But first you'll need to identify a sentence worthy of study.

For instance, if you are working to identify vocabulary you expect your students will need to know in order to be successful with a particular text or topic and then move into planning a sentence dig lesson around it, the first thing you might want to do is consider the question: Is this word critical to understanding this text, this topic, or deeper levels of meaning of the central idea/theme? Does the word reveal more about setting, character, or plot? Does the word clarify the main idea or a key concept? Tune into words that students might be able to decode, and maybe have an idea of its basic meaning, but blow right by without considering the word's impact on the sentence or the mental image the author is trying to create. Sentence digs give students the structure and practice they need to be perspicacious readers.

SHOWCASE SENTENCES LESSONS AT A GLANCE

Lesson	Focus	Literary Element/ Text Feature	Text	Sentence
R1.1	Multiple Meaning Words	Setting	*One Hen* by Katie Smith Milway, illustrated by Eugenie Fernandes	"On market day he walks among **stalls** of fruits, vegetables, meats, kente cloths, and calabash bowls."
R1.2	Connotation	Character Development	*Restart* by Gordon Korman	"I'm not back on the team yet, but no one said I couldn't play a **friendly** game of catch as we make our way to community service. The '**friendly**' part is just for us."
R1.3	Definition Within the Sentence	Process/Sequence	*When Lunch Fights Back: Wickedly Clever Animal Defenses* by Rebecca L. Johnson	"They may **alternate** eyes, shooting first from one and then the other."
R1.4	Context Clues	Problem/Solution Text Structure	*Biodiversity: Eco Facts* by Izzi Howell	"It's important to encourage **sustainable** fishing, in which people can catch enough to support themselves, and fish populations are protected for the future."

SENTENCE DIG R1.1: MULTIPLE MEANING WORDS

Text: *One Hen* by Katie Smith Milway, illustrated by Eugenie Fernandes, page 11

Grades: 2–5

Book summary: Kojo lives in a small town in Ghana with his mother. Like many people in his village, Kojo and his mother are poor and struggle to meet their basic needs - like food. Based on a true story of Kwabena Darko, *One Hen* recalls how Kojo receives a small loan - enough to buy one hen. He buys the hen to have eggs to eat and to sell, and little by little, Kojo grows his business into the largest poultry farm in West Africa. This story demonstrates the power of giving someone a chance and investing not only in our dreams but also in the people around us.

Showcase sentence: On market day | he walks among **stalls** | of fruits, vegetables, meats, kente cloths, and calabash bowls.

Rationale: This sentence has a multiple meaning word: stalls. The use of this word plus the use of the introductory phrase and culture-specific products creates a sentence with quite a bit of complexity for young readers.

How does understanding this sentence help the reader? How does it connect back to the text? Understanding this sentence helps the reader create a stronger mental image of Kojo's culture. The use of the word stalls contrasts with our shopping experience in the United States and many other countries. In addition, this sentence establishes a strong setting that will be revisited through the beginning of the book. It creates a stark contrast to the way Kojo sells eggs by the end of the book. So anchoring this image with this sentence will help readers understand the significance of the overall theme of the book.

Ask: What story element does this sentence describe? *This tells us about the setting. We find out when and where the story is taking place.*

TAKE APART

Remember, your chunks are on sentence strips. Move them around to help students focus on one chunk and then another. You'll move them back together later.

Chunk	Possible Questions to Ask	Possible Answers
On market day,	When is this happening? Why do you think the author described this day as market day?	On market day It's the day Kojo's family went to the market. Markets aren't always open every day – so this is a special day. It's not a market like our grocery stores here in the US. There are many sellers here.

(Continued)

Chunk	Possible Questions to Ask	Possible Answers
he walks among **stalls**	Who is he?	Kojo
	What does stall mean? Can you think of another meaning? Which meaning makes sense for this setting?	Stall: doesn't run/stops working, like a car engine
		Stall: to put off doing something or to not start something – *Stop stalling and get to work.*
	NOTE: You don't need students to say all of these meanings but you should try to get at least two meanings to demonstrate how to determine which one makes the most sense.	Stall: an individual compartment (in a barn, in a restroom)
		Stall: a stand or booth to sell goods
		This last meaning makes the most sense because you would sell goods at a market and Kojo is at the market on market day.
	What does "he walks among stalls" mean?	Among is a preposition that means surrounded by… so Kojo is surrounded by stalls.
	How does this chunk help us visualize the setting?	It's a big market – there are likely a lot of people there and a lot of different things to buy.
of fruits, vegetables, meats, *kente* cloths, and calabash bowls.	What does this list tell us? How does it add to our mental picture of the setting?	This list tells us more about the kinds of goods that are being sold there. It's not just food – cloth and bowls.
		The author is trying to help us envision a lot of different kinds of goods that are being bought and sold.
		NOTE: You may be tempted to unpack *kente* cloths and calabash bowls. However, these are illustrated in the picture in the book for a quick reference.

PUT TOGETHER

During this part, the sentence chunks may be mixed up or off to the side. Invite students to manipulate the chunks when putting the sentence back together and/or while rearranging them.

Ask	Possible Answers	Food for Thought
What is the correct order of this sentence?	On market day	he walks among **stalls**	of fruits, vegetables, meats, *kente* cloths, and calabash bowls.	It's important to remember the author's word order because it was intentional for the reader. Now we'll start to play with this order and think about the sentence in different ways. This work can bring clarity to the reader, and it leans on the writer's process, which we'll want students to emulate.

(Continued)

Ask	Possible Answers	Food for Thought
Is there a way to rearrange this sentence and it still makes sense?	He walks among stalls | of fruits, vegetables, meats, *kente* cloths, and calabash bowls | on market day.	Yes, this works because *on market day* tells us when Kojo is walking among the stalls. In this case, the chunk can go at the beginning or the end of the sentence.
What synonym(s) could we use for **stall**? Why do you think the author chose to stick with the word **stall**?	Booth Stand Kiosk Table	There are many reasons authors choose a particular word. Sometimes it just sounds better in the sentence. Typically, stalls may be seen as temporary and ruggish (think barn stalls) whereas a booth may be thought to be temporary but more polished or professional.
Is there a chunk we can take out? How would that affect the meaning of the sentence?	~~On market day~~ | he walks among **stalls** | of fruits, vegetables, meats, *kente* cloths, and calabash bowls.	Students may say that the sentence's meaning doesn't change. If so, ask *why do you think the author includes that phrase – on market day?* Essentially, it's a note to the reader that Kojo couldn't go to the local market any time he wanted – there was a specific day when the vendors would be there to see their goods. *That* is the day he went to the market.
	Or On market day | he walks among **stalls** | ~~of fruits, vegetables, meats, *kente* cloths, and calabash bowls~~.	Without this phrase the sentence still makes sense, however, the reader would have to rely on only the pictures to know what was being sold at the market.
Why do you think the author included these chunks? How do they help us as a reader?	On market day – tells us when Kojo was there and that the market is available on certain days of the week or month.	As readers, we make sense of what we read through our own experiences. Here the author may be trying to help us connect to the story to see how we are the same across the world. This helps us understand the culture or way of life in this part of Africa. It may be very different from our lives.
	of fruits, vegetables, meats, *kente* cloths, and calabash bowls – this chunk helps us envision the market and how the goods are similar or different from what we see in our community.	Listing the different kinds of products/goods at the market gives the reader insight into the culture and way of life for Kojo. This particular phrase also helps the reader to know that there was a large variety at the market – a lot to see, a lot to buy, and essentially a lot of choices for Kojo. How interesting that he chose to buy a live chicken… which is not mentioned in the sentence.

APPLY

During this part, students quickly apply their new knowledge about the sentence to their reading and writing. These are quick efforts and may be followed up with more practice.

> **Discuss:** In a small group or in partners, discuss how the following setting compares to the setting at the beginning of the story:
>
> > Kojo and his mother live in a mud-walled house with an open fire for cooking. Beside it is a garden where they grow their own food.
>
> **Writing focus:** Invite students to work in partnerships or individually to come up with some of their own sentences using the sentence structure Milway uses to reveal the setting in the showcase sentence from her book *One Hen*. You may note that she uses prepositional phrases to answer the questions when and where.
>
> > **Showcase sentence:** On market day, he walks among stalls of fruits, vegetables, meats, *kente* cloths, and calabash bowls.
>
> **Heavy scaffold:** On _____ day s/he walks among _____.
>   (Which?)   (What? Or where?)
>
> Example: On <u>testing</u> day, she walks among <u>the rows of desks</u>.
>
> **Light scaffold:** On _____ day s/he _____ among _____ of _____,
>   (adj)   (verb)   (What?)   (noun)
>
> _____, and _____.
>   (noun)   (noun)
>
> Example: On <u>game</u> days, he <u>walks</u> among <u>crowds</u> of <u>students, teachers and parents</u> to find a place to sit.
>
> **No scaffold:** Invite students to emulate the showcase sentence within their own writing.

SENTENCE DIG R1.2: CONNOTATION

Text: *Restart* by Gordon Korman, page 111

Grades: 4-6

Book summary: Chase Ambrose fell off a roof. He survived, but he cannot remember *anything*. As he regains his physical health and heads back to school, he has to put the pieces together to learn who he was and decide what kind of person he really wants to be. This sentence is from a chapter when Chase and his two best friends, Bear and Aaron, are walking to their community service assignment. It gives the reader insight into Chase's slow realization that he may not have been a nice guy before his injury.

Showcase sentence: "The **'friendly'** part | is just for us.|"

Rationale: The author uses quote marks for the word friendly in much the same way we might use air quotes when we're talking. He's emphasizing the word and in this case the connotation - the emotion behind the word - isn't friendly. This can be tricky for kids when they're reading. They may not understand that the feeling around the word friendly has changed, giving insight into Chase's perspective.

How does this help the reader? How does it connect back to the text? It will be important for the reader to have the full context of this scene:

> I'm not back on the team yet, but no one said I couldn't play a friendly game of catch as we make our way to community service.
> The "friendly" part is just for us. It doesn't include our fellow pedestrians, who run for their lives when they see us coming.
>
> (111)

As students begin to notice and understand connotations - how a writer may use a word to evoke a certain feeling in addition to the literal meaning of the word - they can better infer literary elements like tone, character motivation, and themes. In this case, understanding this sentence in this scene builds the reader's understanding of how the character, Chase, is changing. He's beginning to see that his old self - with his old friends - may not be as friendly and cool as he once thought. This is key to understanding the theme of the book and the unfolding plot.

Ask: What story element is this section helping us better understand: setting, character, plot, or theme? (NOTE: Students may not know yet, so you may get multiple answers. You can come back to this question at the end after the sentence dig.) *This section gives us insight* into the character of Chase and how he used to be. When the author places Chase with his "old" friends, he tends to act like the old Chase - prior to the accident. The old Chase is rambunctious, self-centered, and inconsiderate.

TAKE APART

Remember, your chunks are on sentence strips. Move them around to help students focus on one chunk and then another. You'll move them back together later.

Chunk	Questions	Possible Answers
The **"friendly"** part	What does the author mean by friendly?	Friendly usually means it's fun – no one gets hurt – everyone is having a good time.
	Why did the author put friendly in quote marks?	One use of quote marks when not used in dialogue is to indicate when an author doesn't agree with a term or wants to indicate sarcasm or disbelief.
	What does the author mean by part? What is the author referring to?	Part refers to the game of catch. In the sentence before this, the boys are playing a friendly game of catch. NOTE: This may be a good time to go back and look at the context of the sentence on page 111: "I'm not back on the team yet, but no one said I couldn't play a friendly game of catch as we make our way to community service. **The 'friendly' part is just for us.** It doesn't include our fellow pedestrians, who run for their lives when they see us coming."
is just for us	Who is *us*? What is the significance of this chunk?	*Us* refers to Bear, Aaron, and Chase. This is significant or important because it shows us that the characters are only thinking about themselves. They're not considering the safety or "friendliness" of anyone else around them.
	How does the next sentence – *It doesn't include our fellow pedestrians, who run for their lives when they see us coming.* – add significance to this chunk?	*Fellow pedestrians* means there are other people on the street while they're playing their game. *Run for their lives* indicates that people are afraid of the way the boys are playing. They're afraid they'll get hurt because the boys are not paying attention to anyone else around them. This lets us know the game isn't friendly. It's a bit wild and people might get hurt.

PUT TOGETHER

During this part, the sentence chunks may be mixed up or off to the side. Invite students to manipulate the chunks when putting the sentence back together and/or while rearranging them.

Ask	Possible Answers	Food for Thought
What is the correct order of this sentence?	The "friendly" part | is just for us.	This is a simple sentence.
Is there a way to rearrange this sentence and it still makes sense?	No	This is a very basic sentence. It's chunked into two parts – the subject and the predicate. If you flip the chunks so the predicate comes first, it doesn't make sense. Most of the time, when we explore several chunks from the sentences it's because there are phrases or clauses that can be moved around. This is not the case here.
Is there a chunk we can take out?	No	One chunk is the subject and one chunk is the predicate. Without both, the sentence doesn't work.
Is there anything you could add to this sentence to make it more effective?	Explore responses that resonate with the group. For example, *The "friendly" part **of our game** is just for us.* Or *The "friendly" part is just for us **not for the people around us**.* OR ***We didn't realize** the "friendly" part was just for us.*	Students may say there is nothing to add to this sentence. It's a pretty good sentence on its own. And it is. Authors often use short sentences to create impact, especially before or after a rather lengthy sentence.

SENTENCE DIGS

APPLY

During this part, students quickly apply their new knowledge about the sentence to their reading and writing. These are quick efforts and may be followed up with more practice.

Discuss: Turn and talk with a partner or a small group. How does this sentence help us understand the main character, Chase? How does it reveal Chase's understanding of himself?

Writing focus: Quotations marks

> With a partner, try writing your own sentence using quote marks around one word – a word you want to emphasize in some way.
>
> Example: Chase is the "nicest" person in school.
>
> _____
>
> _____

CHAPTER 1   Reading: Word Meanings

Thought Partners: _____

Sentence Dig R1.2
THINK SHEET: READING FOCUS

STRATEGY: Sketching

Write the showcase sentence from the sentence dig in the space below:

Directions: Follow the instructions in the sections below.

Draw a sketch of a friendly game of catch.	**Draw** a sketch of *"The **'friendly'** part is just for us. It doesn't include our fellow pedestrians, who run for their lives when they see us coming."*
	Write or Discuss: How does this sentence help the reader understand more about Chase's character?

SENTENCE DIG R1.3: DEFINITION WITHIN THE SENTENCE

Text: *When Lunch Fights Back: Wickedly Clever Animal Defenses* by Rebecca Johnson, page 34

Grades: 4-6

Book summary: *When Lunch Fights Back: Wickedly Clever Animal Defenses* by Rebecca Johnson is an informational book about how animals use defense mechanisms to defend themselves. With a highly engaging topic, Johnson weaves both narrative and expository writing to help readers get a full picture of these amazing animal defense mechanisms. Johnson introduces each animal with a narrative scene - set to show the animal in action. Then she follows up with an in-depth scientific explanation of what is happening and how the animal does what it does.

The focus sentence for this lesson is from Chapter 6 "Here's Blood in Your Eye." In this chapter, Johnson starts off with an engaging scene of a horned lizard defending itself from a coyote attack by shooting blood from its eye into the coyote's eye. Gross! Then the author explains the science behind the mechanism. The showcase sentence explains how the horned lizard keeps the blood squirting when feeling threatened repeatedly.

Showcase sentence: "They may **alternate** eyes, | shooting first from one | and then the other."

Rationale: Aside from the word **alternate**, this sentence is made trickier due to the missing information (ellipsis). *They may alternate eyes, shooting [blood] first from one [eye] and then the other [eye].* We assume students know that the sentence is talking about shooting blood from the lizard's eyes, but struggling readers, readers for whom this is a complex text, and multilingual readers may need this pointed out to them.

How does this help the reader? How does it connect back to the text? This sentence contributes to the understanding of the central idea: *Horned lizards shoot blood to defend themselves from predators.* The showcase sentence demonstrates how the lizard uses its eyes to shoot the blood at the predator. Also, once students understand the lizard can alternate their eyes, they can infer that the lizard can keep up the defense longer than if the blood gushed from both eyes at once. This sentence ultimately helps the reader create a strong mental picture of how this animal's defense mechanism works.

Discuss: Today we'll study this sentence to get a better understanding of how the horned lizard uses its bloody defense mechanism. Our goal is to figure out how this detail adds to our understanding of the central idea: *Horned lizards shoot blood to defend themselves from predators.*

TAKE APART

Remember, your chunks are on sentence strips. Move them around to help students focus on one chunk and then another. You'll move them back together later.

Chunk	Questions	Possible Answers
They may **alternate** eyes,	Who or what is this sentence about? What does the word THEY refer to? What are they doing? Turn and talk with your partner. What is a synonym for *alternate*? Jot your ideas down on a sticky note or white board and hold on to it. (You'll come back to this.)	They is a (subject) pronoun. It's referring to the Texas horned lizard. Alternating eyes (Students will likely say – shooting blood out of their eyes. However, this sentence is about how the lizard *alternates* its eyes while shooting the blood.)
shooting first from one	Let's figure out what this part of the sentence is doing. What are the lizards shooting? How do you know? What does *first from one* mean? *If needed: Draw a line on the board next to the sentence strip to indicate there is a word missing: first from one _____* How do you know?	Blood; it says this earlier in the text. The defense mechanism is shooting blood from its eye. It's shooting blood from one eye. In the first part of the sentence, the author tells us the lizard alternates eyes, so we know it is shooting blood from one [eye].
and then the other.	What does this chunk mean – *and then the other*? If needed, ask what word might be missing: *and then the other _____* What is it doing with this eye? How do you know?	The lizard uses the other eye. Shooting blood We know this because this chunk is connected to the previous one where it says it is "shooting." And we said that shooting was referring to shooting blood.
They may **alternate** eyes,	Now revisit the first chunk again. Reread it while pointing to each eye – one and then the other. What is the author trying to tell us when she says *they may alternate eyes...*? Look at the synonym you wrote with your partner earlier. Turn and talk. Do you still agree that it is a synonym? Do you need a different one? Give me a thumbs up when you and your partner are ready.	Alternate means to take turns or for one to go and then the other. Have students share their ideas and annotate your sentence strip with one or two of their contributions: • Take turns • Rotate • Oscillate • Change • Switch

PUT TOGETHER

During this part, the sentence chunks may be mixed up or moved off to the side. Invite students to manipulate the chunks when putting the sentence back together and/or while rearranging them.

Ask	Possible Answers	Food for Thought
What is the correct order of this sentence?	They may alternate eyes, | shooting first from one | and then the other.	
Can you rearrange the sentence and it still mean the same thing?	Shooting first from one and then the other, they may alternate eyes.	The participle phrase *shooting first from one and then the other*, can be moved to the beginning of the sentence.
Why do you think the author chose not to write the sentence this way?	Students might say the original sentence sounds better. Or The words *shooting first from one and then the other* describe how the horned lizard is alternating its eyes, so it makes sense to put that phrase closer to the word alternate.	Typically when authors are going to put a definition of a word or an example, they try to keep it close to the word it's defining. In addition, because the word "eyes" is missing in the phrase *shooting first from one and then the other*, it makes sense to have it come after the word *eyes* so that readers know from where the animal is shooting blood.
Is there anything you would add to this sentence to make it clearer?	They may alternate eyes, shooting [blood] first from one [eye] and then the other [eye].	Students may want to add in the [implied words] for clarity.

APPLY

During this part, students quickly apply their new knowledge about the sentence to their reading and writing. These are quick efforts and may be followed up with more practice.

Discuss: Turn and talk with a partner or small group. How does this sentence help us better understand the main idea:

> Horned lizards shoot blood to defend themselves from predators.

This helps us understand that the lizard can fight off its attackers by squirting blood at them. The horned lizard can shoot from one eye at a time. This way it can keep defending itself if the predator doesn't go away at first.

Writing focus: Invite students to work in partnerships and/or individually to come up with some of their own sentences using the sentence structure – and vocabulary word *alternate* – that Johnson uses in *When Lunch Fights Back*.

> **Showcase sentence:** They may **alternate** eyes, shooting first from one and then the other.

Heavy scaffold: The swimmers may alternate _____ (What?), starting first with _____ (What?) and then the _____ (What?).

Example: The swimmers alternate <u>arms</u>, starting first with <u>one arm</u> and then the <u>other arm</u>.

Light scaffold: _____ (Subject) alternate _____ (Noun), starting first _____ (With what?) and then _____ (What/noun or noun phrase).

Example: <u>The students</u> alternate <u>line leaders each day</u>, starting first <u>with someone who wears glasses</u> and then <u>someone who does not wear glasses.</u>

No scaffold: Invite students to emulate the showcase sentence within their own writing.

SENTENCE DIG R1.4: CONTEXT CLUES

Text: *Biodiversity: Eco Facts* by Izzi Howell, page 18

Grades: 2-4

Book summary: We're not alone in this world. As a matter of fact, one of the most amazing things about our watery planet is the biodiversity - the variety of life in our world. What's even more amazing than the variety of life in our world is the interrelationship between species. *Biodiversity: Eco Facts* is an informational book that explains how biodiversity is affected by climate change and human activity. The author helps the reader to understand the importance of biodiversity to food chains, habitats, and humans.

Showcase sentence: It's important | to encourage **sustainable** fishing, | in which people can catch enough | to support themselves, | and fish populations are protected | for the future.

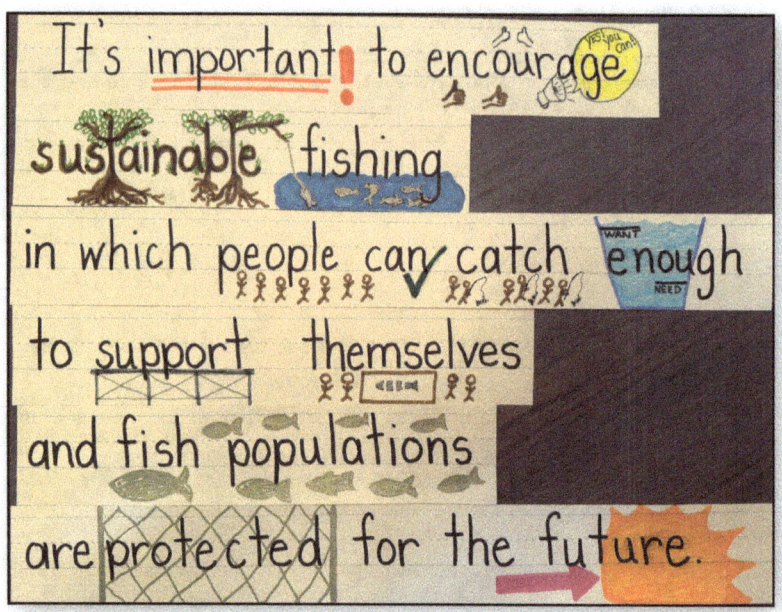

FIGURE 1.1
Annotated sentence dig with sketches to support comprehension

Rationale: I love this sentence because of its structure. It's a complex sentence with a compound dependent clause. This is known as a complex compound sentence. JUICY! Also, it uses the phrase **sustainable** *fishing*, but the word sustainable is never defined throughout the text. This sentence, however, unpacks the definition of what sustainable fishing looks like and supports the reader to infer the definition of sustainable (something that can continue for a long time without harming the environment). In addition, the word sustainable is in bold and is found in the glossary at the back of the book, offering a natural segue to discussions about how the glossary can be used to aid or even check our comprehension work.

How does understanding this sentence help the reader? How does it connect to the text? The section describes the pros and cons of legal fishing for food. The showcase sentence is the last sentence of this section - it summarizes the author's point. Understanding this sentence will help students articulate the author's point, the central message, and the definition of the word sustainable.

Discuss: In the text, the author makes the point that fish are a key resource for feeding people around the world. Today we'll study this sentence to determine how it contributes to the section's overall text structure.

TAKE APART

Remember, your chunks are on sentence strips. Move them around to help students focus on one chunk and then another. You'll move them back together later.

Chunk	Questions	Possible Answers
It's important	What does this chunk mean?	It's – it is important – critical or necessary
	Why do you think the author started with this wording – it's important…?	They're trying to draw our attention to this sentence.
	What is important? What is the big idea the author is leading us to in this sentence?	To encourage sustainable fishing.
to encourage **sustainable** fishing,	Turn and talk: What does it mean to encourage someone? Give an example to your partner.	To cheer someone on. To motivate someone to do something.
	What kind of word is *sustainable*? What is its job in the sentence?	Sustainable is an adjective describing fishing.
	What do you think sustainable means?	Sustainable fishing is when people catch just enough fish to eat *and* leave enough fish in the ocean so the population can recover. (If students don't know, hold that question and return to it later.)

(Continued)

Chunk	Questions	Possible Answers
in which people can catch enough	What do the words *in which* signal to the reader?	*In which* is acting as a relative pronoun to refer to sustainable fishing. The author is signaling to the reader that they are going to tell us what they mean by sustainable fishing.
	What does this chunk mean? What are people catching enough of?	This chunk means that people should only catch the amount of fish they need.
		NOTE: This cohesive device is an ellipsis. The author didn't use the ellipsis punctuation, but they did leave out the word "fish." The author expects the reader to infer the information – *in which people can catch enough fish.*
to support themselves,	How does this chunk help us understand how much fish is enough to catch?	To support themselves means to live – the amount of fish people need to live – food and income ($$$).
		You can also mention that the prepositional phrase tells us how much fish is enough to catch – *to support themselves.*
Look at the chunks: in which people can catch enough / to support themselves	When we put these chunks together, what is the author telling us about sustainable fishing?	Sustainable fishing is when people catch just enough fish that they need to live.
and fish populations are protected	What does this chunk mean?	The amount of fish (the population) is protected – or not in danger of dying out. There are enough fish left in the ocean to reproduce/recover the amount of fish that are caught.
	What is the importance of the word *and* at the beginning of this clause? How does *and* connect this chunk to the idea of sustainable fishing?	The conjunction *and* means in addition to... so it lets the reader know that sustainable fishing is both catching enough fish to live on AND that there are enough fish left in the sea to reproduce.

(Continued)

Chunk	Questions	Possible Answers
for the future.	What does this chunk mean?	This means not only today but also years from now.
	How does it add meaning to the sentence?	This adds meaning to the sentence by letting the reader know this is not about the short term or just today or this month – this is about protecting fish populations for the future – years to come.
If necessary, go back to the chunk: to encourage **sustainable fishing**	Turn and talk to your partner: What does the author mean by sustainable fishing?	Fishing that helps people live and helps to keep the fish population from extinction.
	What does the word sustainable mean?	Sustain means to keep something going – to be able to do something for a long time.
		Students might notice this word is in bold print and is listed in the glossary. If necessary, show them how to double check their inference by using the glossary.
		Sustainable fishing means to be able to fish for a long time – years in the future.

PUT TOGETHER

During this part, the sentence chunks may be mixed up or off to the side. Invite students to manipulate the chunks when putting the sentence back together and/or while rearranging them.

Ask	Possible Answers	Food for Thought
What is the correct order of this sentence?	It's important | to encourage sustainable fishing, | in which people can catch enough | to support themselves, | and fish populations are protected | for the future.	This is the kind of sentence that readers can get lost in due to the way information is layered throughout the sentence. Students may struggle to put this back together. You might consider asking some guided questions if needed. For example, remind students that the simple sentence is *It's important*. Everything else tells us what is important or why it's important.

(Continued)

Ask	Possible Answers	Food for Thought
		What's important? *To encourage sustainable fishing.* What is sustainable fishing? *In which people can catch enough* Catch enough fish to do what? *To support themselves* What else do we know about sustainable fishing – why is it important? *And fish populations are protected* For how long? *For the future.*
Can you rearrange the sentence and it still mean the same thing?	It's important to encourage sustainable fishing, in which *fish populations are protected for the future*, and *people can catch enough to support themselves.* Another way: *For the future*, it's important to encourage sustainable fishing in which people catch enough to support themselves and fish populations are protected.	You can switch the two characteristics of sustainable fishing.
Why do you think the author chose not to write the sentence this way?	The author likely put the part about people first in the sentence because the subheading is "supporting people."	This arrangement does make sense but the movement of "for the future" to the beginning of the sentence implies that the results won't happen right away. We have to do this (sustainable fishing) now so that later (in the future) people have enough to live on and fish populations will be protected. The author wants us to know we can do this right now – we can practice sustainable fishing now so people will have enough to live on (now) and in the future.
Is there anything you can remove from this sentence to make it clearer?	It's important | to encourage sustainable fishing, | ~~in which people can catch enough~~ | ~~to support themselves,~~ | ~~and fish populations are protected~~ | for the future. It's important | to encourage sustainable fishing, | in which people can catch enough | to support themselves, | and fish populations are protected | ~~for the future.~~	This option is clear and to the point, especially if the reader understands what sustainable fishing means. If the reader understands that sustainable means to last a long time, then you might not need the phrase *in the future*, as sustainable implies that.

(Continued)

Ask	Possible Answers	Food for Thought
Can you break this sentence into two or more sentences?	There are a variety of ways to do this. You might encourage students to do this in partnerships and/or on sticky notes. Here are some examples: *It's important to encourage sustainable fishing. Sustainable fishing allows people to catch enough fish to support themselves and the fish populations are protected.* *Sustainable fishing is important because people can catch enough fish to support themselves. It is also important because it protects the fish population.*	When students create two or more sentences, they will need to add words or reword parts of the sentence. As they share their sentences, consider asking them, *what did you need to change or add?* NOTE: Some students might approximate with this: *It's important to encourage sustainable fishing in which people catch enough fish to support themselves. The fish populations are protected.* If students do this, they're likely not recognizing that this is a complex sentence, not a compound sentence. They are simply putting a period where the conjunction "and" is in the original sentence. These students may need extra support recognizing when "and" is joining two independent clauses and when it is combining dependent clauses and/or phrases.

APPLY

During this part, students quickly apply their new knowledge about the sentence to their reading and writing. These are quick efforts and may be followed up with more practice.

> **Reading focus:** Turn and talk with a partner then write your response. How does our showcase sentence contribute to the overall text structure? Explain your thinking.
>
> **Showcase sentence:** It's important | to encourage sustainable fishing, | in which people can catch enough | to support themselves, | and fish populations are protected | for the future.
>
> Sample answers:
>
> This is a call to action sentence. The author is telling us to encourage sustainable fishing as a solution. It supports the text structure because it's in the conclusion.

(Continued)

This is a problem/solution text structure. The problem is overfishing, and the solution is sustainable fishing. Our showcase sentence is the solution, what people need to do.

This sentence shows us the solution to overfishing. We know this because it comes at the end. The beginning of the section talks about overfishing, which is not good. It's a problem.

Our showcase sentence is the author's solution to overfishing. It's a problem/solution text structure. The author starts by saying fishing is how many people survive in the world, but sometimes they overfish. Then the author says why overfishing is bad for the environment and fish populations. Eventually it hurts people because there will be no more fish to catch. So the solution is sustainable fishing – catch enough to live and leave enough fish to reproduce.

Writing focus: The author weaves in information about what sustainable fishing looks like in action – people catch enough to support themselves. Try writing a sentence in which you also show what a word or phrase looks like in action.

> **Showcase sentence:** It's important to encourage **sustainable** fishing, in which people can catch enough to support themselves, and fish populations are protected for the future.

Heavy scaffold: It's important to encourage _____ , in which _____ .
                                                 What?   What happens?

Example: It's important to encourage <u>recycling</u>, in which <u>students separate their trash from paper that can be recycled.</u>

Lighter scaffold: It's important to encourage _____ , in which _____ ,
                                                    noun   clause

and _____ .
         another action clause

Example: It's important to encourage <u>low carbon footprints</u>, in which <u>students walk to school, and schools reduce paper use with technology.</u>

No scaffold: Invite students to emulate the showcase sentence within their own writing.

CHAPTER 2
Important Details

>It's the little details that are vital. Little things make big things happen.
>- *John Wooden, Basketball Coach*

Details matter. They are the difference between a lone sentence and a paragraph. They have the power to make us feel happy, angry, sad, or even inspired. The just-right detail at the just-right time has been known to take readers from a quiet, tear dropping cry to an all-out sob with a runny nose and gasps for breath. Details matter.

Details matter with informational texts as well. They are the difference between an idea and a strong mental image. They have the power to build our understanding from basic ideas to more complex understandings. A just-right detail at the just-right time is like domino toppling - everything just starts clicking into place. They're the difference between a hmmm and an ah-ha! Details matter.

A while back, I was working with some second graders reading the book *Nefertiti The Spidernaut* by Darcy Pattison and illustrated by Valeria Tisnés. We came to this sentence: "But in the microgravity of the International Space Station, she hung almost weightless in mid-air, just as the scientists predicted."

"Readers, let's take a moment to dig into this sentence. Before we start, turn and talk to your partner. What do you think is happening in this sentence? What are you visualizing?"

"I don't get it. How did she hang in mid-air?" asked Issac.

"I'm sure it's on a string - that thread spiders spin," Isa replied as she used her hands to act it out for her partner.

"Where is the string (silk)? What's it attached to?" he wondered.

"The ceiling," Isa stated matter of factly.

"Ceiling? How did it get up there? What's microgravity?"

Details matter: they're the little things that make big things happen not only on a basketball court but in books too! A well-timed sentence dig, which we'll take a closer look at later in this chapter, helped Issac and Isa determine the meanings and effects of *microgravity* and being *almost weightless*. And, once we had a solid mental picture of the scene, we realized hunting was going to be really, really hard for Nefertiti, and some of us had our doubts... just like the scientists.

So when we encounter students who aren't reacting to a text at all, we might begin to wonder if they're missing some important details. It's not only that some students literally skip reading words, but many read a sentence without taking a moment to consider what it means or how it connects back to the text, and then just keep on reading. It's almost as if they mentally shrug their shoulder at the text. But, there's no shoulder shrugging in reading. Details matter.

Details alone don't make the text. Whether reading narratives, informational texts, nonfiction narratives, or even poetry, readers need to rely on their knowledge of the genre to provide a roadmap of sorts. Scarborough refers to this as Literacy Knowledge as its own thread in the reading rope (see Figure I.1 in the Introduction). When we think about the syntax and semantics thread of this rope, it's easy to keep it isolated at sentence-level comprehension. The goal, however, is to weave it together with the other threads, like literacy knowledge, to develop strong comprehension. I mention all of this because in order to build comprehension across a text, readers need discourse comprehension (Moats and Tolman 2019). This means that readers need to develop an understanding of the meanings in longer, cumulative segments of text. This includes developing comprehension of inter-sentence connections and links between larger segments of text. While students will greatly rely on their understanding of genre and text structure to support their comprehension, we can lean into the inter-sentence connections by keeping our sentence digs in context. Though we may pull the sentence out of the story or article to analyze it, we quickly place it back in context to consider its full effect. Our goal is not to understand one sentence; our goal is to build strong readers who comprehend full texts. That means students need to be able to articulate how specific sentences add to different elements of a text.

When we choose sentences for sentence digs, we should keep this in mind. We can think about how the sentences we choose to study add to the text whether it's to support a literary element in a narrative piece or the text structure in an informational piece. Engaging students in conversations around sentences and then making sure we're bringing it back to the context of the text will model a concrete way for them to grapple with details instead of overlooking them.

Across the rest of this chapter, we'll explore some sentence digs from both narrative and informational texts. We'll not only look at the meaning of the sentence standing alone, but we'll also look at that sentence through the lens of the context - how does this detail add to the text? What does it tell us about the character and why is it important? How does this detail support the author's point? What does it tell us about their position and why is it important to us as a reader? And, once we have a handle on these details, what new understanding do we have about the text? Details matter and we're going to dig in!

Before we do, find some sentences from what your students are reading now that are worthy of exploration. As you begin, consider what your students are studying. Are they learning about character motivation, theme, or how events impact each other? Then you might look for some sentence digs within those strong details. Are you studying text structure - compare and contrast or cause and effect for example? Then, consider finding a strong detail sentence that – once understood – will tie back to that structure. We need to scaffold kids into this strong work, so they can practice it with guidance before integrating it seamlessly into their reading strategy repertoire.

		SHOWCASE SENTENCES LESSONS AT A GLANCE		
Lesson	Focus	Literary Element/Text Feature	Title of Text	Sentence
R2.1	Participle phrases to add movement and details	Plot (climax)/ Theme	"The Save" by Joseph Bruchac found in *The Hero Next Door* edited by Olugbemisola Rhuday-Perkovich	"And that somehow Oren found himself **flying – like a big cat – right over the table**, knocking his grandfather to the floor as a shard of sharp metal spun over their heads."
R2.2	Relative pronoun to develop character	Characterization	"The Friend Who Changed My Life" by Pam Munoz Ryan (found on Commonlit.org)	"Indignant and humiliated, I refused to talk to Theresa, **who didn't seem to have any inhibitions about being chatty**."
R2.3	Introductory phrase with a coordinating conjunction	Problem/ solution text structure within a nonfiction narrative	*Nefertiti The Spidernaut: The Jumping Spider Who Learned to Hunt in Space* by Darcy Pattison	"**But in the microgravity of the International Space Station,** she hung almost weightless in mid-air, just as the scientists had predicted."
R2.4	Complex sentence structure – subordinating conjunction	Cause/effect text structure	*When Lunch Fights Back: Wickedly Clever Animal Defense Mechanisms* by Rebecca L. Johnson	"**When seabirds whose feathers are contaminated with fulmar chick vomit land on the ocean's surface**, they may not be able to take off again."

SENTENCE DIG R2.1: PARTICIPLE PHRASES: ADDING MOVEMENT AND DETAILS

Text: "The Save" by Joseph Bruchac, page 132

Grades: 4-6

Book summary: "The Save" is a short story within the collection *The Hero Next Door*. This story is about an Iroquois lacrosse player, Oren, who does not realize his own ability. He plays third string goalie and gets a chance to play in a game. Although nervous, Oren makes an amazing save that he thinks is just a fluke. Later, Oren makes another amazing save - his grandfather's life.

Showcase sentence: And that somehow | Oren found himself **flying - like a big cat - | right over the table,** | knocking his grandfather to the floor | as a shard of sharp metal spun | over their heads.

Rationale: This sentence comes at the climax of the story and is the catalyst to helping the main character, Oren, realize that he has amazing reflexes which makes him a good lacrosse goalie. This sentence uses participle phrases to add details about movement. Also, the sentence uses the word *like* to set off a simile but does not use the word "as" in the same way. In this case, "as" doesn't set off a simile or comparison but rather it acts as a subordinating conjunction connecting a clause to denote something is happening at the same exact time as something else. This can be tricky for readers (and teachers!) who have determined the words *like* or *as* always indicate a simile.

How does understanding this sentence help the reader? How does it connect back to the text? This sentence does a lot of work for the story. First, it's the climax of the story and this detail contributes to the theme of the story that being lucky can help us gain confidence in our skills. Readers can get caught up in Oren's perspective that his big save in the game was a "lucky" accident. However, this sentence shows the reader that Oren has strong reflexes and skills. It connects back to Oren wanting to be like a panther. Oren wanted to be more poised, athletic, and fast. Here, in this sentence, the author provides us with the imagery of Oren flying like a big cat - a panther.

Ask: How does this sentence contribute to the theme? *This sentence gives us another example of how Oren doesn't have to think about reacting to make a save, he just does it. He thinks he's just lucky, but he's actually skilled with his quick reflexes. NOTE: Students may not have a clear idea yet, and you can come back to this question at the end of the sentence dig or later in the text.*

TAKE APART

Remember, your chunks are on sentence strips. Move them around to help students focus on one chunk and then another. You'll move them back together later.

Chunk	Possible Questions to Ask	Possible Answers
And that somehow /	N/A	NOTE: We'll come back to this chunk during the Put Together segment. Students can get a strong mental image of the sentence without this chunk. The power of this part lies when we put this together and think about how it relates back to the text.
Oren found himself **flying** – **like a big cat** –	Who is this sentence about?	Oren
	What did Oren do?	He found himself flying like a big cat.
		Remind students that *Oren found* is the simple sentence – the simple subject with the simple predicate. The rest of the sentence chunks give us details to answer the questions: what, how, where, and when.
	To whom does the pronoun *himself* refer to?	Himself – Oren
	What does the author mean Oren *found* himself *flying*?	When the author uses the word *found* it indicates that Oren didn't really think about doing anything – he just reacted so fast that he realized later what happened.
		The author uses the word *flying* to describe how Oren must have leapt and dove some distance to reach his grandfather. (Consider having a student model this in *slow motion*.)
	Why do you think the author used dashes before and after *like a big cat*?	The author wanted to emphasize the simile because they want the reader to think back to Oren's wish to be more like a panther.
right over the table,	Where did Own fly?	Over the table – meaning he didn't go far. Humans can't really fly – he just was able to move through the air for the distance of the table.
knocking his grandfather to the floor	What does the word knocking mean in this chunk? How do you know?	Knocking means to collide with something or someone, with some force.
		We know this is the meaning because his grandfather was sitting at the table, but Oren was able to push him down to the floor.

(Continued)

44 SENTENCE DIGS

Chunk	Possible Questions to Ask	Possible Answers
as a shard of sharp metal spun	What is a shard? What do you think it means from what is happening in the story? What does the word *as* mean in this chunk? What does it indicate?	A piece or a fragment of metal or glass with sharp edges... usually occurs from something breaking or exploding. Here the word "as" does NOT indicate a comparison or a simile. Instead, it's telling us that this (the shard of sharp metal spun) happened at the same time as Oren knocking his grandfather to the floor.
over their heads.	Why is this chunk important to the sentence?	It tells us that the shard flew just over Oren and his grandfather's heads as they were on the floor. It just missed them. If Oren hadn't reacted, the shard would have hit his grandfather.

PUT TOGETHER

During this part, the sentence chunks you separated out for discussion earlier may be mixed up or off to the side. Invite students to manipulate the chunks when putting the sentence back together and/or while rearranging them.

Ask	Possible Answers	Food for Thought
What is the correct order of this sentence?	And that somehow | Oren found himself flying – like a big cat – | right over the table, | knocking his grandfather to the floor | as a shard of sharp metal spun | over their heads.	Some students may hesitate to start the sentence with *And that somehow*. They'll know from the capital letter that it starts the sentence, but many children have been taught to never start a sentence with *and*. You may note that this use of a conjunction helps the reader connect this sentence to the whole scene and that one small phrase lets us know that Owen was reacting not thinking. Sometimes writers do that – intentionally start a sentence with a coordinating conjunction. If your students are weary of the beginning of this sentence, be sure to ask the next question on this chart.

(Continued)

Ask	Possible Answers	Food for Thought
Why do you think the author started this sentence with *And that somehow*?	This chunk connects the phrase back to the paragraph. The word *And* at the beginning tells us there were other things happening at the same time or before this. The word *somehow* lets us know that Oren didn't think about his reaction – he just did it.	This sentence appears in a paragraph that starts off with "What happened next was hard for even Oren to explain." The word *And* does indicate another event in the list of things that happened. And the word *somehow* refers back to the topic sentence – this was hard for Oren to explain. Everything happened very fast... he reacted to a situation instead of thinking about it.
If you removed the transition phrase – *And that somehow* – is there a way to rearrange the sentence and it still makes sense?	As a shard of sharp metal spun over their heads, Oren found himself flying – like a big cat – right over the table, knocking his grandfather to the floor. Like a big cat, Oren found himself flying right over the table, knocking his grandfather to the floor as a shard of sharp metal spun over their heads. Knocking his grandfather to the floor, Oren found himself flying – like a big cat – right over the table as a shard of sharp metal spun over their heads.	Remember, this is a complex sentence. The subordinating conjunction and the clause following it can be moved from the end of the sentence to the beginning. The simile can also be moved to the beginning of the sentence. It's still comparing Oren to a big cat. The participle phrase, knocking his grandfather to the floor, is also movable in the sentence. It doesn't have the same clarity of the order of events as the original sentence, however.
Can you separate this sentence into two sentences? What do you have to do to make that work?	And that somehow Oren found himself flying – like a big cat – right over the table! He knocked his grandfather to the floor as a shard of sharp metal spun over their heads.	One way to create two sentences is to end the sentence after the word *table*. Add the subject *he* and change the participle *knocking* into the past tense *knocked*.
Why do you think the author chose to have one long sentence rather than two sentences?	The one sentence sounds like a lot is happening all at once.	The author may have opted for a longer sentence because a lot happened in this moment and it happened fast. Breaking the sentence into shorter ones may create a calmer and slower mood.

46 SENTENCE DIGS

APPLY

During this part, students quickly apply their new knowledge about the sentence to their reading and writing. These are quick efforts and may be followed up with more practice.

> **Discuss:** Turn and talk with a partner or small group. This sentence is at the climax of the story – the part of the story with the most tension and/or the turning point when the action begins to resolve the conflict. Remember, Oren is conflicted because he isn't confident in his athletic ability. He still thinks his great save in the game was a fluke – an accident. How does this sentence at the climax of the story begin to help Oren – and the reader – know that he is more capable than he realizes?
>
> Be sure to refer to other parts of the story as needed to support your ideas.
>
> **Writing focus:** We can use a simile set off by dashes to add emphasis to our writing too. Write a sentence about the picture you sketched using dashes to set off a simile.
>
> > **Showcase sentence:** And that somehow Oren found himself flying – **like a big cat** – right over the table, knocking his grandfather to the floor as a shard of sharp metal spun over their heads.
>
> **Heavy scaffold:** I leapt – like a _____ – off the bus, _____ through
>   noun or phrase to complete the simile   verb with -ing
>
> puddles as the rain fell over my head.
>
> *Example: I leapt – like a <u>grasshopper</u> – off the bus, <u>hopping</u> through puddles as the rain fell over my head.*
>
> **Light scaffold:** I _____ – like a _____ – off the bus, _____ _____
>   action (verb)   noun   -ing verb   Where?
>
> as the _____.
>   dependent clause – what else is happening?
>
> **No scaffold:** Invite students to emulate the showcase sentence within their own writing.

SENTENCE DIG R2.2: RELATIVE PRONOUNS: DEVELOPING CHARACTER

Text: "The Friend Who Changed My Life" by Pam Muñoz Ryan, paragraph 36

Grades: 4-6

Book summary: This memoir by Pam Muñoz Ryan is about a time when she was new in school and was bullied by another girl. Pam was encouraged to stand up for herself. This plan backfired as she ended up fighting her bully. Through their punishment of missed recess and a shared love for the library, the two forge a close friendship.

Showcase sentence: Indignant and humiliated, | I refused to talk to Theresa, | **who didn't seem to have any inhibitions about being chatty.**

Rationale: I love the contrast the author sets up between the two characters within one sentence. Using carefully placed verbs and a key appositive phrase, the author not only establishes some key characteristics of Pam and Theresa but also begins to hint at Theresa's motivation for bullying Pam in the first place. Later in the story, readers will again see Theresa react differently than expected which will help Pam come to a realization about Theresa's intentions.

How does understanding this sentence help the reader? How does it connect back to the text? This sentence helps the reader identify some big differences between the two characters. Pam is feeling angry and that her punishment is unjust - she didn't ask to be bullied and have to defend herself. While Theresa seems to not have a care in the world and uses the time to be chatty. The reader gets the impression that Pam will not want to be friends with Theresa, and the reader may find Theresa's character confusing as she acts like a bully and then like a friend. This confusion fuels the story for the main character as well until its resolution.

Ask: Today we'll study this sentence to think more deeply about character dynamics (how they interact with each other) and how they affect the story.

TAKE APART

Remember, your chunks are on sentence strips. Move them around to help students focus on one chunk and then another. You'll move them back together later.

Chunk	Possible Questions to Ask	Possible Answers
Indignant and humiliated, I refused to talk to Theresa, who didn't seem to have any inhibitions about being chatty.	NOTE: Start with the whole sentence before taking it apart. Who is the subject of the sentence? How do you know?	Students should note that the sentence is about Pam, the main character. We know this because the text is a memoir and the author uses the pronoun "I." NOTE: Some students will say the sentence is about both Pam and Theresa. Although we find out information about Theresa, the subject of the sentence is Pam. If students struggle with this, take away the extra phrases *Indignant and humiliated* and *who didn't seem to have any inhibitions about being chatty.*
Indignant and humiliated,	This chunk is telling us how Pam is feeling. Even if you don't know the definition of these words, based on the text, how is she feeling right now? What are some synonyms we can use for each of these words?	She is mad and upset. She may feel embarrassed to have to sit on the bench during recess for two weeks. She might feel like the situation isn't her fault – she was being bullied and she was just standing up for herself. As students mention these feelings, attach them to the words *indignant* and *humiliated*. For example, you might say, "Yes, she is mad because she thinks the situation is unfair. That's what indignant means – to be upset about being treated unjustly or unfairly." Indignant: upset about injustice, angry, mad Humiliated: ashamed, embarrassed
I refused to talk to Theresa,	Authors sometimes use shades of meaning to get their point across. Here, the author uses the phrase *refused to talk* rather than *ignored* or *turned away from*. What is the message or the connotation *refused to talk* gives the reader?	The phrase *refused to talk* seems to be laced with anger. When we ignore someone, we might be angry but we also might be disinterested or nonplussed with the situation. Here the author wanted us to know she was still hurt and mad and humiliated and she was going to do what she had the power to do – REFUSE to talk.

(Continued)

Chunk	Possible Questions to Ask	Possible Answers
who didn't seem to have any inhibitions about being chatty.	Who is this chunk talking about? How do you know?	This is talking about Theresa because the phrase is right next to her name. NOTE: Remind students that this chunk is an appositive. It is a part of a sentence that gives extra information about someone or something. Here, we find out how Teresa is acting. Or you can take the opportunity to remind students that *who* is a relative pronoun introducing a relative clause. It is referring back to Theresa. Theresa didn't seem to have any inhibitions about being chatty.
	What does this chunk tell us about Theresa?	She is talking a lot.

PUT TOGETHER

During this part, the sentence chunks may be mixed up or off to the side. Invite students to manipulate the chunks when putting the sentence back together or while rearranging them.

Ask	Possible Answers	Food for Thought
What is the original order of this sentence?	Indignant and humiliated, | I refused to talk to Theresa, | who didn't seem to have any inhibitions about being chatty.	Notice that the verbs referring to Pam are at the front of the sentence where the subject "I" is located. The appositive – the extra information about Theresa – is at the end of the sentence, closer to where Theresa is mentioned.
What are some synonyms we can use to replace *inhibitions*? What words would make sense here?	Indignant and humiliated, I refused to talk to Theresa, who didn't seem to have any _____ about being chatty. • Problem • Worries • Qualms	To avoid a long vocabulary lesson about the etymology of the word *inhibitions*, you can either tell students the definition or have someone quickly look it up in the dictionary. However, many students will be able to use the context and tone of the sentence to appropriately replace the word with a synonym.
How could you rewrite this sentence if you didn't use the word "who"?	Indignant and humiliated I refused to talk, but Theresa didn't seem to have any inhibitions about being chatty.	In order to keep this as one sentence, students will need a conjunction.

(Continued)

Ask	Possible Answers	Food for Thought
Work in partnerships if needed.	Indignant and humiliated, I refused to talk, while Theresa didn't seem to have any inhibitions about being chatty. Although Theresa didn't seem to have any inhibitions about being chatty, I refused to talk, feeling indignant and humiliated at the same time.	Consider giving the students a few minutes to work on this with a partner while writing their ideas on a sticky note. If time permits or on another day, sort the sticky notes with grammatically correct sentences into the type of sentence written: simple, compound, complex, or complex-compound, and ask students to defend their category choice. Giving students opportunities to analyze sentence structure, categorize them, and explain their choices helps them develop their understanding of different ways sentences are put together.

APPLY

During this part, students quickly apply their new knowledge about the sentence to their reading and writing. These are quick efforts and may be followed up with more practice.

> **Discuss:** Pam and Theresa are in trouble for fighting. What do their reactions tell us about each character? Why do you think Pam might find Theresa's reaction confusing?
>
> **Writing focus:** We can use a relative pronoun to add more information about a character. Try writing a sentence using the relative pronoun who to tell the reader more information.
>
> > **Showcase sentence:** Indignant and humiliated, I refused to talk to Theresa, **who didn't seem to have any inhibitions about being chatty.**
>
> **Heavy scaffold:** _____ and _____, I sat down next to my
>   *feeling*   *feeling*
> teacher, who _____.
>   *Something about the teacher*
> *Example:* <u>Eager</u> and <u>excited</u>, I sat down next to my teacher, who <u>chose me to read my story</u>.
>
> **Light scaffold:** _____ and _____, I _____ to
>   *feeling*   *feeling*   *verb phrase*
> _____, who _____.
>   *who?*   *a detail about the person*
> *Example:* <u>Queasy</u> and <u>tired</u>, I <u>stumbled</u> over to <u>my mom</u>, who <u>is a registered nurse</u>.
>
> **No scaffold:** Invite students to emulate the showcase sentence within their own writing.

SENTENCE DIG R2.3: COORDINATING CONJUNCTIONS: STARTING AN INTRODUCTORY PHRASE

Text: *Nefertiti The Spidernaut: The Jumping Spider Who Learned to Hunt in Space* by Darcy Pattison, page 14

Grades: 2-4

Book summary: This book chronicles the journey of Nefertiti, a jumping spider who is taken into outer space! Scientists wondered if a jumping spider, like Nefertiti, could adapt to a zero gravity atmosphere. The book outlines the spider's journey, the conditions she had to adapt to in outer space, and then her return back home. Although the book is illustrated, there are photographs and videos of Nefertiti readily available online to add to the reading experience.

Showcase sentence: But | in the microgravity of the International Space Station, | she hung almost weightless in mid-air, | just as the scientists had predicted.

Rationale: There are a lot of things I love about this sentence. For a reader, it's essential because the sentence indicates the setting and its effect on the spider. I also chose this sentence because students are taught **not** to start a sentence with the word *but*. However, when a published writer does it, they are signaling a change.

How does understanding this sentence help the reader? How does it connect back to the text? This sentence not only reflects the new setting in space, it also magnifies the problem of the book. The problem is Nefertiti doesn't know how to hunt without gravity. Can she adapt? The reader needs to understand this sentence to understand how hard this is for the spider. This sentence connects back to the text with the word *but*. The author is signaling a big change. The sentence before reads, "On Earth, Nefertiti jumped in an arc and almost never missed her prey." So what is the big change? There are two - one, Nefertiti is now in space at the International Space Station and two, ... she's going to miss her prey!

Ask: Looking at this sentence and thinking about the story, what has changed for Nefertiti? How do you know? (If students struggle to answer this, you can come back to it at the end of the sentence dig.)

52 SENTENCE DIGS

TAKE APART

Remember, your chunks are on sentence strips. Move them around to help students focus on one chunk and then another. You'll move them back together later.

Chunk	Possible Questions to Ask	Possible Answers
But	NOTE: Come back to this chunk when putting the sentence back together.	
in the microgravity of the International Space Station,	What does this chunk tell us about the sentence? Where do you think the International Space Station is? What do you think microgravity means?	It tells us where this is happening. It's in outer space, orbiting Earth. Someone may say *micro* means small and so it means small gravity or where there isn't a lot of gravity. Microgravity is what we call it when astronauts seem to be floating around while in space. They appear to be weightless because there is no gravity in outer space. You may need to explain that gravity is the force that holds us on the ground. It's why we don't float around on Earth.
she hung almost weightless in mid-air, /	Who is this sentence about? (Who is she?) How do you know? What is she doing? How does this chunk of the sentence connect to the previous one [in the microgravity of the International Space Station,]?	The sentence is about Nefertiti because the author uses the pronoun *she*. Also, a couple of sentences earlier, the author mentions Nefertiti by name. She is hanging in mid-air. Mid-air means with nothing around her – almost like she is floating. These connect because when we put the chunks together we know who the sentence is about, what she is doing, and where this is happening. Both chunks refer to being in outer space. Microgravity means to appear weightless, and the next chunk tells us that Nefertiti hung almost weightless.
just as the scientists had predicted.	What did the scientists predict? The experiment is to see if Nefertiti can adapt to hunting in outer space. Why would hanging almost weightless be a problem for a jumping spider?	That Nefertiti would just hang in the air. You can't jump if you're floating around. You have to be able to pop off the ground.

PUT TOGETHER

During this part, the sentence chunks may be mixed up or off to the side. Invite students to manipulate the chunks when putting the sentence back together and/or while rearranging them.

Ask	Possible Answers	Food for Thought
What is the original order of this sentence? Why do you think the author started this sentence with the conjunction *But*?	**But** | in the microgravity of the International Space Station, | she hung almost weightless in mid-air, | just as the scientists had predicted. The author is telling us Nefertiti isn't on Earth. The author is hinting that unlike on Earth, Nefertiti is going to struggle catching her prey.	The author uses the conjunction *but* to show contrast. The prior sentence tells us Nefertiti never missed her prey while hunting on Earth. *But...* NOTE: The author could have joined the two sentences together for a compound sentence. However, it would be terribly long. Also, by starting a new sentence with the conjunction *but*, the author seems to be emphasizing the contrast between the two worlds.
Is there a way we can rearrange this sentence?	Just as the scientists had predicted, | she hung almost weightless in mid-air, | in the microgravity of the International Space Station. [Remove the conjunction *but*] But, | she hung almost weightless in mid-air, | in the microgravity of the International Space Station, | just as the scientists had predicted. But, | just as the scientists had predicted, | she hung almost weightless in mid-air, | in the microgravity of the International Space Station. But, | just as the scientists had predicted, | in the microgravity of the International Space Station, | she hung almost weightless in mid-air.	Notice that students can rearrange the clauses and phrases to make different sentences that are grammatically correct. You might ask students which sentence they like the best and why they think the author chose to go with the order in the book. In most cases, students will want to keep the phrase – just as the scientists predicted – close to the prediction – she hung almost weightless in mid-air. In the final sentence offered, it's unclear if the scientists made the prediction while they were in the microgravity of the International Space Station or if their prediction is about the spider being in the microgravity of the International Space Station.
Is there a phrase or clause we can take out of the sentence and it still makes sense with the story? Follow up: Why do you think the author wanted these phrases/clauses in the sentence?	**But** | in the microgravity of the International Space Station, | she hung almost weightless in mid-air, | ~~just as the scientists had predicted~~. **But** | ~~in the microgravity of the International Space Station,~~ | she hung almost weightless in mid-air, | just as the scientists had predicted.	Although you can remove these from the sentence, each of these chunks give the reader important information. These phrases also help the reader to understand how important this moment was for the experiment – the scientists predicted correctly – while in space she would be weightless. This lets us know Nefertiti's hunting ways will have to change.

54 SENTENCE DIGS

APPLY

During this part, students quickly apply their new knowledge about the sentence to their reading and writing. These are quick efforts and may be followed up with more practice.

Discuss: Turn and talk to your partner: What has changed for Nefertiti? Why is this a problem for the spider? You can use details from the text (pages 14–15) to support your answer. (Sample answer: Nefertiti is now in space and not on Earth. It says she is in the International Space Station. This is a problem for her because now she is hanging in mid-air and can't jump in the same way. How will she get her prey?)

Writing focus: Writers can tell readers where something is happening at the beginning of the sentence. Practice telling the reader where something is happening by using the preposition in.

> **Showcase sentence: But** in the microgravity of the International Space Station, she hung almost weightless in mid-air, just as the scientists had predicted.

Heavy scaffold: But in _____ (Where?), she/he/they _____ (Do what? Action).

Example: But in <u>school</u>, she <u>read books</u>.

Light scaffold: But in _____ (noun), she/he/they _____ (verb) just as _____ (Who?) had _____ (verb).

Examples: But in <u>the football game</u>, he <u>ran faster than anyone</u> just as <u>the coach</u> had <u>taught him</u>.

But in <u>the war</u>, <u>George Washington led the troops</u> just as <u>the Continental Congress</u> had <u>asked him</u>.

No scaffold: Invite students to emulate the showcase sentence within their own writing.

SENTENCE DIG R2.4: COMPLEX SENTENCES: ESTABLISHING CAUSE AND EFFECT DETAIL

Text: *When Lunch Fights Back: Wickedly Clever Animal Defense Mechanisms* by Rebecca Johnson, page 25

Grades: 4-6

Book summary: *When Lunch Fights Back: Wickedly Clever Animal Defenses* by Rebecca Johnson is an informational book about how animals use defense mechanisms to defend themselves. The focus sentence is from Chapter 4 "Master Blasters." In the section "The Fulmar's Flipside," the author starts with a strong narrative scene of a fulmar chick defending itself as it vomits on its predator. The author then explains the science behind this defense mechanism. This showcase sentence shows the effect the vomit has on the predator - seabirds.

Showcase sentence: When seabirds | whose feathers are contaminated with fulmar chick vomit | land on the ocean's surface, | they may not be able | to take off again.

Rationale: This is a doozy. This is a good example of a sentence where I might have one focus for the whole group discussion and then have another focus for a small group discussion. As you read through the lesson, you might consider which questions are most important for your whole group and which questions are better left for small group instruction.

I chose this sentence because it represents a cause/effect text structure. The sentence itself has the structure, plus the detail is an effect of the fulmar chick's defense mechanism. Win-win! This is also a solid example of complex sentence structure, which includes a subordinating conjunction with a dependent clause starting the sentence and an independent clause following it. Finally, there is a relative pronoun - whose - that adds specific details about which seabirds the sentence is about. When kids read this sentence, they often do not know what the sentence is about or how many different kinds of birds are actually in the sentence. (There is only one but some students think there are at least two.) From this confusion and seemingly chaotic sentence structure comes clarity for readers who take the time to figure it out.

How does understanding this sentence help the reader? How does it connect back to the text? This supports the topic sentence, "In studying the effects of fulmar vomit on bird-feathers, scientists were surprised to discover it can be a potentially deadly defensive weapon." It also supports the main idea of the section: Fulmar chicks use vomit to protect themselves. Naturally, a reader should be asking themselves *How? How does vomit protect the chick? How does vomit on feathers potentially kill another bird?* This sentence is key to understanding the potential danger. In doing so, the reader now understands that the fulmar chick's vomit is not only gross but deadly as well.

Ask: 1) In nonfiction, we know that text structure can happen at the sentence, paragraph, and text levels. Zeroing in on this sentence, what type of text structure is it? How do you know? *Students may not be able to answer this question yet. If so, come back to it at the end of the lesson.*

2) Who or what is this sentence about? How do you know? *Students may reply seabirds because it is named first in the sentence. They may say seabirds and fulmar chicks because they see both birds named. Confirm that the subject is "seabirds" and we know because they are the ones that may not be able to take off again. You may also note that in this sentence, "fulmar chick" is an adjective phrase to describe what kind of vomit is on the seabirds' feathers.*

TAKE APART

Remember, your chunks are on sentence strips. Move them around to help students focus on one chunk and then another. You'll move them back together later.

Chunk	Possible Questions to Ask	Possible Answers
When seabirds	What does this subordinating conjunction (*when*) indicate? What is the author trying to signal?	At a certain time
	Who or what is the author talking about?	Seabirds
whose feathers are contaminated with fulmar chick vomit	How does this chunk connect to the first one – when seabirds…?	This tells us which seabirds – the ones with vomit on their feathers.
	What mental image does this chunk create for you?	Feathers have vomit (throw-up) all over them. A bird with vomit on it.
	What do you think the word contaminated means?	Students might use the words sick, poison, dirty. Contaminated means to soil, stain, or infect by contact.
	How many different kinds of birds are in this clause? How do you know?	One – seabirds, and not all seabirds just the ones with vomit on them. Fulmar chick is actually an adjective here describing what kind of vomit. There are no fulmar chicks (noun/animal) in the sentence.
land on the ocean's surface,	When we add this chunk to the two we have discussed, what does it tell us?	It tells us what the seabirds are doing at this time (when). NOTE: If students are confused by this idea of landing on water, consider using a duck as an example. A duck can "land" and sit on water as it paddles with its feet below the surface. Other birds can do this at sea as well.

(Continued)

Chunk	Possible Questions to Ask	Possible Answers
	Looking at these three chunks together *When seabirds whose feathers are contaminated with fulmar chick vomit land on the ocean's surface...* is this a complete sentence? Why or why not? (Turn and talk.)	Although the clause has a subject (seabirds) and a predicate (land on the ocean's surface), it is not a complete sentence. The word WHEN at the beginning keeps this from being a complete thought. We call this a dependent clause. This means it needs to be attached to a complete sentence to make sense.
they may not be able to take off again.	Is this a complete sentence? How do you know?	Yes. It has a subject, a predicate, and it is a complete thought. It can stand alone.
	Who or what is the pronoun *they* referring to? How do you know?	The pronoun *they* is referring to the seabirds. We know this because that is the subject of the dependent clause.
	What is happening in this part of the sentence?	The birds can't take off again.
	What does that mean – they *may not be able to take off again*?	*Take off* means to start flying (like a plane takes off).
	What can we infer will happen if the birds can't fly again?	If they can't take off again, they'll likely drown.

PUT TOGETHER

During this part, the sentence chunks may be mixed up or off to the side. Invite students to manipulate the chunks when putting the sentence back together and/or while rearranging them.

Ask	Possible Answers	Food for Thought
What is the original order of this sentence from the text?	When seabirds | whose feathers are contaminated with fulmar chick vomit | land on the ocean's surface, | they may not be able to take off again.	When a sentence has a dependent clause and an independent clause like this one, we call this a complex sentence.
Is there another subordinating conjunction we can use instead of the word *when*? Does it change the meaning of the sentence?	Subordinating conjunctions include: after, although, because, before, if, when, where, once… For example: ~~When~~ **Once** seabirds | whose feathers are contaminated with fulmar chick vomit | land on the ocean's surface, | they may not be able to take off again.	Talk through a couple of examples and discuss how it may change the meaning of the sentence. The word "once" would substitute nicely and "after" will work. Other conjunctions either won't make sense or change the meaning of the sentence. Allow students this inquiry opportunity to discover the effects of how one word can change a sentence.

(Continued)

SENTENCE DIGS

Ask	Possible Answers	Food for Thought
If time permits or on another day… If we took off the word *When*, what conjunction could we use to make this a compound sentence? Which conjunction will emphasize that the bird can't take off again as it usually would?	Seabirds whose feathers are contaminated with fulmar chick vomit land on the oceans' surface, **and/but/yet** they may not be able to take off again. …**but** they may not be able to take off again.	Students may realize there are three coordinating conjunctions that make sense in the sentence. Also note that this is a compound sentence because you now have two independent clauses. The conjunction *but* provides contrast and lets the reader know this is not normal for the bird. It can't take off again because of the vomit on its feathers.
Is there a phrase that we can take out of this sentence and have it still make sense? How does it change the meaning of the sentence?	When seabirds | ~~whose feathers are contaminated with fulmar chick vomit~~ | land on the ocean's surface, | they may not be able to take off again.	This chunk starts with a relative pronoun and gives extra information about the seabirds. Even though the sentence makes sense after removing this information, the removal does impact the meaning of the sentence. Now the sentence reads: When seabirds land on the ocean's surface, they may not be able to take off again. This sentence refers to all seabirds, which is not the author's intent.

APPLY

During this part, students quickly apply their new knowledge about the sentence to their reading and writing. These are quick efforts and may be followed up with more practice.

Discuss: Turn and talk: Why is the fulmar chick's vomit potentially deadly for some birds?

Writing focus: Writers often use complex sentence structure to combine ideas. Try writing some complex sentences using the sentence structure in the showcase sentence.

> **Showcase sentence: When seabirds whose feathers are contaminated with fulmar chick vomit land on the ocean's surface,** they may not be able to take off again.

Heavy scaffold: When _____ (Who or what?), whose _____ (detail about who or what) _____ (verb or verb phrase) _____ (Where/when/or how?), they may not be able to _____ (Do what? action).

Example: When <u>fulmar chicks</u>, whose <u>wings are not yet strong enough to fly</u>, <u>are attacked in their nests</u>, they may not be able to <u>protect themselves</u>.

Or When <u>students</u>, who <u>have been studying all day</u>, <u>talk loudly in the cafeteria</u>, they may not be able to <u>hear the fire alarm</u>.

Light scaffold: When _____ (plural noun) _____ (relative pronoun phrase/clause) _____ (verb or verb phrase) _____ (prepositional phrase/where?), they _____ (verb (with or without a preposition phrase)).

Example: When <u>fulmar chicks whose parents are gone are attacked in their nests</u>, they <u>vomit on their predator</u>.

Or When <u>students</u> <u>whose shoes are untied</u> <u>run</u> <u>on the playground</u>, they <u>may trip and fall</u>.

No scaffold: Invite students to emulate the showcase sentence within their own writing.

Thought Partners: _____

Sentence Dig R2.4
THINK SHEET: WRITING FOCUS

STRATEGY: Sentence Combining

Write the showcase sentence from the sentence dig in the space below:

Directions:

1. Cut out the sentence strips for each round.
2. In each round, work with a partner or small group to create 1 complex sentence using the sentences from the text, *When Lunch Fights Back: Wickedly Clever Animal Defense Mechanisms* by Rebecca L Johnson.
3. Take time to discuss the different subordinating conjunctions you could use and how it affects the sentence.
4. Discuss in which order the sentence should go.
5. Write one complex sentence for each round on your recording sheet. Color code the sentence: Green for the subordinating clause and yellow for the independent clause.

Subordinating Conjunctions Word Box					
after	as if	although	as long as	as	as though
when	whereas	whenever	wherever	where	while
unless	until	because	before	if	if only
in order that		since	so that		

Sentence Strips for Round 1:

The fulmar chick opens its mouth wide.
It's going to scream.

Sentence Strips for Round 2:

Scientists have discovered that fulmar chicks can defend themselves with vomit while hatching.
They are completely free of their shells!

Sentence Strips for Round 3:

The vomit gets on another bird's feathers.
No amount of cleaning and preening will remove it.

Recording Sheet:
Write a complex sentence from each round of your group discussions. Then color code the sentence: Color the dependent clause green and the independent clause yellow.

Round 1:

Round 2:

Round 3:

CHAPTER 3
Figurative Language

Some People

By Rachel Field

Isn't it strange some people make
You feel so tired inside,
Your thoughts begin to shrivel up
Like leaves all brown and dried!

But when you're with some other ones,
It's stranger still to find
Your thoughts as thick as fireflies
All shiny in your mind!

I was working with some fourth graders and showed them this poem. They weren't impressed. As one boy lamented, "We get it. Don't make people feel bad like an old dried up leaf. Be nice." Then I asked them to reread the poem, but instead of reading the word *people*, I asked them to substitute the word *books*. That same boy who was so bored with the idea of how people make us feel, that same boy who was ready to dismiss the poem, that boy's eyes lit up and he said, "YES! Books do that to me all of the time!" I then posed a few questions for their groups to discuss:

- Which books would you put with the first stanza? Why?
- Which books would you put with the second stanza? Why?

What I found to be so interesting as I walked around and listened to the groups is that the books they put with the second stanza weren't always easy to read. As one group said, "*The Library Dragon* (1998) goes with the second stanza. Not because we loved the story... it was okay. But we liked figuring out how the author was using the words to create a dragon-feel to the story." Another group added the Harry Potter (1997) books because they couldn't always figure out where Snape really stood throughout the series. Another group loved the book *Odder* by Katherine Applegate (2022) because it was written in poems and they got to imagine a lot of the story.

As I walked around and listened into these conversations, I thought I was going to be pulled into the talk around the first stanza. But what caught my attention was the talk around the second stanza. Students did love a good story, but they also loved the way these stories are written. Whether they could word it clearly or not, these young readers had expectations for a book that sparked their minds - and a good story wasn't enough.

Part of the fun of reading a juicy novel or an engaging informational text is thinking deeply about it. Don't you just love that *ah-ha!* feeling when a hidden layer of meaning is unraveled in a poem or a surprising theme emerges in a novel or even when a seemingly basic detail adds kapow to the overall article? This often happens when an author uses some sort of figurative language and we, the readers, figure out its hidden meaning for ourselves and in relation to the text.

We tap into these hidden layers by inferring. Learning to infer is a key reading skill.

Part of learning to infer involves a lot of language work with connectives and cohesive ties. It also involves integrating what's on the page with our relevant background and vocabulary knowledge. It's this integration that is necessary when unraveling the author's meaning behind the use of figurative language. Authors want us to stop and say - *wait a minute... what does this really mean? How does this add to the story? How does this help me understand the author's perspective?*

Figurative and nonliteral language are clues embedded in the text to help readers make inferences. Typically figurative language is used to express emotion, create the tone or mood of the piece, or may even express nuances in connotation. Sometimes the author will use it to symbolize bigger ideas or to layer details that add up later. The bottom line is that authors *want* readers to pay attention. In *The Reading Comprehension Blueprint* (2021, 170-171), Hennessy explains:

> the author expects that the students will mine the words of the text and tap into their inferential processes and skills to make sense of what is being read. IF the ultimate goal of proficient reading is a deep understanding of the author's intended meaning, then students must go beyond the surface code of the text. Understanding the underlying meaning and developing a situation or mental model depend on inferential processes.

Readers, once they get a hold of this work, often thrive on not only finding pockets of this kind of writing but also the challenge of cracking the code.

Using sentence digs for this work will help students build a routine for when they encounter language phrases that hold additional meaning. Understanding the author's meaning depends on reading the text and keeping the text in mind while digging into the sentence. It will also require students to pull from their own background knowledge and understanding of vocabulary to work out the meaning. Students with backgrounds that are different from the author or who are learning an additional language may struggle with this work. Sentence digs will help with this, but if more support is needed, you might consider doing more frequent and shorter digs in small groups.

SHOWCASE SENTENCES LESSONS AT A GLANCE

Lesson	Focus	Literary Element/Text Feature	Title of Text	Sentence
R3.1	Literal vs nonliteral language comparisons	Mood	*Juana & Lucas* by Juana Medina	"My **day is going downhill** faster **than** an *elefante* on a skateboard, and there is still more **than** half a day of school left."
R3.2	Simile	Plot/event	*Jovita Wore Pants: The Story of a Mexican Freedom Fighter* by Aida Salazar	"Jovita, her sisters, and Abuela **were scattered like pollen** across Mexico, forced to live with different relatives so they could be safe."
R3.3	Metaphor	Author's perspective	*What if There Were No Bees? A Book About the Grassland Ecosystem* by Suzanne Slade and Carol Schwartz	"But bees do **the work of giants**."
R3.4	Repetition for emphasis	Character development	*The Boy Who Drew Birds: A Story of John James Audubon* by Jacqueline Davies and Melissa Sweet	"**Every** shelf, **every** tabletop, **every** spare inch of floor, was covered with nests **and** eggs **and** tree branches **and** pebbles **and** lichen **and** feathers **and** stuffed birds: redwings **and** grackles, kingfishers, **and** woodpeckers."
R3.5	Simile	Event / character development	*Beauty and the Beak: How Science, Technology, and a 3D-Printed Beak Rescued a Bald Eagle* by Deborah Lee Rose, Jane Veltkamp et al.	"She clenched her talons tightly around it and swam to the shore, **using her wings like oars to row**."

SENTENCE DIG R3.1: LITERAL VS NONLITERAL PHRASES

Text: *Juana & Lucas* by Juana Medina, page 19

Grades: 2-4

Book summary: Juana lives in Bogotá, Columbia and loves to play with her dog Lucas, to draw, and to be with her abuelo. She does not like dancing, or getting in trouble, and she especially does not like learning English. However, her grandfather wants to take her to Spaceland in Orlando, Florida; in order to talk to the characters, Juana decides to try her best to learn English. In the end, she decides she wants to travel the world and learn many languages.

Showcase sentence: My **day is going downhill** | faster **than** an elefante on a skateboard, | and there is still more **than** half a day of school left.

Rationale: This sentence uses comparisons in three different ways, which can be challenging for readers. First, the author uses an idiom - my day is going downhill - to mean it's getting worse. Then she uses the comparison - faster than an elephant on a skateboard. This is to be taken nonliterally, as we would not see an elephant on a skateboard. However, it adds some dramatic flair to the sentence to emphasize how fast her day is souring. Finally, we have the literal comparison - there is still more than a half day of school left. I love the use of the word "still" as if the day isn't really going that fast - there is a lot more time for things to go wrong.

How does understanding this sentence help the reader? How does it connect back to the text? This sentence is building some tension. Already in the text, the character has had a couple of things happen that would upset most of our days. However, this sentence is saying there is more to come - the day gets worse. It's a sentence that, when understood by the reader and within the context of the text, will heighten the tension of the story and anticipation of the reader. What else can possibly go wrong? How bad are things going to get?

Ask: Looking at this sentence, what do you think it means? (Ask kids to turn and talk and then discuss as a group.) *Possible responses: Juana is having a bad day. Juana is going to have a bad day. Juana's day is going to get worse.*

Today, we're going to dig into this sentence and think about why the author used figurative language instead of just saying Juana is having a bad day. Why did the author go to the trouble of adding figurative language?

CHAPTER 3   Reading: Figurative Language   67

FIGURE 3.1
Annotated sentence dig with sketches to support comprehension

TAKE APART

Remember, your chunks are on sentence strips. Move them around to help students focus on one chunk and then another. You'll move them back together later.

Chunk	Possible Questions to Ask	Possible Answers
My day is going downhill /	Who is talking in the sentence? How do you know?	Juana – the personal pronoun MY reminds us that the narrator is the main character.
	What is this sentence about?	It's about Juana's day.
	What does this idiom mean – going downhill?	The idiom going downhill means things are worsening or going badly. So in the context of this sentence, Juana's day is getting worse.
faster than an elefante on a skateboard, /	What do you think elefante means?	Elephant
	Imagine an elephant on a skateboard going down a hill. Is that elephant moving fast or slow?	The weight of the elephant would make it go very fast. NOTE: Explain that this comparison is an example of nonliteral language. The author doesn't mean there is actually an elephant on a skateboard going down a hill. They're asking the reader to imagine that to understand how fast bad things are happening for Juana… faster than that imaginary elephant!
and there is still more than half a day of school left.	What does this chunk tell us?	How much time there is left in her school day – more than half. Plenty of time for a lot of things to go wrong.
	What time of day – morning or afternoon – is it? How do you know?	It's likely still morning. She has only been on the bus and has had math class.

PUT TOGETHER

During this part, the sentence chunks may be mixed up or off to the side. Invite students to manipulate the chunks when putting the sentence back together and/or while rearranging them.

Ask	Possible Answers	Food for Thought
What is the original order of this sentence?	My **day is going downhill** | faster **than** an elefante on a skateboard, | and there is still more **than** half a day of school left.	This is a compound sentence. Sometimes the order in a compound sentence doesn't matter; the placement of the conjunction *and* will help your students figure out the correct order.
Can this sentence be rearranged? If so, does it affect the meaning?	Faster than an elefante on a skateboard, | my day is going downhill, | and there is still more than a half a day left of school. There is still more than a half a day left of school, | and my day is going downhill | faster than an elefante on a skateboard. There is still more than a half a day left of school, | and faster than an elefante on a skateboard, | my day is going downhill.	This is a compound sentence and the two independent clauses happen at the same time. This means either can be first or second in the compound sentence. The comparison *faster than an elefante on a skateboard* needs to be next to what it's being compared to – her day going downhill.
Rearrange the sentence back to its original order: Why do you think the author decided to write the sentence this way?	My day is going downhill | faster than an elefante on a skateboard, | and there is still more than | half a day of school left.	It sounds more like a child. She is complaining about her day and then realizes that there is more than half a day left.
What can you remove from this sentence and it still has the same meaning?	My day is going downhill | ~~faster than an elefante on a skateboard,~~ | and there is still more than | half a day of school left.	You can remove the elephant comparison and the sentence holds the same meaning.
Can you make this one sentence into two sentences? Why do you think the author combined them?	My day is going downhill faster than an elefante on a skateboard. There is still more than half a day of school left.	The author might have combined the sentences to help the character sound exasperated and/or forlorn.

APPLY

During this part, students quickly apply their new knowledge about the sentence to their reading and writing. These are quick efforts and may be followed up with more practice.

Discuss: The author could have said: *My day is going poorly.* Or *I'm having a bad day and it's getting worse.* Instead she uses figurative language to say: *My day is going downhill faster than an elephante on a skateboard, and there is still more than a half a day of school left.* Why do you think she used figurative language? How does that help you, the reader, to better understand the character and what's happening in the story?

Writing focus: Authors often use comparisons in their writing to help readers visualize their words. In this showcase sentence, the author uses the word **than** to compare things. Try writing your own sentences with comparisons that use the word than.

> **Showcase sentence:** My **day is going downhill** faster **than** an elefante on a skateboard, and there is still more **than** half a day of school left.

Heavy scaffold: My _____(What?)_____ is going downhill faster than

_____(comparison – what?)_____ .

Example: My picnic is going downhill faster than a jaguar runs.

Light scaffold: My _____(noun)_____ is going downhill faster than

_____(comparison)_____ ,

and there's still _____(amount of time)_____ left.

Example: My picnic is going downhill faster than a jaguar runs, and there's still two hours left.

Thought Partners: _____

Sentence Dig R3.1
THINK SHEET: WRITING FOCUS

STRATEGY: Write & Sketch

Write the showcase sentence from the sentence dig in the space below:

[   ]

Directions: Using the sentence frame below, write a sentence like the showcase sentence. Then sketch the literal and nonliteral meanings.

My _____ is going downhill faster than _____,
         (event)   (comparison)

and there's still _____ left.
                        (amount of time)

Sketch the literal meaning of your sentence:	**Sketch** the figurative language of your sentence. What did you really mean?

SENTENCE DIG R3.2: SIMILE

Text: *Jovita Dreamed of Wearing Pants! The Story of a Mexican Freedom Fighter* by Aida Salazar and illustrated by Molly Mendoza, page 19

Grades: 3-6

Book summary: This is the true story of Jovita Valdovinos, a Mexican heroine in the 1930s. This story tracks back to the 1920s when her father commanded a battalion in the Cristero Revolution. As a child, the revolution took a deep toll on Jovita's family. At this time girls - women - did not wear pants nor fight on horseback - but Jovita eventually did. Jovita's story is an inspiring tale about family, survival, independence, and community written by her great-niece.

Showcase sentence: Jovita, her sisters, and Abuela/**were scattered like pollen**/across Mexico,/forced to live with different relatives/so they could be safe.

FIGURE 3.2
Annotated sentence dig with sketches to support comprehension

Rationale: This sentence has a subject with multiple people. Often, students will hold a subject like this as one entity. However, in this sentence the women are scattered like pollen - the subjects go different places. The sentence also provides a bit of an explanation for the simile, which is different. I also chose this sentence because it answers so many questions readers have, making it easy to break down: Who? Did what? How? Where? Why?

How does understanding this sentence help the reader? How does it connect back to the text? Understanding this sentence helps the reader track the chronology of Jovita's experiences. It also gives us another peek at how Jovita often felt helpless during her childhood and how those experiences built her determination to take action. This connects back to the text as it reveals to the reader how war affects everyone - and even today, people must flee their homes for safety.

Ask: Begin by asking students two general questions about the sentence:

- Who is this sentence about, and what happened to them? (*Jovita, her sisters, and Abuela were sent to live with different relatives so they could be safe.*)
- Do you think they went together to different relatives or did they each go separately to different relatives? (*Students may have conflicting answers and that's what we're going to discover through the sentence dig.*)

TAKE APART

Remember, your chunks are on sentence strips. Move them around to help students focus on one chunk and then another. You'll move them back together later.

Chunk	Possible Questions to Ask	Possible Answers
Jovita, her sisters, and Abuela were	What does this chunk tell us?	Who the sentence is about: Jovita, her sisters and Abuela.
were scattered like pollen	This is a simile – it is describing what happened to the women. What does scattered like pollen mean literally? What does the author really mean by this simile? How does it connect to the subject of our sentence: Jovita, her sisters, and Abuela?	Literally, scattered like pollen means to separate or break apart. Like when you blow a white, puffy dandelion and the seeds and pollen scatter. It means that Jovita, her sisters, and Abuela are scattered in different directions – they're separated.
across Mexico, NOTE: Leave this and the rest of the chunks off to the side and ask the questions first. Then pull out the correct chunk.	Which chunk of the sentence tells us *where* the women were scattered? Do you think the girls were near each other? What makes you think this?	Across Mexico No they were not near each other. Mexico is a large country. The word *across* means from one side to the other.
forced to live	Which chunk tells us what else happened to the women? What kind of feeling does the word *forced* bring to this sentence?	Forced to live It's harsh; it feels bad. They likely didn't want to be separated and live somewhere else.
with different relatives	Who did these women go to live with? What are some examples of relatives?	Different relatives Family: aunts, uncles, or cousins
so they could be safe.	What does this final part of the sentence tell us? Which word signals to the reader that this tells us *why* they left?	It tells us why they had to go live with other relatives. The coordinating conjunction *so* means *for this reason*. It answers the question *why*?

CHAPTER 3   Reading: Figurative Language

PUT TOGETHER

During this part, the sentence chunks may be mixed up or off to the side. Invite students to manipulate the chunks when putting the sentence back together and/or while rearranging them.

Ask	Possible Answers	Food for Thought
What is the original order of the sentence?	Jovita, her sisters, and Abuela | were **scattered like pollen** | across Mexico, | forced to live with different relatives | so they could be safe.	Some students will be tempted to put | so they could be safe | after the comma near the word Mexico. This signals that students are relying on punctuation to tell them where to put conjunctions rather than using the meaning of the sentence. Although punctuation is a great clue, with longer sentences, it shouldn't be relied on as the only clue. Meaning matters.
What if we took out the simile *scattered like pollen* – how does this change the meaning of the sentence?	Now the reader may think that the women stayed together – moving to live with relatives.	This simile carries an important detail. You might help students understand how difficult it was first to flee their home and second to have to be separated from the people you love.
Is there another way we can arrange this sentence?	Scattered like pollen | across Mexico, | Jovita, her sisters, and Abuela | were forced to live with different relatives | so they could be safe. So they could be safe, | Jovita, her sisters, and Abuela | were scattered like pollen, | forced to live with different relatives | across Mexico.	This sentence has a lot of different options for arranging the phrases and clauses. You might begin this activity with students in small groups using small paper strips with the chunks written on them for students to manipulate and discuss. Then have the groups bring their favorite back to the whole class and discuss why the order they created helps them understand the sentence, character, and/or story better.

SENTENCE DIGS

APPLY

During this part, students quickly apply their new knowledge about the sentence to their reading and writing. These are quick efforts and may be followed up with more practice.

Discuss: Let's focus on the last part of this sentence: *so they would be safe*. Why do you think it was important to Papá for Jovita, her sisters, and abuela to live apart? How do you think that kept them safe?

Write: The author uses a simile with a prepositional phrase to tell us what happened to the girls, how it happened, and where. Let's try it.

> **Showcase sentence:** Jovita, her sisters, and Abuela **were scattered like pollen** across Mexico, forced to live with different relatives so they could be safe.

Heavy scaffold: _____ were _____ like
                              Who?   Subject (plural)

_____ across _____.
  What happened? (noun)   Where?

Example: The chickens were chased like mice across the farmyard.

Light scaffold: _____ were _____ like
                              Who? Subject (plural)   Verb

_____ _____,
    Noun   Where? (prepositional phrase)

_____ to _____ so
  What else happened? (verb)   Do what? (verb)

_____.
  Why? (independent clause)

Example: The chickens were chased like mice across the farmyard, panicked to escape the fox so they could lay their eggs in peace.

My friends and I were attached like velcro in the amusement park, determined to stay together so we wouldn't get lost in the crowds.

SENTENCE DIG R3.3: METAPHOR

Text: *What If There Were No Bees? A Book About the Grassland Ecosystem* by Suzanne Slade and illustrated by Carol Schwartz, page 2

Grades: 2-4

Book summary: The grassland is an ecosystem found all over the world. Bees are one species within that ecosystem. They famously carry pollen from plant to plant and make honey. But, how does this small insect affect the world around them? Are they really *that important* to the ecosystem? What would happen if they disappeared? This text looks at the chain reaction if bees were to disappear and the giant effect it would have on the entire ecosystem.

Showcase sentence: But bees do|the work of giants.

Rationale: This is a short but powerful sentence. It is a metaphor that students often read past without much consideration. The beauty of the metaphor lies within the size of the things being compared. Bees, being so small, can only do small amounts of work. Giants, who are big and strong, can do big, grand things. Yet, this metaphor lets the reader know the work bees do is not what you'd expect of a small insect. The work they do is massive - giantlike.

How does understanding this sentence help the reader? How does it connect back to the text? It establishes the author's perspective that bees are not a pesky insect or simply honey makers. They are a *huge* part of the ecosystem. This sentence at the beginning of the book sets the reader up to think *big*. What is the big deal about bees? What is BIG about their work? This sentence quickly establishes the impact the author hopes to make by the end of the book that bees are essential and worth saving.

Ask: Depending on your students' background knowledge, explain that a metaphor is a type of figurative language that compares without the words *like* or *as*. Display the showcase sentence and ask - what is being compared? *Students may answer - bees are being compared to giants. If so, ask them to pause on that question and come back to it after the dig.* The sentence is actually referring to the impact bees have on the ecosystem - the bees' work is big, huge, giant.

TAKE APART

Remember, your chunks are on sentence strips. Move them around to help students focus on one chunk and then another. You'll move them back together later.

Chunk	Possible Questions to Ask	Possible Answers
But bees do	Who or what is the sentence about? What is the verb in this sentence? What does the conjunction *but* signal at the beginning of this sentence?	Bees Do The conjunction *but* signals a contrast. The sentences before this one talk about the bee being tiny compared to other animals. Its size is small, but...
the work of giants.	This is a metaphor. What is it about? What is the bees' work being compared to? What do you know about giants? What does that word make you think? NOTE: Authors sometimes use the word *giant* as an adjective to describe things as being mighty or big. What are some other synonyms for the adjective *giant*?	The work bees do NOTE: If students just say *the work* then ask them – *what work? ... whose work?* – to help them connect it back to the subject of the sentence. The work of giants They're big. They're strong. They can do big things. Massive, huge, gigantic, colossal, large

PUT TOGETHER

During this part, the sentence chunks may be mixed up or off to the side. Invite students to manipulate the chunks when putting the sentence back together and/or while rearranging them.

Ask	Possible Answers	Food for Thought
Can we rearrange this sentence?	No	This is a simple sentence that needs to keep its order. In addition, the conjunction *but* needs to start the sentence because it is connecting the sentence to previous ideas in the paragraph.
What if we changed the word *giants* to... ...grasshoppers ...babies ...100 humans ...how does the meaning change?	...*grasshoppers* – Grasshoppers don't do work; they just jump around. This would make it sound like the bees' work is playful and without purpose. ...*babies* – Babies are helpless. They don't do any work and need someone to take care of them. This would change the meaning to mean the bees' work is to make others work for them. That doesn't make sense. ...*100 humans* – 100 humans is a lot of people. They can do a lot of work. This makes it sound like the bees' work is a lot... they do a lot.	By substituting the word *giants* with other antonyms and synonyms, we can help students realize the impact of the metaphor and why the author compared the bees' work to giants'.

(Continued)

Ask	Possible Answers	Food for Thought
How can you say this sentence in your own words?	*Bees do big work.* *Bees have a giant job to do.* *Bees do important work.*	Listen for students to keep the same idea that the metaphor establishes – bees do important or big work.

APPLY

During this part, students quickly apply their new knowledge about the sentence to their reading and writing. These are quick efforts and may be followed up with more practice.

Discuss: After reading the whole book, come back to this sentence. How does this sentence (metaphor) reveal the author's perspective? Use examples from the text to support your ideas.

Writing focus: Writers often use a metaphor to make a comparison. Practice creating some metaphors.

> **Showcase sentence:** But bees do the work of giants.

- Create a word bank of other words authors might use in metaphors for BIG. Students can work with partners or small groups to create their own word bank by thinking of nouns that are big or huge.

Example word bank:

> mountain   skyscraper   elephant   giraffe   boulder   monster   truck

- Together, create a poster that shows some examples using these nouns in metaphors and draw a quick sketch beside them.

Example: Staying up late, I finally finished folding **the mountain of laundry** *on my bed.*
In front of the door, **the guard was a boulder** *letting no one in.*

SENTENCE DIG R3.4: REPETITION FOR EMPHASIS

Text: *The Boy Who Drew Birds: A Story of John James Audubon* by Jacqueline Davies and Illustrated by Melissa Sweet, page 10

Grades: 3-5

Book summary: Birdwatching. It's a favorite pastime of many - young and old. John Audubon contributed significantly to what we know about birds in North America through his drawings and observations. So much so that the Audubon Society was named in his honor. This is a nonfiction narrative that describes the early life of John Audubon, his passion for birdwatching, and the things he learned from watching these flying creatures.

Showcase sentence: Every shelf, **every** tabletop, **every** spare inch of floor, | was covered | with nests **and** eggs **and** tree branches **and** pebbles **and** lichen **and** feathers **and** stuffed birds: | redwings and grackles, kingfishers, and woodpeckers.

Rationale: This sentence holds a lot of information for the reader to process. It's long with a lot of different kinds of punctuation. Students can often get overwhelmed with a sentence this long and glaze over it. Yet the artful use of repetition (every, and) helps the reader build a dizzying yet accurate mental image. In addition, the author uses repetition to form a list to create a feeling of being overwhelmed and then uses a colon to indicate a list that will be more like a shopping list - straightforward and to the point.

How does understanding this sentence help the reader? How does it connect back to the text? Not only does it help us envision the setting - his living space - but it gives us a stronger insight into the obsession John Audubon has with birds. He doesn't just like watching them in nature, he brings artifacts into his home to roost. And they're everywhere!

This connects back to the text in two ways. First, it connects to the sentence before it that says, "He climbed straight to his attic room - his musée, he called it." The author tells us *where* the character is and then in the next sentence, our showcase sentence, describes the room. This is tricky because the author doesn't mention the room in the next sentence; kids need to infer that's the space the author is describing.

Also, it establishes that John Audubon is looking very closely, he's studying and analyzing the birds, their habits, and their habitats. Further in the text, we find John questioning the bird "experts" at that time. As readers, we trust John's perspective because he has spent so much time studying birds. So this sentence also helps us build our mental image around the character John Audubon.

Ask: Who or what is this sentence about? How do you know?

CHAPTER 3 Reading: Figurative Language

TAKE APART

Remember, your chunks are on sentence strips. Move them around to help students focus on one chunk and then another. You'll move them back together later.

Chunk	Possible Questions to Ask	Possible Answers
Every shelf, every tabletop, every spare inch of floor,	What is this sentence focused on in the attic room?	Every shelf, tabletop, and spare inch of floor.
	Do you think there is more than one shelf, tabletop, and spare inch of floor? Why or why not?	Yes there are more than one. The repeated word *every* indicates not just one but every single one… meaning there is more than one in the room and they're all involved!
was covered	How does this verb phrase connect to the previous sentence chunk?	It's telling us the shelf, tables, and floor are covered with something.
		There is something on the shelves, table tops and floor.
		Covered means you can't see what's underneath. So whatever is on the shelves, tabletops, and floor is so much that you can't see the surface of them.
with nests and eggs and tree branches and pebbles and lichen and feathers and stuffed birds:	What does this chunk tell us?	What is on the shelves, tabletops, and floor.
	How does this make you feel as a reader? What does it make you think about the room?	It makes me feel like there is a lot (overwhelmed) in the room. It makes me think the room is a mess – that there is too much.
		It gives a mental image of being disorderly.
	How does the author establish this feeling for the reader?	The author repeats the word *and* over and over. This makes the reader feel like things are being piled on and on.
	The author uses a colon (:) at the end of this phrase. Why do you think they did that?	The colon is used to signal a list. Using it right after the word *birds* indicates that now the author is going to add another list of the stuffed birds in the room.
		In this sentence, the colon is like the end of an infomercial – *but that's not all – he also has these stuffed birds…!*
redwings and grackles, kingfishers, and woodpeckers.	What is this a list of? What in the sentence helps you know this?	It's a list of stuffed birds in John's room.
		The colon after *stuffed birds* tells us that the list will tell us more about the stuffed birds.

PUT TOGETHER

During this part, the sentence chunks may be mixed up or off to the side. Invite students to manipulate the chunks when putting the sentence back together and/or while rearranging them.

Ask	Possible Answers	Food for Thought
What is the correct order of this sentence?	Every shelf, every tabletop, every spare inch of floor, | was covered | with nests and eggs and tree branches and pebbles and lichen and feathers and stuffed birds: | redwings and grackles, kingfishers, and woodpeckers.	Due to its length, students may need a few moments (or tries) to reorder this sentence as the punctuation may not be helpful.
What if we took out all of the repetition? Would that change the meaning or the connotation (feeling) of the sentence? NOTE: Use sticky notes to quickly cover the repeated words.	Every shelf, ~~every~~ tabletop, ~~every~~ spare inch of floor, | was covered | with nests ~~and~~ eggs ~~and~~ tree branches ~~and~~ pebbles ~~and~~ lichen ~~and~~ feathers and stuffed birds: | redwings ~~and~~ grackles, kingfishers, ~~and~~ woodpeckers.	It doesn't change the meaning, but it doesn't feel as overwhelming. You still get the sense that there is a lot there. The repeated words – *every* and *and* add emphasis and a bit of rhythm.
How can you say this sentence in your own words? Challenge students to use fewer words.	The room was filled with bird items. The shelves, tables, and floor were covered with everything having to do with birds. The room was a mess with bird stuff and stuffed birds.	In order to trim this sentence, students will need to use collective nouns or nouns that encompass the vast variety of items to reign in the description.

APPLY

During this part, students quickly apply their new knowledge about the sentence to their reading and writing. These are quick efforts and may be followed up with more practice.

Discuss: Why do you think the author included this sentence in the story? What do they really want us to know about John Audubon?

Writing focus: When authors use repetition, they want us to pay attention. In this case, Jacqueline Davies wants us to pay attention to the setting because it reveals information about the main character.

> **Showcase sentence: Every** shelf, **every** tabletop, **every** spare inch of floor, was covered with nests **and** eggs **and** tree branches **and** pebbles **and** lichen **and** feathers **and** stuffed birds: redwings and grackles, kingfishers, and woodpeckers

Try it: Write a sentence about a scene/setting using repetition.

Heavy scaffold: Every _____ (something big), every _____ (something medium), every _____ (something small) was _____ (verb) with _____ (What?) and _____ (What?) and _____ (What?) and _____ (What?).

Example: Every <u>wall</u>, every <u>bookcase</u>, every <u>desk</u> was <u>layered</u> with <u>charts</u> and <u>posters</u> and <u>paper</u> and <u>notebooks</u>.

Light scaffold: Every _____ (noun), every _____ (noun), every _____ (noun) was _____ (verb) with _____ (noun) and _____ (noun) and _____ (noun) and _____ (noun) and _____ (noun) and _____ (noun) and _____ (noun – category) : _____ (noun (example of category)) and _____ (noun (example of category)), _____ (noun (example of category)), and _____ (noun (example of category)).

Example: Every <u>wall</u>, every <u>bookcase</u>, every <u>desk</u> was <u>layered</u> with <u>anchor charts</u> and <u>posters</u> and <u>paper</u> and <u>notebooks</u> and <u>rulers</u> and <u>pencils</u> and <u>textbooks</u>: <u>reading</u> and <u>math</u>, <u>social studies</u>, and <u>science</u>.

SENTENCE DIG R3.5: SIMILE

Text: *Beauty and the Beak: How Science, Technology, and a 3D-Printed Beak Rescued a Bald Eagle* by Deborah Lee Rose, Jane Veltkamp, et al., page 9

Grades: 2-4

Book summary: Beauty is the perfect moniker for this bald eagle. Filled with majestic grace and overwhelming strength, Beauty thrives in her natural habitat in Alaska. Until one day, she is shot and left for dead. But she wasn't dead, and she summoned the strength to survive despite losing the top half of her beak. Found, she was taken to a wildlife center and then to a raptor center. Here, Beauty's life would change again as a raptor biologist and a bioengineer worked together to recreate her beak using a 3D printer. This amazing true story will capture the hearts and minds of readers and writers of all ages.

Showcase sentence: She clenched her talons tightly around it | and swam to the shore, | **using her wings** | **like oars to row.**

Rationale: Tucked into the participle phrase is a simile that gives readers a strong mental image of the eagle's wing strength. In addition, this sentence is loaded with pronouns with different antecedents. This can be difficult for students to track what is happening in the sentence.

How does understanding this sentence help the reader? How does it connect back to the text? This simile, this scene in the book, helps the reader develop a clear picture of just how strong and able this eagle is in the wilderness. It builds the readers' understanding of how the eagle uses all of its body parts for survival. Creating this sense of awe for the bird will help the reader feel the shock and anguish over the bird's injury and losing the use of its beak. Finally, the sentence sets the reader up to truly marvel at the solution - a prosthetic beak - and how the eagle adapts to its new parts.

Ask: Before we dig into this sentence, let's clarify the pronouns: *she, her, it, her.* Who or what is *she* in this sentence? Who or what is *it* in this sentence? How do we know?
She - Beauty, the eagle - The very first sentence in the paragraph specifically says "the eagle" is swooping down to get the fish. So we know "she" is Beauty, the eagle.
her - Beauty, the eagle - Both times "her" is next to a bird body part (talons, wings), so we know the author is referring to Beauty, the eagle.
it - large fish - The sentence right before this one refers to the fish being too heavy to lift. So we know "it" refers to the fish; the eagle clenched the fish in her talons.

Consider writing or drawing a quick sketch above these words to help students remember what/who we are referring to in the sentence as we dig into it.

TAKE APART

Remember, your chunks are on sentence strips. Move them around to help students focus on one chunk and then another. You'll move them back together later.

Chunk	Possible Questions to Ask	Possible Answers
She clenched her talons tightly around it	What are talons? What does clenched mean? Act this out: show me how you can clench with your hands. Now do that with your toes without taking off your shoes.	The bird's claws (feet). Clenched means to grab tightly – like making your hand into a fist.
and swam to the shore,	Who/what swam to shore? How do you know? What is another word or synonym for *shore*? What does this chunk mean?	Beauty swam to shore. We know this because the conjunction *and* signals that Beauty did two things: she clenched the fist *and* swam to shore. Land, beach, coast, edge of lake The eagle swam to shore.
using her wings	What does this participle phrase tell us? (What does this describe?) Act it out: With your arms, show me how an eagle might use its wings to swim.	This describes how the eagle swam to shore – she used her wings.
like oars to row.	What does this chunk describe? What is the author referring to when they say *oars to row*? What is the author trying to tell us?	This tells us how the eagle is using its wings. She is referring to a paddle you can use with a rowboat. The bird isn't really rowing a boat, but she has her back to the land and she is moving her wings backwards – moving water away from her – as if she was in a rowboat. Act it out for clarity.

84 SENTENCE DIGS

PUT TOGETHER

During this part, the sentence chunks may be mixed up or off to the side. Invite students to manipulate the chunks when putting the sentence back together and/or while rearranging them.

Ask	Possible Answers	Food for Thought
What is the original order of this sentence?	She clenched her talons tightly around it | and swam to the shore, | using her wings | like oars to row.	This is a beautiful example of a simple sentence with some complexity. This sentence has a compound predicate with a participle phrase and a simile. But it's not a compound sentence, nor a complex sentence. Because this is a longer sentence and has some different kinds of phrases, students may have trouble identifying it as a simple sentence.
Is there another way we can write this sentence? What do you have to change to rearrange the sentence?	Using her wings | like oars to row, | she swam to the shore | clenching her talons tightly around it.	Using her wings like oars to row has to stay close to the verb swam, as it describes how she is swimming. In doing so, you need to change clenched to a participle or you can put it in a prepositional phrase – as she clenched her talons tightly around it.
What happens if we remove the chunks *using her wings like oars to row*? Does the sentence still make sense? Why do you think the author included that last comparison?	She clenched her talons tightly around it | and swam to the shore, | ~~using her wings | like oars to row.~~	The sentence still makes sense and means the same thing. The author includes the comparison so the reader can visualize how the eagle was swimming. Most people don't know eagles can do that.

APPLY

During this part, students quickly apply their new knowledge about the sentence to their reading and writing. These are quick efforts and may be followed up with more practice.

> **Discuss:** Why do you think the author took time to tell us this about Beauty? What does the author want us to know about this eagle? (Use evidence from the text to support your answers.)
>
> **Writing focus:** The authors, Rose and Veltkamp, teach us that we can use a simile in a participle phrase. We have also learned a lot about Beauty the bald eagle. Try writing another sentence about Beauty, using a simile in a participle phrase.
>
> | **Showcase sentence:** She clenched her talons tightly around it and swam to the shore, using her wings like oars to row. |
> |---|
>
> **Heavy scaffold:** Beauty _____, _____ like
>   Does what?   How? participle (verb + ing) phrase
>
> _____.
>   What?
>
> *Example: Beauty <u>flew from her nest</u>, <u>taking off</u> like <u>a rocket</u>.*
>
> **Light scaffold:** Beauty _____ and _____,
>   verb or verb phrase   verb or verb phrase
>
> _____ like _____.
> How? participle phrase   What? (comparison)
>
> *Example: Beauty <u>perched in the tree</u> and <u>looked around the forest</u>, <u>thinking about her next meal</u> like <u>a hungry teenager.</u>*
>
> **No scaffold:** Invite students to emulate the showcase sentence within their own writing.

SECTION 2
Digging into the Craft of Writing

*The ear demands some variety. Now listen. I vary the sentence length,
and I create music. Music. The writing sings.*
- Gary Provost (2019)

Have you ever had a student who can tell you (orally) what they want to write with such excitement that their face lights up and their hands move this way and that? You send them off and check in a few minutes later... to find they've only been able to draft a couple of sentences. Or maybe you've had a student who writes and writes and writes but you realize they have repeated and repeated and repeated because they can't seem to figure out how to express the big ideas they have? Yup. Me too. And like me, you've likely come to realize that, while students have lots of great ideas in their heads, they often don't have the language structures to express them. When we think about syntax and semantics through the lens of writing, we consider how we can intentionally apply a variety of language structures to put sentences together in ways that engage readers while reflecting big ideas. Sometimes these sentences will be short. Sometimes they'll be medium length. And sometimes, when the ideas are big and the writing juices are flowing, students will be able to build sentences that make the writing teacher in us say - I taught them to do that! - while, deep in our hearts, marveling at the talent it took to compose such a delicious sentence.

In this section, we'll approach sentence digs from a writer's perspective. We'll still consider the work of the author and its effects on the reader. We'll still use sentences from texts students are studying. We'll still use the same routine to take the sentence apart, put it together, and apply it to our writing. However, as we explore sentences through our writer's eye, we'll focus more on the impact the author's choices have to support the meaning of the overall text as we look for opportunities to transfer those same craft moves to enhance student writing projects.

It's important to note that we'll be keeping this work in context by doing two things. First, we're leveraging sentences directly from the texts students are reading. Throughout each lesson, we'll be referring back to the whole text and/or text element where the sentence is found. This will help students consider the writer's choices and the impact syntax and semantics have at the sentence level as well as on the whole piece of writing. In addition, we'll keep this work in context by leveraging student conversations. Students need opportunities to talk to each other - whether with partnerships, triads, or small groups. Encourage lively, ongoing conversations throughout the lesson and as students move to apply the work. Finally, we'll keep everything grounded in context by giving students opportunities to apply their learning directly to their own writing - whether they are drafting or revising a piece. Keeping the work in context in this way enhances the explicit instruction during the dig or any direct support you may follow up with while conferring. This grounding is essential, because it serves as a bridge from instruction to application.

As with everything in this book, the sample lessons that follow are just a sampling of how this work might unfold. To be sure, your sentence digs will reflect your writers' needs, the books you are reading, the authors you are studying, and... yes, even the standards of your grade level. I encourage you to adopt and adapt ideas from this chapter in ways that directly support your students' current writing projects. What kinds of sentences will support the writing they are trying to do? For instance, if you're studying compare and contrast essays, you'll want to make sure you're showcasing well-crafted sentences that will help young writers express comparisons and - as importantly - differences between subjects. If we're involved with narratives, you may choose to dig into sentences where writers layer prepositional phrases to add details to form a strong mental image in the reader's mind. Or if you're working on informational pieces, you might decide this is the perfect opportunity to highlight sentences that expertly use an appositive, a phrase that gives more information about the noun before it, instead of just listing fact after fact after fact. In this way, your sentence digs can help you meet writers' needs and the requirements of their current writing projects in an intentional and timely manner.

Recall that reading and writing are reciprocal in nature. And we'll continue to leverage that relationship in this section - always connecting the showcase sentence back to the context of the text. We'll quickly consider the meaning of the sentence - as a reader - and we'll linger longer with questions about the author's purpose. Why did they write this sentence, this way, at this time? What were they thinking? What prompted this craft choice over any others? What impact does this writer's choices have on how their reader makes meaning of the text?

In this section of the book, we'll explore sentence digs around three areas of study: word choice, important details, and text structure. As in previous lessons, you'll find some Think Sheets included along the way that give students an opportunity to delve more into the work of sentence combining. Remember, these sheets are designed to be utilized strategically with your students' needs in mind. Some writers may not require much practice, while others will need more. What's most important is that this work transfers to student writing... the blank page. In the end, small and consistent amounts of sentence-level work - over time - will yield strong writers.

CHAPTER 4
Word Choice

> Words are sacred. They deserve respect.
> If you get the right ones, in the right order,
> you can nudge the world a little.
> - *Tom Stoppard*

There is a huge difference between how readers and writers wrestle with words. For readers, the words are there - they're already chosen, arranged, and set. They're in context and carry meaning - adding to the mental image the reader creates in their mind. As readers, we wrestle with decoding and pronunciation and intonation. We grapple with phrasing and meaning from the semantics the writer created. And in doing so, we're rewarded with new knowledge that ignites our minds or a story that moves our hearts. As readers, we receive the words, mix them with our experiences, and create meaning.

Writers wrestle with words in a somewhat more spectacular manner. Writers have a routine tussle with the blank page - knowing they'll fill it with words, words, words. But it's not enough to write down word after word. Writers craft those words. They arrange them in such a way that a reader might delight in reading them aloud. In fact, if we're lucky, the semantics of the carefully chosen words and the cleverly crafted sentences lead readers from a movie in their mind to an experience of the heart. And sometimes, sometimes the way a writer arranges and rearranges the words and sentences, they bring out such a gust of emotion - from weeping to laughter - that the reader craves reading that section aloud over and over again. (Here's to you Dav Pilkey!)

But, beyond the romance of word choice and semantics there is a pragmatism in syntax worth considering. Without syntax, the structure of language (aka grammar and usage), writers are at a loss. We first learn syntax through oral language. We pick up on it naturally as we learn to listen and are taught to communicate. In the jump to the written word, we can see students' approximations as they attempt to order words and structure sentences. This too is word choice. Writers choose structures through which to write: words, phrases, and clauses. And it's worth our time to analyze sentences through a writers' lens and think: *how* did they write this sentence? Which grammatical structures made this possible? How can this be such a long, long sentence and *not* be a run-on? Why did the author write this sentence in this way at this point in the text? How does this sentence, written this way, affect the reader's experience?

These are some of the questions we'll ask as we dig into the work of this chapter. We'll look at the beautiful word choices authors make, but we'll also examine key grammatical structures that allow us to layer in details and meaning - packing a sentence to its full capacity. In this way, students will not only marvel at the beauty of language, but they'll learn how to take their big ideas and express them with robust sentences in their own writing.

SHOWCASE SENTENCES AT A GLANCE

Lesson	Focus	Author's Purpose/ Grammatical Structure	Text	Sentence
W4.1	Layering clauses and phrases to expand a sentence	Writing small	"One Hot Mess" by Carmen Deedy in *Funny Girl: Funniest Stories Ever* edited by Betsy Bird	But all eyes watched **as** she struck the match and tossed it **in** a perfect flaming arc **into** the bathtub.
W4.2	Verb choice	Mood Character reactions	*Playing the Cards You're Dealt* by Varian Johnson	Before Ant **even touched** the knob to the back door, his mom **appeared** in the kitchen with hands on her hips, lips **pursed,** and eyeballs **zeroed** in on him.
W4.3	Word choice with subordinating conjunctions, prepositions, and verb phrases	Creating mental images	*Next Time You See a Spiderweb* by Emily Morgan	**When** an insect flies **into** or walks **over** this kind of web, it **becomes entangled** in the silk threads, making it easy for the spider to **catch** the insect.
W4.4	Novel word choice; conjunction choice Academic vocabulary	Character development	*Whoosh! Lonnie Johnson's SUPER-SOAKING Stream of Inventions* by Chris Barton and Don Tate	They **flowed whether** Lonnie was working with hundreds of people at NASA or up late tinkering with his own inventions in – finally! – his own workshop.

SENTENCE DIG W4.1: CLAUSES AND PHRASES: WRITING SMALL

Text: "One Hot Mess" by Carmen Deedy, page 45

Grades: 3-5

Book summary: "One Hot Mess" is a short story by Carmen Deedy. When Carmen was growing up, her family moved often. Her father, Papi, finally made and saved enough money to move them into the biggest apartment they had ever lived in. Carmen's mother, Mami, hated germs and planned to deep clean the apartment when they moved in, as she always did. One thing Mami did to get rid of germs in a cast iron tub was to set it on fire. Carmen thought it was a good idea to sell tickets for neighborhood kids to come watch the spectacle. Many children came and Mami lit the tub on fire... except it wasn't a cast iron tub. It was fiberglass... and fiberglass doesn't react well to fire.

Showcase sentence: But all eyes watched | **as** she struck the match and tossed it | **in** a perfect flaming arc | **into** the bathtub.

Rationale: I love this sentence because it's a great example of writing small - the idea that you lean into small details to increase the anticipation of the reader. The characters are anxious to see this woman set a bathtub on fire - on purpose! Carmen Deedy holds the reader's attention for just a moment longer by drawing attention to the match from strike, to toss, to the perfect flaming arc in the air and into the bathtub. She does this by layering details using clauses and phrases.

How does understanding this sentence help us as writers? What can we learn from the author's craft? How does it connect back to the text? This sentence reminds its readers who is doing what in this moment just before the fire, that there are kids watching (all eyes) but they're not in the room, and that one person is in the middle of this action (Mami/she). And because of the author's word choices, readers are reminded that Mami has done this before. It's not a big deal to her - she tosses the match *and* it's a *perfect* arc. This craft move builds the tension and fuels the next event (the massive fire) into a big bang!

As writers, we can learn the effect of slowing down a moment. That slowing down even the ten to twenty seconds right before the big event can create a huge impact. And choosing just the right words will help us manage the readers' anticipation. This is a powerful writing move.

Ask: Who or what is this sentence about? *Many students will say it's about Mami throwing the match in the bathtub. But really, the way it's written, it's about the eyes (the children) watching what Mami is doing.*

TAKE APART

Remember, your chunks are on sentence strips. Move them around to help students focus on one chunk and then another. You'll move them back together later.

Chunk	Possible Questions to Ask	Possible Answers
But all eyes watched	Why did the author use the phrase "all eyes" as the subject of her sentence?	She's referring to the children who came to watch Mami set the tub on fire. The children are not in the bathroom, so maybe the author wants us to know the children are not there but they're watching.
		This may give the reader the sense that it was quiet. There are a lot of people in the apartment but the author only refers to the eyes… eyes don't make noise.
as she struck the match and tossed it	The word *as* can start a clause or a phrase. Is this a clause or a phrase? How do you know?	This is a clause because there is a subject (she) and a predicate (struck and tossed). This makes the word *as* a subordinating conjunction.
	Why did the author include this in the sentence? How does it connect to the simple sentence *all eyes watched*?	The author wanted to help the reader see what the kids in the story were seeing. So she adds this clause to answer the question: what *did all eyes watch*?
	Why do you think the author chose the verbs struck and tossed to describe what Mami did to the match? What effect does this word choice have on the reader?	This gives the reader the sense that Mami does this a lot. They're not fancy verbs and it makes it seem like this is not a big deal. "Toss" gives the feeling that Mami is being a bit cavalier; she's not concerned at all. She does this all of the time.
in a perfect flaming arc	What does this prepositional phrase tell us more about?	It tells us *how* she tossed the match.
	What effect does this word choice have on the reader?	It helps the reader form a mental picture.
		It slows the writing down so it feels like you're watching it in slow motion.
into the bathtub.	How does this prepositional phrase connect to the sentence? What does it tell us?	It tells us *where* Mami threw the match.

PUT TOGETHER

During this part, the sentence chunks may be mixed up or off to the side. Invite students to manipulate the chunks when putting the sentence back together and/or while rearranging them.

Ask	Possible Answers	Food for Thought
What is the original order of this sentence?	But all eyes watched | **as** she struck the match and tossed it | **in** a perfect flaming arc | **into** the bathtub.	You might discuss why this sentence starts with the conjunction *but*. It connects this sentence to the one previous: *Again, no one moved.*
What would the sentence be if Carmen Deedy had combined this one with the previous sentence: *Again, no one moved.* (Students can write their combination on a personal whiteboard or sticky note.)	Again, no one moved, but all eyes watched as she struck the match and tossed it in a perfect flaming arc into the bathtub.	Note that this creates a compound-complex sentence.
Why do you think the author decided *not* to combine these sentences?	By using two sentences, Carmen puts a pause between them. This seems to emphasize no one moved. The pause also seems to add a little drama to the next sentence *All eyes watched...*	This type of analysis is important for young writers to realize that authors think about not just the syntax but the semantics of their words like how they bring the meaning to the reader through vocabulary while creating literary elements like mood, tone, and tension. Writers think about the readers' experience when crafting scenes.
Is there anything we can take out of the sentence? How does it affect the meaning and/or tone?	But all eyes watched | **as** she struck the match and tossed it | ~~in a perfect flaming arc~~ | **into** the bathtub. But all eyes watched | **as** she struck the match and tossed it | ~~in a perfect flaming arc~~ | ~~into the bathtub.~~	The absence of the phrase: *in a perfect flaming arc* still leaves a sound sentence. However, the sentence sounds more dramatic and adds a sense of skill to her toss with the phrase added in. By deleting the last two phrases, the sentence still makes sense and lets us know what the children saw. However, the reader misses the details that create a much richer image.
What is the effect if we replaced | *all eyes* | with | *the children* |?	But the children watched as she struck the match and tossed it in a perfect flaming arc into the bathtub.	Some students will like this change, thinking it is clearer to the reader about who is watching. Some students will say it's not as dramatic as saying "all eyes."

APPLY

During this part, students quickly apply their new knowledge about the sentence to their reading and writing. These are quick efforts and may be followed up with more practice.

Reread this excerpt from the story:

My mother unscrewed the top of the bottle of [rubbing] alcohol.

She moved the bucket of water closer to the tub.

She upturned the bottle and drained the contents with great care.

She reached into her apron pocket and drew from it a small box of wooden matches.

The crowd pressed forward.

"¡Tranquilos!"

Again, no one moved. But all eyes watched as she struck the match and tossed it in a perfect flaming arc into the bathtub.

(49)

Discuss with your group: Why didn't the author just say – Mami set the bathtub on fire? Why did she take time to show the reader – step by step – what Mami did? What was the effect on you as a reader?

Writing focus: As Carmen Deedy composed this sentence, she may have used some questions to help her layer the details. Authors often ask themselves: Who? What? When? Where? Why? and How? to add details.

> **Showcase sentence:** But all eyes watched **as** she struck the match and tossed it **in** a perfect flaming arc **into** the bathtub.

Heavy scaffold: All eyes watched, as _____
                                              What else was happening? What were they watching?

_____ _____ .
How did this happen?   *Where did this happen?*

Example: All eyes watched, as <u>my teacher pulled out the final exam and passed it out</u> <u>with a serious thud on each desk.</u>

Light scaffold:

1. Write a basic sentence.
2. Ask yourself a question: What? When? Where? How?
3. Write a prepositional phrase that answers that question.

(Continued)

4. Ask yourself another (different) question: What? When? Where? How?
5. Write another prepositional phrase that answers that question.

Example:

The soccer player scored a goal.
How? The soccer player scored a goal with a shot in the corner of the net.
When? The soccer player scored a goal with a shot in the corner of the net just before half-time.

No scaffold: Invite students to emulate the showcase sentence within their own writing.

Apply to your writing: Find a place in your writing - just before a big event - where you can slow the reader down and show the action step by step. Take turns orally composing scenes from your writing in this slow, step by step method. How does it change your story? How does it affect your reader?

SENTENCE DIG W4.2: VERB CHOICE: CHARACTER REACTION

Text: *Playing the Cards You're Dealt* by Varian Johnson, page 9

Grades: 4-6

Book summary: Ant is a fifth grader who is struggling not only to live up to his dad's expectations at the card table but also to understand the complex relationships between fathers and sons and the grown up problems that affect families. He wants to prove himself to be tough and grown up by winning a local junior Spades tournament, but his card partner gets in trouble and cannot participate. Ant needs to find a new partner; his best chance is with the new girl in town, Shirley. But what will his dad think?

Showcase sentence: Before Ant **even touched** the knob to the back door, | his mom **appeared** in the kitchen with hands on her hips, | lips **pursed,** | and eyeballs **zeroed** in on him.

Rationale: This sentence demonstrates a basic writing technique that students can quickly accomplish. The author has created a mental image where the reader turns around to see Ant's mom - and then the author walks our eyes up from her waist to her face by giving us specific details from hands to lips to eyes. The verb choices in this sentence also reveal not just the mom's perfect timing but also her mood. This will resonate with any reader who has been caught *almost* doing something they shouldn't. In addition, the phrase *lips pursed* and *eyeballs zeroed in on him* are great opportunities to introduce multilingual learners to new English phrases that might be confusing.

How does understanding this sentence help us as writers? What can we learn from the author's craft? How does it connect back to the text? This sentence is toward the beginning of the book but quickly establishes that Ant's parents are involved... they're paying attention, especially mom. As the story continues, Ant is going to go through some challenging situations involving his best friend and his dad. His mom will always be there to support him. This first encounter the reader has with his mother is essential toward building that foundation of her character.

Ask: Who is this sentence about? Students may say Ant and his mom, but it really focuses on his mom. The independent clause answers this question. The dependent clause tells the reader *when* it happened. When did his mom appear? - before he even touched the knob. *Busted.*

TAKE APART

Remember, your chunks are on sentence strips. Move them around to help students focus on one chunk and then another. You'll move them back together later.

Chunk	Possible Questions to Ask	Possible Answers
Before Ant **even touched** the knob to the back door,	What is the significance of the word choice *even touched*? What is the author trying to tell us?	She's conveying that Ant almost made it out of the house but before his hand touched the door knob she was in the kitchen. The word "even" emphasizes the word touch. So the author is trying to say that Ant didn't even get his hand on the door.
his mom **appeared** in the kitchen with hands on her hips,	Why do you think the author chose the word *appeared*?	The word "appear" may make readers think his mom appeared like magic. She was just suddenly there – no fanfare or noise. It's early in the morning and Ant is trying to be very quiet. So *appeared* is a word choice that fits this mood.
lips **pursed**,	What part of speech is *pursed*? How do you know? If it's not a handbag, what does *pursed* mean in this sentence? What does this tell us about his mom?	It's a verb. Students may know this because of the past tense ending. Or they may know this because it follows a noun (lips) and it's what the lips are doing. It means to pucker one's lips in disapproval. She doesn't like that he's trying to leave early. Invite students to act this out by pursing their lips in disapproval.
and eyeballs **zeroed** in on him.	Why do you think the author chose the phrase *eyeballs zeroed in on him*?	She's looking right at him. She's paying close attention. Her eyes weren't looking anywhere else. They were locked on him. She was giving him a look of disapproval.

PUT TOGETHER

During this part, the sentence chunks may be mixed up or off to the side. Invite students to manipulate the chunks when putting the sentence back together and/or while rearranging them.

Ask	Possible Answers	Food for Thought
What is the original order of this sentence?	Before Ant **even touched** the knob to the back door, | his mom **appeared** in the kitchen with hands on her hips, | lips **pursed,** | and eyeballs **zeroed** in on him.	You may point out that this is a complex sentence. You can also point out that the mom did three things: appeared, pursed, and zeroed. Notice all of the verbs in this sentence are in the past tense because the narrator is retelling this story.
How would it change the sentence if we removed the word *even*?	**Before** Ant ~~even~~ touched the knob to the back door, his mom appeared in the kitchen with hands on her hips, lips pursed, and eyeballs **zeroed** in on him.	The word *even* places some emphasis on a small action – touching the door knob – and creates a "surprise" tone that Ant's mother had caught him sneaking out. By removing the word *even* the sentence seems to lose its focus on the action and the sense of surprise.
What other words might replace *before*? How do they change the sentence? Why do you think the author chose the word *before*?	Since Although Because	Allow students to try some different subordinating conjunctions and think about how they change the sentence. The author may have chosen the word *before* because it gives a sense that he *almost* made it outside. And which kid hasn't been busted just before they got away with something? It's a great word choice to connect with the reader.
What are some other words we can use to replace the verbs? How do these word choices affect the sentence?	Before Ant **grabbed** the knob to the back door, / his mom **ran to** the kitchen with hands on her hips, lips **pursed,** and eyeballs **zeroed** in on him.	Using the words *grabbed* and *ran to* give the sentence energy. It changes the mood from sneaking quietly while his mother sleeps to rushing around and making some noise, causing his mom to run to the kitchen. (Allow for other responses.)

CHAPTER 4   Writing: Word Choice

APPLY
During this part, students quickly apply their new knowledge about the sentence to their reading and writing. These are quick efforts and may be followed up with more practice.

Discuss: This scene is when Ant wants to walk to school by himself because he is in fifth grade now. What are some other examples in the text of Ant trying to grow up? How does the author's word choice describe what Ant is going through?

Writing focus: When you work on your writing, consider how characters interact with each other. You don't have to use dialogue as your only tool to show how a character reacts. You can write like Varian Johnson and show the readers how characters react.

> **Showcase sentence:** Before Ant **even touched** the knob to the back door, his mom **appeared** in the kitchen with hands on her hips, lips **pursed,** and eyeballs **zeroed** in on him.

Heavy scaffold: Before I could even get out of bed, my dog _____ with paws

Did what?

_____, tongue _____, and tail _____.
How?   *How?/Doing what?*   *How?/Doing what?*

Example: Before I could even get out of bed, my cat <u>pounced on my bed</u> with paws <u>spread out,</u> tongue <u>stuck out,</u> and tail <u>standing straight up and alert</u>.

Light scaffold: Before _____, _____ _____
Dependent clause – what happened?   *subject*   *verb with phrase about body*

_____, and _____.
phrase about the mouth or another body part   *phrase about eyes or another body part*

Example: Before <u>I could make dinner,</u> <u>my son flung open the pantry door with his arms outstretched,</u> <u>eyes locked on the cookies,</u> and <u>his fingers wiggling to reach them!</u>

After <u>I refused to take her out for ice cream,</u> <u>my sister stomped up the stairs with heavy feet,</u> <u>her pigtails swung,</u> and <u>her lips folded into a frown.</u>

SENTENCE DIG W4.3: VERB CHOICE: CREATING MENTAL IMAGES

Text: *Next Time You See a Spider Web* by Emily Morgan, page 12

Grades: 2-5

Book summary: Typically, we try to avoid spiderwebs and cobwebs. We use brooms to sweep them away from our homes and porches. We scream and rapidly try to rid ourselves of them when we accidentally walk through one on a nature trail. Spiderwebs are icky… until they're not. *Next Time You See a Spider Web* invites readers to take a close look at this sticky mess to recognize it for what it is - an amazing spider skill! Alongside photographs, Emily Morgan gives readers a close view of how spiders spin their silky webs without getting stuck themselves and how those webs help them catch, trap, and snare prey.

Showcase sentence: When an insect **flies into |** or **walks over |** this kind of web, | it **becomes entangled |** in the silk threads, | making it easy for the spider | to **catch** the insect.

Rationale: There are a lot of decisions the author makes while writing this particular sentence. From the specific subordinating conjunction to start it off to the exact prepositions used to place the insects on the web to the verb phrases, these word choices create a specific mental image for the reader. We often think of word choice being about fancy verbs or choosing the just-right shade of meaning, but sometimes it's about making all the phrases work together to load a sentence up with information.

How does understanding this sentence help us as writers? What can we learn from the author's craft? How does it connect back to the text? This sentence helps the reader understand how the tangled cobweb, which looks like a mess of threads thrown together, works to help the spider and helps the reader differentiate between the different kinds of webs and how they trap prey.

Analyzing this sentence can help us as writers think about how we, too, can be specific in our writing with the words we choose. In addition, this particular sentence has three big chunks: a dependent clause telling us when… an independent clause telling us an insect is entangled in the web… and a participle phrase explaining why this is useful. We can help kids build this kind of sentence within their own writing by modeling some sentence building work around it.

Ask: As readers, let's make sure we understand this sentence. The pronoun *it* is used twice. Who or what is *it* referring to and how do you know? (Both times *it* is referring to an insect. If necessary, use sticky notes or a sketch to note this on the sentence strips so students remember as they talk about the writing.)

What does this sentence mean to us as readers? *Students may say something like - this sentence tells us how an insect gets caught in the tangled web or cobweb. An insect flies into (crashes into or tries to go through) the web or an insect walks over it and finds itself trapped in it. Then the spider can eat it.* If some students are having trouble with this sentence, consider sketching and/or annotating with synonyms to anchor the meaning and help them analyze the writing.

TAKE APART

Remember, your chunks are on sentence strips. Move them around to help students focus on one chunk and then another. You'll move them back together later.

Chunk	Possible Questions to Ask	Possible Answers
When an insect flies into or walks over	Why do you think the author started the sentence with *when*?	The author is saying at this time – this action happens first.
	Why do you think the author chose to use the word "or" and include two verb phrases: *flies into* or *walks over*?	There are different kinds of insects that get caught in this web. Some will fly and some don't fly, they walk.
	What does the author's phrase "flies into..." make you think?	The insect is trying to enter the web. The insect is crashing into the web.
	Let's think about the author's word choice for *walks over*. She could have said *walks into*. Take a moment to act out an insect *walking over* a sticky web. What is the author trying to help us envision?	Students might find themselves picking up their legs in exaggerated movements as if their feet are sticking to the "web." Their arms may flail a bit for balance. The author may want us to envision an insect walking over this web, its feet getting stuck and as it struggles its other body parts become stuck too.
this kind of web,	What is the word *this* referring to? What kind of web?	In the sentence before this one, the author names this kind of web as a tangled web or cobweb.
	How does this phrase connect to the first?	It tells us **where** the insect is flying into or walking over.
		When we add this phrase to the first we have a dependent clause: when an insect flies into or walks over this kind of web. The author is letting us know something is going to happen because of this.
it becomes entangled	What do you think the word *entangled* means? How do you know?	Some students may say: stuck or caught or tangled. Help students understand that entangled means twisted together or caught up in – help them think about the first part of the sentence: the insect isn't just stuck – it's twisted up in this web – full body. You might note that this is an independent clause. It can be a sentence on its own.

(Continued)

Chunk	Possible Questions to Ask	Possible Answers
in the silk threads,	What kind of phrase is this? What does this phrase do in this sentence? How does this clause connect to the dependent clause *when an insect flies into or walks over this kind of web*?	This is a prepositional phrase that tells us where the insect is entangled. This clause tells us what happens when an insect tries to fly or walk through this web.
making it easy for the spider to catch the insect.	Why did the author choose to include this participle phrase at the end of the sentence?	The author wanted us to know that the silk threads worked because they are wrapped around the insects.

PUT TOGETHER

During this part, the sentence chunks may be mixed up or off to the side. Invite students to manipulate the chunks when putting the sentence back together and/or while rearranging them.

Ask	Possible Answers	Food for Thought
What is the original order of this sentence?	When an insect flies into or walks over	this kind of web,	it becomes entangled	in the silk threads,	making it easy for the spider	to catch the insect.	It might be helpful to remind students that there are three big parts of this sentence – a dependent clause, an independent clause, and a participle phrase. Together this makes a complex sentence.
This sentence has a lot of specific verbs that make the action pop. What would happen if we changed some of these verbs? How does that affect the sentence? NOTE: Consider allowing students to work in pairs with a white board to discuss the word choices for verbs the author made and any changes they would make.	Flies: swoops/crashes/zips Walks: crawls, trudge, tiptoes Becomes entangled: becomes trapped, becomes snared, becomes twisted-up Catch: jump on, eat, imprison	As students make changes – zeroing in on word choice – it's important to keep asking them *how does this affect the sentence?* For example, the picture shows a sticky cobweb that is vertical, if an insect trudges over it, it gives the effect that the insect is walking slowly and intentionally or with difficulty. Whereas the word *walks* gives the sense of nonchalance – the insect doesn't realize the web is sticky and... whoops... it's now stuck... Or if a student were to try out "become twisted-up" that is a bit of a mouthful to read that sentence aloud. Kids may find different words they like better for the sentence, but we want them to see how a writer considers a word's effect before solidifying their choice.

(Continued)

Ask	Possible Answers	Food for Thought
How would the meaning of the sentence change if we used a different conjunction than *when*?	**Because** an insect flies into or walks over | this kind of web, | it becomes entangled | in the silk threads, | making it easy for the spider | to catch the insect.	If the author used the word *because*, the meaning still holds. It doesn't fit in the text, though, as it would need a prior sentence about the insect moving into the web.
	After an insect flies into or walks over | this kind of web, | it becomes entangled | in the silk threads, | making it easy for the spider | to catch the insect.	Using the word *after* will work. This is a shade of meaning situation. *When* means at the same time or as it is happening. *After* would mean that the insect flew into the web and *then* moments after it's entangled. To be more precise, the author used *when*.
	If an insect flies into or walks over | this kind of web, | it **will become** entangled | in the silk threads, | making it easy for the spider | to catch the insect.	The author could use the word *if* to give a similar message to the reader. However, the word *if* implies that an insect might *not* come along. Whereas *when* implies it's only a matter of time and the spider is willing to wait... Again a slight difference but one the author needs to consider.

APPLY

During this part, students quickly apply their new knowledge about the sentence to their reading and writing. These are quick efforts and may be followed up with more practice.

> **Discuss:** Go into your own writing. Find your favorite sentence, a sentence you're excited for others to read and one that you really like the way it sounds when you read it aloud.
>
> **Partner A:** Read your sentence aloud and explain your thinking behind your word choices. Use this sentence frame to help you: I used the word _____ because _____.
>
> **Partner B:** Listen to your partner's writing. Add to his/her thinking with your own comments about their word choice for that sentence. Use these sentence frames to help you:
>
> *Compliment:* I noticed you used the word _____. I think that's effective because _____.
>
> *Suggestion:* I noticed you used the word _____. I wonder if it would make your sentence stronger if you used the word _____.
>
> Repeat giving Partner B a chance to share and Partner A a chance to listen and respond.

Thought Partners: _____

Sentence Dig W4.3
THINK SHEET: WRITING FOCUS

STRATEGY: Sentence Extension

Write the showcase sentence from the sentence dig in the space below:

[   ]

Directions:
Studying this sentence has helped us think about word choice, and it has demonstrated for us how to build longer and stronger sentences. Our showcase sentence has three large chunks - a dependent clause, an independent clause, and a participle phrase.

With a partner, build onto these independent clauses by adding a dependent clause. Start with a subordinating conjunction.

Subordinating Conjunctions:					
after	although	as	as long as	because	before
despite	even if	even though	if	in order that	rather than
since	so that	that	though	unless	until
when	where	whereas	whether	while	as if

a. _____, the spider waits nearby.

b. _____, the spider feels the vibrations on the threads.

c. _____, the insect struggles to get loose.

Choose one of the sentences above and rewrite it below ending it with a participle phrase. Remember a participle phrase starts with a verb ending with -ing.

[   ]

Copyright material from Aimee Buckner Haisten (2026), *Sentence Digs*, Routledge

SENTENCE DIG W4.4: THE JUST-RIGHT CONJUNCTION: DEVELOPING CHARACTER

Text: *Whoosh! Lonnie Johnson's SUPER-SOAKING Stream of Inventions* by Chris Barton and Don Tate, page 14

Grades: 3-5

Book summary: This biography exemplifies perseverance. Lonnie Johnson was always building and inventing things. When he was young, he invented a robot. When he worked for NASA, he built a jet propulsion laboratory. He liked to tinker, invent, and build. One day, while working on a new cooling system for air conditioners and refrigerators, he accidentally invented the first super soaker water gun!

Showcase sentence: They **flowed** | **whether** Lonnie was working with hundreds of people at NASA | **or** up late tinkering with his own inventions | in - finally! - his own workshop.

Rationale: I chose this sentence because of the word choices the author made. The use of multiple pronouns in a sentence is always interesting to note and unpack. The author also chose to use the verb *flowed* in a novel way. It's a beautiful way to connect the text to the invention of a water gun. Finally, the author chose the correlative conjunctions *whether... or*. The conjunctions *whether... or* offer two different instances when the ideas are flowing - creating the overall meaning that the ideas were always flowing.

How does understanding this sentence help us as writers? What can we learn from the author's craft? How does it connect back to the text? This sentence continues to build the readers' understanding of Lonnie's work ethic and personality. He was always thinking of new ideas. This summarizes the text so far, as the story tells us about times Lonnie worked on ideas at home and at work (NASA). This sets up how he will work through the ups and downs of the super soaker.

Ask: Why do you think the author put dashes around the word finally and used an exclamation point right in the middle of a sentence? *This is the first time we see Lonnie in his own private workshop, so this was a big deal. The author uses dashes to let the reader know that he is <u>interrupting the thought to add this celebration word</u> about the workshop. Lonnie has wanted one since he was a kid.*

TAKE APART

Remember, your chunks are on sentence strips. Move them around to help students focus on one chunk and then another. You'll move them back together later.

Chunk	Possible Questions to Ask	Possible Answers
They flowed	Who or what is this sentence about? Who or what does the pronoun "they" refer to? What did the ideas do? What does it mean that ideas flowed?	They The pronoun "they" refers to ideas in the previous sentence. NOTE: If students say the sentence is about *ideas*, ask *how do you know? The word ideas isn't in this sentence.* The students should be able to link the pronoun to the word ideas in the sentence before it. They flowed. Help students understand this means the ideas seemed to come to Lonnie quickly and without much trouble.
whether Lonnie was working with hundreds of people at NASA	Why do you think the author included "with hundreds of people"? How does it connect to the chunk before it – *They flowed*?	The author wanted the reader to know that Lonnie was around a lot of people. The author is letting us know that the ideas came easily to Lonnie when he was working at NASA with a lot of people around him. Even if the problems were difficult, he had an idea.
or up late tinkering with his own inventions	What does tinker mean? In this part of the sentence, is Lonnie with hundreds of people or alone? What makes you think this? Why is this part of the sentence important to us as a reader?	Tinker means to try to fix something in a casual way, usually to no useful effect. Lonnie is likely alone because it's late at night and he's tinkering. It tells us where Lonnie was late at night when he worked on his own inventions; he was in his own workshop. It also lets us know his ideas didn't stop when he left work.
in – finally! – his own workshop.	How does this chunk add meaning to the sentence?	It tells us where Lonnie is at night. The noun phrase "private workshop" helps the reader to imagine that Lonnie is working alone in a quiet place – the exact opposite of working at NASA during the day. By setting off the word "finally!" with dashes, the author reminds us that Lonnie had been wanting a workshop in his home for a long time.

PUT TOGETHER

During this part, the sentence chunks may be mixed up or off to the side. Invite students to manipulate the chunks when putting the sentence back together and/or while rearranging them.

Ask	Possible Answers	Food for Thought
What is the original order of this sentence?	They flowed | whether Lonnie was working with hundreds of people at NASA | or up late tinkering with his own inventions | in – finally! – his own workshop.	This is a longer sentence and students may have trouble putting it back together. You can ask questions like: Which chunk should we start with? Why? Looking at the first word in each chunk, which one do you think comes next? Why? NOTE: This is where you can talk about the relationships between conjunctions. The conjunction "whether" will always come before the conjunction "or" when they are working together.
I'm still intrigued by the word "flow." Why do you think the author used the word flow instead of saying, Lonnie had lots of ideas whether...?	Answers will vary, but someone will say that flow sounds like water does, and Lonnie invents the super soaker – a water toy!	Authors often use words that are related to the bigger topic of the book. In this case, the big topic of the book is Lonnie's invention – the super soaker water toy. So, using the word flow here helps the reader associate the ideas Lonnie has with water. Another example is in the title: *Whoosh! Lonnie Johnson's SUPER-SOAKING Stream of Inventions*. Soaking – getting things all wet. Stream of Inventions – a stream of water is a lot of water that is constantly flowing... the inventions were numerous.
Let's go back to the words *whether... or*. These are called correlative conjunctions. What are these words doing in this sentence? What is an example of how you might use *whether... or* in a sentence?	They are pointing out two different situations when the ideas are flowing. Examples kids might come up with: You might have to decide *whether* to wear a light jacket *or* a heavy coat outside in the winter. You might have to eat your dinner *whether or* not you like it.	The words *whether... or* are correlative conjunctions that give two equally plausible situations. So, in this sentence, the author is saying "They (ideas) flowed" in these situations – being at work with hundreds of people or up late tinkering. It didn't matter when or where, Lonnie had lots of ideas.

(Continued)

SENTENCE DIGS

Ask	Possible Answers	Food for Thought
Can we rearrange this sentence so it still makes sense? Has the meaning changed?	Whether Lonnie was working with hundreds of people at NASA | or up late tinkering with his own inventions | in - finally! - his own workshop, | they flowed.	This makes sense, and if the author used this sentence, they might use the word "ideas" instead of "they" since the pronoun is so far from its antecedent. Because whether is a subordinating conjunction it – along with its clause – can be placed at the beginning of the sentence.
Is there any part of the sentence that we can take out and it would still make sense?	They flowed | ~~whether Lonnie was working with hundreds of people at NASA | or up late tinkering with his own inventions | in - finally! - his own workshop.~~ They flowed | ~~whether Lonnie was working with hundreds of people at NASA | or up late tinkering with his own inventions~~ | in - finally! - his own workshop. They flowed | whether Lonnie was working with hundreds of people at NASA | or up late tinkering with his own inventions | ~~in - finally! - his own workshop.~~	These are preposition phrases that tell us where Lonnie is working (with hundreds of people at NASA) and where he is tinkering (with his inventions in - finally! - his own workshop. The sentence can still stand without these prepositional phrases: They flowed whether Lonnie was working or tinkering.
Why do you think the author chose to tell us more about where he was working and tinkering?	• To let us know the ideas were flowing day and night • To help us picture him having ideas in different places • To help us understand he had ideas if he was with a lot of people or alone	Authors often extend their sentences by telling the reader when and where something is happening. This helps readers to create a mental picture of the story.

APPLY

During this part, students quickly apply their new knowledge about the sentence to their reading and writing. These are quick efforts and may be followed up with more practice.

> **Discuss:** We talked a lot about the author's word choices today. We discussed the choice of the words flow and *whether… or*. We also talked about why the author used prepositional phrases to tell us more about where Lonnie had his ideas.
>
> **Talk with your partner:** Which word choice do you think had the biggest impact on you as a reader? How did it help you better understand Lonnie and/or the story?
>
> **Writing focus:** Writers can extend sentences with prepositional phrases to tell us when and where something happened.
>
> > **Showcase sentence:** They flowed **whether** Lonnie was working with hundreds of people at NASA **or** up late tinkering with his own inventions in – finally! – his own workshop.
>
> **Heavy scaffold:** The children played whether they were playing _____ (When?) _____ (Where?) or playing _____ (When?) _____ (Where?).
>
> Example: *The children played whether they were playing <u>before school at the bus stop</u> or playing <u>after dinner on their Xbox.</u>*
>
> **Light scaffold:** _____ (subject) _____ (verb) whether _____ (Who or what?) was _____ (participle) ing _____ (When?) _____ (Where?) or _____ (participle) ing _____ (When?) _____ (Where?).
>
> Example: *<u>Sharks</u> <u>swim</u> whether <u>they</u> are hunting <u>in the morning</u> <u>in the deep sea</u> or swimming <u>in the afternoon sun</u> <u>by a boat of fishermen</u>.*
>
> **No scaffold:** Invite students to emulate the showcase sentence within their own writing.

Thought Partners: _____

Sentence Dig: W4.4
THINK SHEET: READING & WRITING FOCUS

STRATEGY: Sketch and Revise

Write the showcase sentence from the sentence dig in the space below:

[   ]

Sketch:

On your own, draw a quick sketch and jot the words from the showcase sentence that show two times the ideas flowed:

1.	2.

Discuss: The author could have written: Lonnie had a lot of ideas. He had ideas at work. He had ideas at home. *Why is the author's final choice - as shown in the showcase sentence - more effective?*

Word Play:

Here are some other correlative conjunctions:

| both… and | neither… nor | either… or | rather… than | not only… but also |

With your partner, try using these in the showcase sentence instead of *whether… or*. Decide which pair you can use and the sentence will still make sense. Write it below:

_____

_____

_____

Now, come up with some of your own example sentences using correlative conjunctions. After practicing with your partner, write your favorite example below.

_____

_____

_____

Digging In

Reread the piece of writing you are working on now. Identify a sentence that you can extend or two sentences you can combine using correlative conjunctions. Make the revision in your writing.

CHAPTER 5
Important Details

> Good writing is supposed to evoke sensation in the reader.
> Not the fact that it is raining, but the feeling
> of being rained upon.
> - *E.L. Doctorow*

My favorite time of year has always been the preplanning week after summer break, when I could go into my classroom and breathe. I used this time to set up my classroom - from the overarching design and room arrangement to the finest details of where materials will go, where the best place for tissues is, and where students will line up to transition in and out of the classroom. I need these important details set - set for me and for my students - before the fast pace of the school year takes over. As you know, what may seem like unimportant details a non-educator might never notice are make or break details to a teacher.

Details matter to writers too. They breathe life and reality into our settings, characters, and plot. They bring reliability and accessibility to our informational topics. Details are what draw the readers into our writing to experience the text. Because of that, writers don't leave details to chance: they think about them, draft them, and revise them throughout the writing process. Just like a teacher setting up the classroom, the writer knows the way the details are laid out will make a world of difference to the reader... even if they never notice. Details make the structure of our writing work - they bring our readers into the text and hold their attention as we delve into our story, our characters, our theme. These same details build - sentence after sentence - to create the paragraphs that ground our readers' understanding of our topic, main idea, and perspective.

Studying detail or supporting sentences isolated from the text is dangerous. Dangerous because we know these sentences lack any heavy significance on their own. They need context. For example, if we were to study the sentence "Silence filled the arena" (Nelson and James 2019): isolated from the text, we are left wondering - what arena? Who is silent? Are people even there? What's happening? Is it early morning or late at night? We just don't know and so studying this sentence as a standalone focus will have little impact. However, when you have the context of its story, *Let 'Er Buck* (Nelson and James 2019), you know that the character George Fletcher, an African American cowboy, has felt the sting of racism his whole life. As a cowboy, he became a bronco riding phenomenon. And this sentence lies at the end of a dramatic bucking competition, in front of a packed arena, in which George was the clear winner and yet lost... most likely due to his race:

> After the ride, everybody stood rapt, waiting for the winner to be announced.
> In due time, one of the judges called through the megaphone, "John Spain, first. George Fletcher, second." Silence filled the arena.

Now we have something to talk about! These details, these seemingly simple details fill us with disbelief, injustice, and offense. They voice the crowd's dismay: in a split second of time when there should have been roars of cheering and celebration... there was silence. It's a powerful sentence - when presented in context. The author knows it, and the reader feels it.

As always, when we do this kind of sentence decomposition work, we want to pull from texts we are currently reading with our students. We want our students to have the context, which may require us to revisit a page or paragraph together before leading the sentence dig routine. This isn't cheating. It's leveraging the reciprocity of reading and writing. If understanding how a sentence is written can help us comprehend it, then the reverse is true - understanding the sentence in context can help us go back and unpack how the writer created the sentence and why its impact on the text is strategic. With this in mind, we want to continue to find sentences that juggle the syntax of words in such a way that complex ideas are written clearly and are accessible to the reader. In this way, we can study how to bring our big ideas from our minds and our oral language into a formal written piece.

As you move students to write with important details, you're really inviting them to craft strong paragraphs. Sentences full of effective details build up the paragraphs and paragraphs build the text. So you might naturally start to ask yourself, why don't we just decompose a whole paragraph? To be sure, there is value in this type of practice when students can understand the whole paragraph and grasp the work of the sentences within it. As your young learners become more knowledgeable about the contributions sentences make to build meaningful paragraphs, you might think about a mini-study over the course of a few days that dives into a full paragraph and looks at how its sentences work collectively to build the main idea from one sentence to the next. Don and Jenny Killgallon have done some exemplary work in this area in their book *Paragraphs for Elementary School* (2014). However, in this book, we'll keep our work focused on sentence-level composition. But have no fear - by decomposing key sentences *and* determining their impact on the overall text, you'll be helping students to not only write effective supporting sentences but also to layer in their many details in ways that ultimately develop a strong paragraph.

There are times when the details of my own writing just seem to flow and plop right out of my head onto the paper. But many times, like many writers, I rely on grammatical structures to nudge my details into existence. For example, when I am revising at the sentence level, I often think - can I add a prepositional phrase? Would an introductory clause be good here? Which subordinate conjunction will push my point front and center? In this way, relying on grammar helps me craft stronger sentences. So as we talk about details and we think about ourselves and our students as writers, we'll also take this opportunity to explore how we can use grammar and grammatical structures as energy drinks for our sentences: a little boost to our thinking process to help us write more and to write well. As you consider this idea – of using grammar structures to push our sentence development – you'll notice some Think Sheets with sentence extension and combining work included with several of the sentence digs in this chapter. This grammar-focused combining work is incorporated to give students additional opportunities to practice constructing stronger sentences with more complex structures.

The lessons that follow include a sampling of different kinds of detail sentences that support a specific writing purpose – from developing character and plot to developing a main idea and perspective. With sentence digs, we can explore common grammatical structures authors use and consider how they leverage them to work for their readers. As always, you're invited to try out the lessons as they're written, tweaking their components and complexity based on your students' needs. Or, simply study the lessons as a model to emulate using key sentences pulled from texts your students are currently reading.

SHOWCASE SENTENCES LESSONS AT A GLANCE

Lesson	Focus	Author's Purpose/ Grammatical Structure	Text	Sentence
W5.1	Prepositional phrases	Characterization	*Mexikid: A Graphic Memoir* by Pedro Martín	He ran a mule train **between the two warring sides** to make sure all the people had food to eat.
W5.2	Appositive phrase	Theme	*Ruth Bader Ginsburg: The Case of R.B.G. vs Inequality* by Jonah Winter, illustrated by Stacy Innerst	She did so because she wanted people – **especially young women** – to see at least one woman on the Supreme Court.
W5.3	Compound predicate	Theme	*Let 'Er Buck: George Fletcher the People's Champion* by Vaunda Micheaux Nelson, illustrated by Gordon C. James	In the warm glow of the setting sun, spirited spectators **lifted George onto their shoulders and paraded around the arena.**
W5.4	Comparison	Main idea Author's perspective	*The Magnificent Migration: On Safari with Africa's Last Great Herds* by Sy Montgomery, photos by Roger and Logan Wood	And **though lions may seem more glamorous**, it's wildebeests who drive the ecology and evolution of the largest savanna ecosystem in the world.

SENTENCE DIG W5.1: PREPOSITIONAL PHRASES: DEVELOPING CHARACTER

Text: *Mexikid: A Graphic Memoir* by Pedro Martín, page 26

Grades: 4-6

Book summary: Published in 2023, this award-winning graphic memoir invites us into the life of Pedro Martín, who is a Mexikid - a kid born in the US to parents from Mexico. Pedro and his family take a thousand mile road trip from California to Mexico to pick up his abuelito and bring him back to California. During the road trip to Mexico, Pedro learns more about his heritage and his family history. Filled with strong characters, dramatic retellings of family history, and humor, Pedro Martín takes his readers on a trip they won't soon forget.

> **Showcase sentence:** He ran a mule train | **between the two warring sides** | to make sure all the people had food to eat.

Rationale and notes: This sentence has a couple of places that will give readers pause. First, the phrase *mule train* may not be part of students' background knowledge. Yet, this is an important detail within the sentence, as it sets up the simplicity of Abuelito's operation in a very difficult and complicated war. In addition, the author uses a well-placed prepositional phrase to add depth and intensity to the sentence.

How does understanding this sentence help us as writers? How does this detail connect back to the text? This sentence develops the character, Abuelito. The reader learns about Abuelito along with the character Pedro, as people along the road trip tell stories of this man who Pedro first describes as "an old widower living with one relative or another." We come to find out that this man didn't just live through the Mexican Revolution but he was an active participant. This showcase sentence tells us just how he participated and the immense courage and compassion it took for him to do so.

Ask: What does this detail tell us about Abuelito's character?

Students may tell you the basics: *he runs a mule train and he helps feed people that are hungry.* They may struggle with gleaning that this sentence implies he is courageous and compassionate. You can come back to that - adding on to this question - at the end of this sentence dig. If your students are clear that Abuelito is courageous and compassionate, then you can adapt the sentence dig to include questions like: Which chunk tells us he is brave? How do you know?

TAKE APART

Remember, your chunks are on sentence strips. Move them around to help students focus on one chunk and then another. You'll move them back together later.

Chunk	Possible Questions to Ask	Possible Answers
He ran a mule train	Who is this sentence about? How do you know?	This sentence is about Abuelito. We know this because the sentence starts with the pronoun *he*. We know that the pronoun refers to Abuelito because this sentence comes in the middle of a conversation between Pedro and Apa about Abuelito.
	Turn and talk: What is a mule train?	A mule train is a line of mules or mules with wagons that carry cargo.
	What kind of cargo do you think the mules were carrying? What makes you think this?	It's likely the mules were carrying food products because the last chunk refers to people having food to eat.
	What does this chunk mean: he ran a mule train?	In this case, the word *ran* means organized or led. So Abuelito organized or led a mule train.
between the two warring sides	What does the word *between* mean? Why did the author choose this preposition?	The word *between* means the space separating two objects, places, or groups of people. The author uses this word to let us know Abuelito's mule train ran in that space.
	What does the author mean by *two warring sides*? How do we know?	We know that Abuelito was in the Mexican Revolution – or between it, as Apa said. A revolution is a war; the two warring sides will be the two groups of people fighting against each other (the Conventionistas and the Constitutionalistas).
	If Abuelito ran his mule train *between* the two warring sides, what does that tell us about the kind of person Abuelito was during this time?	Students might say he was courageous. They may say he was neutral – choosing to help both sides.
to make sure all the people had food to eat.	This is an adverbial phrase with the infinitive *to make*. It tells us more about why Abuelito ran his mule train. Who did he want to help?	He wanted to help *all* the people. In this case, "all the people" means people on both sides of the war.
	What does this tell us about Abuelito's character? How do you know?	He's compassionate because he risked his life to help all the people so they would have food.

PUT TOGETHER

During this part, the sentence chunks may be mixed up or off to the side. Invite students to manipulate the chunks when putting the sentence back together and/or while rearranging them.

Ask	Possible Answers	Food for Thought
What is the original order of this sentence?	He ran a mule train | between the two warring sides | to make sure all the people had food to eat.	This sentence can be tricky for students due to the number of phrases that follow the verb.
Is there another way to arrange the sentence? Does it affect the meaning?	To make sure all the people had food to eat, | he ran a mule train | between the two warring sides. He ran a mule train | to make sure all the people had food to eat | between the two warring sides.	Here the meaning is similar to the original sentence. The syntax of this sentence – the order of the phrases – can be confusing to the reader. By putting the phrase *between the two warring sides* at the end, it can lead a reader to think the people who need food are literally in the space between the two sides as they fight... in the middle of a battlefield! Whereas the author's intent is to say that Abuelito led his mule train through battlefields to get to the people who needed the food.
What if we were to take out the prepositional phrase *between the two warring sides*? How would that affect the meaning of the sentence?	He ran a mule train ~~between the two warring sides~~ to make sure all the people had food to eat.	The sentence still tells us what Abuelito did during the Revolution. It still helps the reader understand that he was compassionate. It does not help the reader realize how dangerous the job was – and therefore doesn't lead us to understand that Abuelito was also courageous.

(Continued)

Ask	Possible Answers	Food for Thought
Is there anything else we could take out of this sentence?	He ran a mule train ~~between the two warring sides to make sure all the people had food to eat.~~	You could also remove *to make sure all the people had food to eat*. The sentence *He ran a mule train* still tells us what Abuelito did in the war but we lose the character development the author is going for.
What questions would you have as a reader if the writer simply wrote: He ran a mule train.	Students might respond with: • Where did he run a mule train? • Why did he run a mule train? • What is a mule train?	Notice and discuss how the author anticipated these questions. He answered them with the different chunks.
Which chunk answers the question where?	He ran a mule train **between two warring sides.**	Yes, this prepositional phrase gives us more information about the location of where something happens.
Which chunk answers the question of why he ran a mule train?	He ran a mule train | between two warring sides | **to make sure all the people had food to eat.**	The adverbial phrase *to make sure all the people had food to eat* tells us more about Abuelito's motivation to run a mule train between warring sides.
Sometimes authors answer all of the questions readers may have. How did the author answer our question – what is a mule train – in this graphic novel?	There are a few pictures that illustrate this sentence.	Part of the complexity of a graphic novel is that the author is interweaving the text and pictures together to create meaning. Students may need to be reminded that pictures often carry context for the reader.

SENTENCE DIGS

APPLY

During this part, students quickly apply their new knowledge about the sentence to their reading and writing. These are quick efforts and may be followed up with more practice.

Discuss: Turn and talk: What does this detail reveal about Abuelito's character?

Writing focus: Lengthen your sentences with a prepositional phrase to tell your reader where something is happening.

> **Showcase sentence:** He ran a mule train between the two warring sides to make sure all the people had food to eat.

Heavy scaffold: He led _____ (Who or what?) between _____ (Where?).

Example: He led <u>the children</u> between <u>the rows of tables to make sure they found their seats</u>.

Light scaffold: He ran a _____ (noun) between _____ (noun – where?) to make sure _____ (What happened?).

Example: He ran an <u>ice cream stand</u> between <u>two baseball fields</u> to make sure <u>he had plenty of customers</u>.

No scaffold: Invite students to emulate the showcase sentence within their own writing.

Thought Partners: _____

Sentence Dig W5.1
THINK SHEET: WRITING FOCUS

STRATEGY: Sentence Extension

Write the showcase sentence from the sentence dig in the space below:

[   ]

Directions:

Extend each of the following sentences by adding a prepositional phrase. A prepositional phrase starts with a preposition and ends with a noun.

You start a prepositional phrase with a preposition such as:

above	across	against	along	among	around	at	before
behind	below	beneath	beside	by	down	from	in
into	near	of	off	on	to	onto	with

1. Pedro enjoyed reading comics.
   _____

2. Pedro likes to draw.
   _____

3. When we heard our dad whistle, we knew it was time to go.
   _____

Challenge: Extend one of your sentences above by adding an infinitive phrase. An infinitive is the word *to + a verb*. Example: *He ran a mule train between the two warring sides **to make** sure all the people had food to eat.*

_____

_____

_____

SENTENCE DIG W5.2: APPOSITIVE PHRASE: THEME

Text: *Ruth Bader Ginsburg: The Case of R.B.G. vs Inequality* by Jonah Winter, illustrated by Stacy Innerst, page 34

Grades: 3-5

Book summary: *Ruth Bader Ginsburg: The Case of R.B.G. vs Inequality* reveals the everyday inequities Ruth faced due to her gender and religion. Through her tenacious spirit and unwavering dedication to her own goals, Winter and Innerst tell the story of this modern day hero - Ruth Bader Ginsburg: her quest for an education, her fight to be seen and treated equally, and her desire to inspire women everywhere. With so much rich writing and historical detail, you'll want to return to this book again and again, as we do in this sentence dig.

> **Showcase sentence:** She did so | because she wanted people | - **especially young women** - | to see at least one woman | on the Supreme Court.

Rationale: This text is rich with sentences to savor and study. In this part of the story, the author continues to build toward their theme that Ruth Bader Ginsberg is a symbol for justice, and in this sentence, they do so by adding information using an appositive phrase. An appositive phrase gives more information about a noun it follows. It's often set apart with commas, but in this case, the author chose to use dashes to give extra emphasis to the phrase.

How does understanding this sentence help us as writers? How does this detail connect back to the text? This sentence helps the reader understand that Ruth was determined to be a role model for young women. Also, it reminds us she was the only woman on the Supreme Court at the time, so her mental and physical toughness mattered as she symbolized justice and what it meant to overcome gender inequality.

Ask: How does this sentence support the theme: Ruth Bader Ginsburg was a symbol of justice for many people? *This sentence shows that R.B.G. understood that her work mattered to others, especially women.*

NOTE: If students struggle with this, return to this discussion at the end of the sentence dig.

TAKE APART

Remember, your chunks are on sentence strips. Move them around to help students focus on one chunk and then another. You'll move them back together later.

Chunk	Possible Questions to Ask	Possible Answers
She did so	Who or what is this sentence about? How do you know? What did Ruth do? What word or words does the author use to tell us this?	Ruth is the subject of the sentence because the author uses the pronoun she, which refers to Ruth. She returned to work only 19 days after having major surgery to treat cancer. The word so is used as a pronoun to refer to this situation or action referred to prior to this sentence.
because she wanted people	What does the word *because* signal to the reader? What "people" is this referring to?	The word *because* signals to the reader that the author is going to tell us what was motivating Ruth. The people of the United States of America.
– **especially young women** –	How does this chunk connect to the rest of the sentence? What does the word *especially* mean? What is its effect in this sentence?	It's an appositive phrase, which gives more information about the noun – people. The word *especially* singles out something as being special or for emphasis. In this sentence, Ruth wants other women to see that women belong on the Supreme Court.
to see at least one woman	What does this chunk mean? Why is it important to the sentence?	At least means no less than. This chunk reminds us that Ruth was the only woman on the court, so she felt she had to be there. This is important to the sentence because it explains why Ruth returned to work so quickly. There were no other women on the Supreme Court... yet!
on the Supreme Court.	What type of phrase is this? What does this tell us? Why is the Supreme Court capitalized?	This is a prepositional phrase that tells us WHERE we should see at least one woman. It's capitalized because it is a proper noun. There is only one US Supreme Court.

PUT TOGETHER

During this part, the sentence chunks may be mixed up or off to the side. Invite students to manipulate the chunks when putting the sentence back together and/or while rearranging them.

Ask	Possible Answers	Food for Thought
What is the original order of this sentence? What kind of sentence is this: simple, compound, complex, or compound-complex?	She did so because she wanted people – **especially young women** – to see at least one woman on the Supreme Court.	This is a complex sentence. There is an independent clause: *she did so* followed by a dependent clause with a subordinating conjunction: *because she wanted people – especially young women – to see at least one woman on the Supreme Court.*
If you take out the appositive phrase – *especially young women* – does the sentence still make sense? Does it have the same effect?	She did so because she wanted people – ~~especially young women~~ – to see at least one woman on the Supreme Court.	It does make sense and is still a strong sentence. It doesn't have the same effect because it doesn't single out young women. By having the appositive phrase, especially young women, the author is reminding us of the theme that R.B.G. is a symbol for justice. Being the *first* and *only* woman on the Supreme Court breaks a gender barrier, especially for women.
If you removed the phrase *at least*, how does that change the sentence?	She did so because she wanted people – especially young women – to see ~~at least~~ one woman on the Supreme Court.	The sentence still means the same thing but loses a little of its emphasis. The phrase *at least* reminds us that there were no other women on the Supreme Court at the time… that gender inequality was still something women were fighting against.

APPLY

During this part, students quickly apply their new knowledge about the sentence to their reading and writing. These are quick efforts and may be followed up with more practice.

Discuss: How does the showcase sentence support the theme: Ruth Bader Ginsburg was a symbol of justice for many people? What are some other examples from the book where Ruth is a symbol of justice?

Writing focus: Writers use appositives to add more information about a noun.

> **Showcase sentence:** She did so because she wanted people – **especially young women** – to see at least one woman on the Supreme Court.

Heavy scaffold: My mom _____ because she wanted _____ – especially
                            Did what?   *Who?*

_____ – to _____.
    Who?   *Do what?*

Example: My mom <u>cheered loudly</u> because she wanted <u>the players</u> – especially <u>me</u> – to <u>hear her</u>.

Light scaffold: _____ _____ because _____ wanted _____
                      subject   *verb (predicate)*   *pronoun*   *Who/what?*

– especially _____ – to _____.
                Who/what?   *infinitive verb phrase*

Example: <u>The trap-door spider dug its burrow near the pond</u> because <u>it</u> wanted <u>prey</u> – especially <u>small frogs and lizards</u> – to <u>wander into its trap</u>.

No scaffold: Invite students to emulate the showcase sentence within their own writing.

Thought Partners: _____

Sentence Dig W5.2
THINK SHEET: WRITING FOCUS

STRATEGY: Sentence Extension

Write the showcase sentence from the sentence dig in the space below:

[   ]

Directions:

Extend each sentence below by adding an appositive phrase to rename (or clarify) one of the nouns. Use the information in parentheses to help you.

Example:

Ruth Bader Ginsberg overcame many obstacles. (The second woman on the Supreme Court)

Ruth Bader Ginsberg, **the second woman on the Supreme Court**, overcame many obstacles.

1. Martin Ginsberg was a lawyer. (Ruth's husband)
   _____

2. Jimmy Carter appointed Ruth to be a judge on the US Court of Appeals. (The President of the United States)
   _____

3. Ruth tied for first in her class. (One of only a few women in Harvard Law School)
   _____

Challenge: Go into your own writing work. Extend some of your sentences by adding appositive phrases to give readers more information about important nouns.

CHAPTER 5   Writing: Important Details   **127**

SENTENCE DIG W5.3: COMPOUND PREDICATE: THEME

Text: *Let 'Er Buck: George Fletcher the People's Champion* by Vaunda Micheaux Nelson, illustrated by Gordon C. James, page 29

Grades: 3–5

Book summary: *Let 'Er Buck: George Fletcher the People's Champion* is the story of George Fletcher, an African-American cowboy, and his ride to the Hall of Fame. In 1911, George made it to the finals of the Pendleton Round-Up saddle bronc competition. But when a white man was declared the winner over George, the rowdy crowd was stunned to silence and action. Quickly they collected a monetary prize and made George the People's Champion. This delightful book is full of cowboy sayings and will engage readers who love reading true stories and finding new heroes.

Showcase sentence: In the warm glow of the setting sun, | spirited spectators | **lifted George onto their shoulders** | and paraded around the arena.

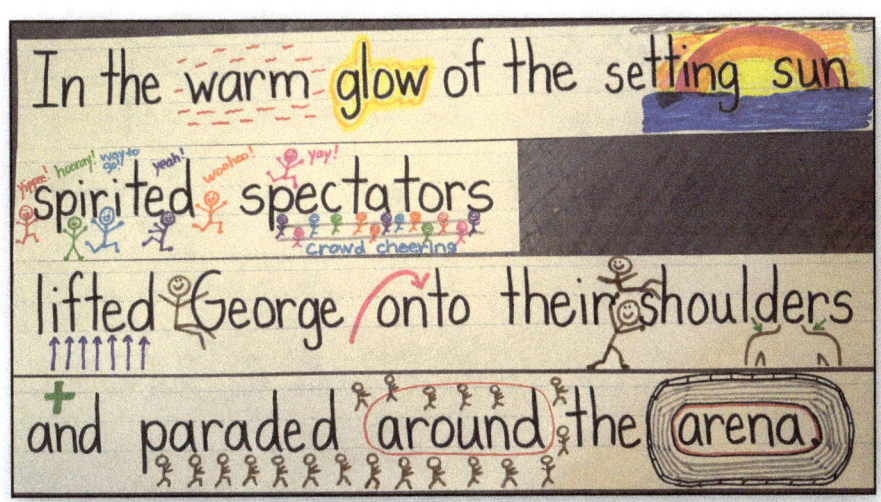

FIGURE 5.1
Annotated sentence dig with sketches to support comprehension

Rationale: This sentence is a great example of a compound predicate. The spectators didn't just parade around the arena – they did so with George on their shoulders. George was being paraded around the arena. Helping young writers understand that the subject of their sentence – spirited spectators – can do more than one thing in a sentence will empower them to write longer and stronger sentences.

How does understanding this sentence help us as writers? How does this detail connect back to the text? This sentence is the resolution of the story. George wasn't declared the winner, although he was clearly the best rider. The crowd was stunned at the climax of the story. The story is resolved when the spectators claim George as their champion - lifting him on their shoulders and marching him around as if he had won the contest. This adds to the theme of the story that we can all contribute to racial justice.

Discuss: Who is this sentence about?

The sentence is about the spirited spectators - the people who were watching the event. Because there are several nouns in the sentence - glow, sun, spectators, George, shoulders, arena - many children will assume George is the subject because it's the only proper noun. Others may say sun because it appears early in the sentence. It's important to be clear that the spectators are the subject of the sentence. Clarify this if students are confused.

TAKE APART

Remember, your chunks are on sentence strips. Move them around to help students focus on one chunk and then another. You'll move them back together later.

Chunk	Possible Questions to Ask	Possible Answers
In the warm glow of the setting sun, /	What does this chunk tell us?	This chunk tells us the time of day – it's evening, the sun is setting.
	What kind of phrases are *in the warm glow* and *of the setting sun*?	Students may say these are descriptive phrases. They're correct, the phrases are describing the setting and helping us understand the time.
		But these are also prepositional phrases. They start with a preposition (*in, of*) they end with a noun (*glow, sun*) and they give the reader information about "when" something is happening.
spirited spectators /	What does this phase mean?	Spirited = excited, full of energy
		Spectators = people watching an event
	Who or what is this sentence about?	This phrase refers to the excited people in the arena who saw the event.
		The spirited spectators
lifted George onto their shoulders /	Who lifted George onto their shoulders?	The spirited spectators
	What is George doing in this chunk?	He's being carried on people's shoulders.
and paraded around the arena.	What does it mean to parade?	To march and celebrate in public

PUT TOGETHER

During this part, the sentence chunks may be mixed up or off to the side. Invite students to manipulate the chunks when putting the sentence back together and/or while rearranging them.

Ask	Possible Answers	Food for Thought
What's the original order of this sentence?	In the warm glow of the setting sun, | spirited spectators | lifted George onto their shoulders | and paraded around the arena.	If students struggle putting the chunks back together, remind them they can use capitalization and punctuation as clues.
How does the writer tell us what the spirited spectators did?	In the warm glow of the setting sun, | spirited spectators | **lifted** George onto their shoulders | and **paraded** around the arena.	This is a compound predicate – when the writer includes two actions or verbs / verb phrases. Sometimes writers include two verb phrases because the subject of the sentence is doing more than one thing at the same time – or two actions happen very quickly one after the other.
Can we change the order of the verbs in this sentence? Why or why not?	No; the sentence won't make sense. One has to lift George first and then parade or march with him on shoulders. In the warm glow of the setting sun, | spirited spectators | **paraded** around the arena | and **lifted** George onto their shoulders.	Sentences are often told in order. So the order of verbs do matter when a writer creates a compound predicate or even a list of verbs. Typically, what happens first goes first in the sentence.
The author leverages shades of meaning in this sentence. For example, she uses *glow* instead of light and *spirited* instead of wild. Why do you think the author used the word *paraded* instead of marched?	**paraded** around the arena vs **marched** around the arena Students may say parade sounds more fun and out of control like a spirited spectator may be. March sounds more formal and orchestrated.	The author may have chosen parade because it is a form of celebration and the crowd was celebrating their champion – George Fletcher.
How would one write this as two sentences?	In the warm glow of the setting sun, spirited spectators lifted George onto their shoulders. They paraded around the arena.	A compound predicate shares the same subject. So when writers reread their drafts and see two sentences in a row that have the same subject, they can choose to combine those sentences with a compound predicate.

APPLY

During this part, students quickly apply their new knowledge about the sentence to their reading and writing. These are quick efforts and may be followed up with more practice.

Discuss:

- Who is this sentence about?
- What are they doing? How do we know?
- Draw a quick sketch of this sentence. Label your sketch using the words from the sentence.

Writing focus: Writers can combine sentences with a compound predicate. This is a sentence that has one subject but two or more predicates (verbs).

> **Showcase sentence:** In the warm glow of the setting sun, spirited spectators **lifted** George onto their shoulders and **paraded** around the arena.

Heavy scaffold: In the warm glow of the setting sun, the children _____ and _____.
                                                                                     Did what?   Did what?

Example: In the warm glow of the setting sun, the children <u>put away their toys</u> and <u>went inside for the night</u>.

Light scaffold: _____, _____ _____ and
                 prepositional phrase: When   Who or what? (subject)   verb/verb phrase

_____.
verb/verb phrase

Example: <u>Ahead of my morning alarm</u>, <u>my dog jumped on my bed</u> and <u>licked my face to wake me up</u>!

No scaffold: Invite students to emulate the showcase sentence within their own writing.

Thought Partners: _____

Sentence Dig: W5.3
THINK SHEET: WRITING FOCUS

STRATEGY: Sentence Combining

Write the showcase sentence from the sentence dig in the space below:

[   ]

Directions:
Combine the following sentences by creating a compound predicate.

Example:

George **worked as a cowboy**.

George **competed in competitions**.

*George **worked as a cowboy** <u>and</u> **competed in competitions**.*

1. George pulled a horse's name from the hat.
   George hoped for a hard-bucking horse.

   _____

   _____

2. The horse, Lightfoot, leaped around the arena.
   The horse, Lightfoot, snorted around the arena.

   _____

   _____

3. The horse, Sweeney, reared on his hind legs.
   The horse, Sweeney, bucked wildly.

   _____

   _____

Challenge: Combine these sentences to create a compound sentence with a compound predicate.

The spectators crowded the arena.

The crowd cheered loudly.

The crowd shouted themselves hoarse.

_____

_____

_____

_____

SENTENCE DIG W5.4: COMPLEX SENTENCE: MAIN IDEA

Text: *The Magnificent Migration: On Safari with Africa's Last Great Herds*, by Sy Montgomery, photos by Roger and Logan Wood, page 18

Grades: 3-5

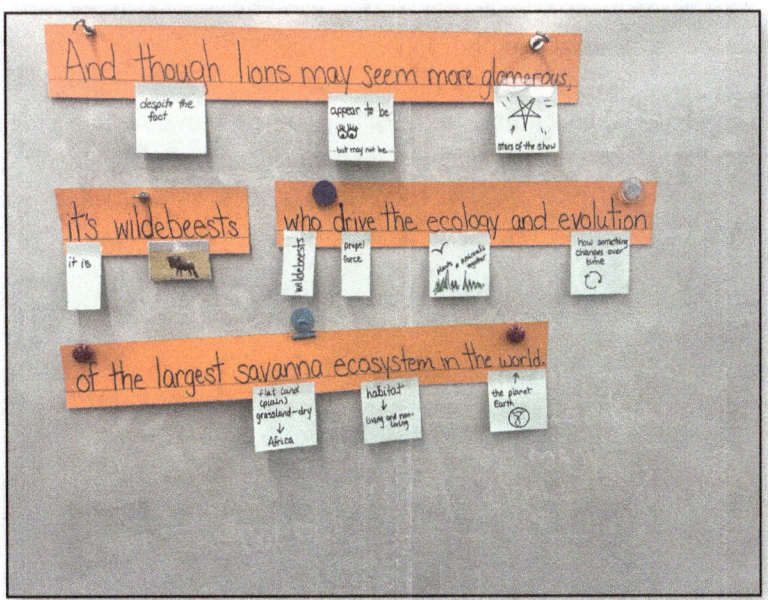

FIGURE 5.2
Annotated sentence dig with sketches to support comprehension

Book summary: This informational book describes the great migration that happens each year in Africa... the migration of the wildebeests. Their migration is not one they take alone, but with them they bring an entourage of other animals, changing the ecosystem as they go. Coupled with photographs, the text ripples with information about this unusual animal, its herd, and the amazing journey they take across the African savanna. Look out lions - there is a new king in town!

Showcase sentence: And **though lions may seem more glamorous,** | it's wildebeests | who drive the ecology and evolution | of the largest savanna ecosystem | in the world.

Rationale: I love this sentence for how the author seems to know their audience. When I think of an African safari, I think of lions and elephants and maybe zebras. I don't even register wildebeests as an animal on the safari. Yet, this sentence grabs a reader's attention by naming the glamorous status lions have while letting us know the true rock stars of the savanna are the wildebeests. In doing so, the author piques our interest and pulls us further into the text. This is the kind of writing we want students to do.

How does understanding this sentence help us as writers? How does this detail connect back to the text? This sentence sets up the main idea for the entire book. Throughout the text, the author continues to reflect on how the wildebeests' journey impacts other animals and the land. With this one sentence, the author establishes that lions may reign in our hearts but wildebeests deserve our attention.

Discuss: Who or what is this sentence about? How do you know? *It's important for students to establish that the sentence is about wildebeests. The subject of the sentence is the pronoun "it" referring to wildebeests. Understanding this sets students up for success while decomposing the rest of the sentence.*

TAKE APART

Remember, your chunks are on sentence strips. Move them around to help students focus on one chunk and then another. You'll move them back together later.

Chunk	Possible Questions to Ask	Possible Answers
And **though lions may seem more glamorous,**	What is this chunk about?	Lions
	What is the author saying about lions in this chunk?	The author is saying that lions seem more glamorous.
	What does the author mean by glamorous?	The lions are attractive or exotic. People tend to be interested in lions.
	Why did the author start the chunk with *And though*... what does though mean?	*Though* means however or despite the fact.
		The author grabs our attention in the text by focusing on what the lions are doing. Then they shift to the main scientist and why he studies wildebeests. Using the connector – And though – allows the author to connect the excitement of seeing lions to the reason Dick Estes studies wildebeests.
	Why do you think the author uses the phrase *may seem* in this chunk?	By using the phrase *may seem*, the author indicates that readers who think this haven't considered another animal. The author relies on thinking the audience knows about lions and are impressed by them. But this chunk lets us know that the author has another animal in mind that is even more impressive than lions.

(Continued)

Chunk	Possible Questions to Ask	Possible Answers
Discuss the question before displaying the chunk: it's wildebeests	Which chunk is the kernel sentence (also known as the simple sentence)? Which chunk has the main subject and predicate? How does this chunk connect to the first one we talked about – *and though lions may seem more glamorous*?	"it's wildebeests" Consider unpacking the contraction to say – it is wildebeests. This is the independent clause, and it can stand alone. Everything else in the sentence is growing our understanding about this chunk. The first chunk leaves us wondering – more glamorous than what? This chunk completes the comparison: lions may seem more glamorous than wildebeests.
Ask the question before pulling out the chunk: who drive the ecology and evolution	Which chunk tells us what the wildebeests do that makes them more glamorous than lions? What is the relative pronoun *who* referring to? What does ecology mean? What does evolution mean? What does this chunk mean?	"who drive the ecology and evolution" Who refers to the wildebeests. We know relative pronouns follow the nouns they reference. So this chunk is about the wildebeests. Ecology is the study of how living things interact with their environment. In this case, it means changes in populations (of animals) over time. Wildebeests propel (or direct) the way living things interact with the savanna and changes in different animal populations over time. (Lions just hunt and eat other animals.)
of the largest savanna ecosystem	How does this chunk help readers understand the sentence?	It tells us where the wildebeests drive the ecology and evolution.
in the world.	What impact does this chunk have on the rest of the sentence?	This lets us know more about where this is happening. It's not just the largest savanna ecosystem in a country or on a continent... it's the largest in the entire world. The impact of this tells the reader that the wildebeests are extremely important and deserve our attention.

PUT TOGETHER

During this part, the sentence chunks may be mixed up or off to the side. Invite students to manipulate the chunks when putting the sentence back together and/or while rearranging them.

Ask	Possible Answers	Food for Thought
What is the original order of this sentence?	And **though lions may seem more glamorous,** | it's wildebeests | who drive the ecology and evolution | of the largest savanna ecosystem | in the world.	You might note or point out the relative pronoun *who* follows the noun that it references. When we see relative pronouns like who, that, which, when, or where, it introduces a clause and should follow the noun it describes. So in this case, *who drive the ecology and evolution* needs to come right after *it's wildebeests* because *who* refers to and tells more about *wildebeests*.
What kind of sentence is this?	It's a complex sentence. It has one independent clause linked to a dependent clause.	Note that *and though lions may seem more glamorous* is a dependent clause. It doesn't stand on its own because it doesn't hold a complete thought.
How could we rewrite this as two separate sentences?	Lions may seem more glamorous. It's wildebeests | who drive the ecology and evolution | of the largest savanna ecosystem | in the world.	By removing the connectors "and though," *lions may seem more glamorous* becomes an independent clause – a complete sentence. When you remove *and though* the sentence about lions seems disconnected. A reader may find themselves wondering *more glamorous than what?* By using the connecting phrase *and though*, the author delivers the idea that lions may seem glamorous but wildebeests are the driving force on the savanna.
How can we make this a compound sentence?	Lions may seem more glamorous, | **but** it's wildebeests | who drive the ecology and evolution | of the largest savanna ecosystem | in the world. OR Lions may seem more glamorous, | **yet** it's wildebeests | who drive the ecology and evolution of the largest savanna ecosystem | in the world.	The conjunction matters in this compound sentence. The author is comparing our attraction to lions vs wildebeests. We need a conjunction (but/yet) that shows these two ideas are different or even opposite.
Why do you think the author chose to write the sentence as a complex sentence?	Answers will vary.	It's important to note that authors make sentence structure choices based on several factors such as wanting to create a fluent paragraph, or creating a mood or tone for the text.

APPLY

During this part, students quickly apply their new knowledge about the sentence to their reading and writing. These are quick efforts and may be followed up with more practice.

Discuss: What purpose does this sentence serve in this text?

Some students will say that this sentence grabs our attention as readers. Or they may say that it challenges our beliefs as readers, making us want to read on. This sentence is the main idea of the book and gives the author's perspective on wildebeests. The rest of the text will connect back to this sentence over and over again.

Writing focus: Practice writing a complex sentence like the author by starting it with *And though…*

> **Showcase sentence:** And **though lions may seem more glamorous**, it's wildebeests who drive the ecology and evolution of the largest savanna ecosystem in the world.

Heavy scaffold: And though _____ (an animal) may seem _____ (adjective to describe the animal), it's _____ (another animal) who _____ (Does what?).

Example: And though <u>puppies</u> may seem <u>energetic</u>, it's <u>ferrets</u> who <u>race around the house and climb the furniture</u>.

Light scaffold: And though _____ (noun) may seem _____ (adjective), it's _____ (noun) _____ (relative pronoun) _____ (Do what (that reflects the adjective you used earlier)) _____ (prepositional phrase (of, in, over, after, before…)).

Example: And though <u>bacon</u> may seem <u>unhealthy</u>, it's <u>cereal</u> <u>that</u> <u>has a lot of sugar</u> <u>in one serving</u>.

No scaffold: Invite students to emulate the showcase sentence within their own writing.

Thought Partners: _____

Sentence Dig W5.4
THINK SHEET: WRITING FOCUS

STRATEGY: Sentence Combining

Write the showcase sentence from the sentence dig in the space below:

Directions:

Combine the following sentences into a complex sentence by using a subordinate conjunction to connect the two sentences. Some subordinating conjunctions include:

| after | although | as | when | while | until | because | before | if | since | though |

Example:

    The wildebeests travel a thousand miles through the savanna each year.

    The wildebeests encounter different animals on their journey.

Because *the wildebeests travel a thousand miles through the savanna each year, they encounter different animals on their journey.*

1. Lions are known as predators who stalk, attack, and eat their prey.

    Lions spend most of their time resting.

_____

_____

_____

_____

2. Wildebeests move across the savanna.
   The land is trampled.

   _____

   _____

3. Wildebeest run in large herds.
   A wildebeest on its own is easy prey.

   _____

   _____

Challenge: Extend this sentence by adding an independent clause.

Although wildebeests are large animals, _____.

CHAPTER 6
Crafting Language

Writing is an act of faith, not a grammar trick.
- E.B. White

I am not a runner. Though I have run in the past - 10ks and half marathons - I really don't enjoy any part of running. My sister-in-law is a runner. And she's fast! She loves zipping around her neighborhood and the "runner's high" she gets from the adrenaline that pulses through her body. This is something I've never experienced. A runner's high? Nope. Not me. My sister-in-law swears this is because I simply haven't run far enough yet. But I'm left to wonder - 13 miles isn't enough? Although I am skeptical about this "runner's high," I do know there is a wonderful feeling that comes from writing a well-crafted sentence. A writer's high, perhaps? Regardless, one thing I know for sure is that with intentional instruction, we can guide every student toward that feeling of pride and success that comes from writing well-crafted sentences.

When I was teaching sixth grade, I had a student named Chase. Chase was one of those students who teachers loved to have in class. He seemed to like learning, got along with the other children, and worked hard to do his best work. Writing, however, was his least favorite subject. He often complained, "I'll never write like Julius Lester or Cynthia Rylant!" The only response I had for him was "Good. We already have Julius Lester and Cynthia Rylant. We need a Chase in our literary world!" He'd roll his eyes in that way a middle schooler does and would get back to work. I'll admit, he wasn't winning any writing contests any time soon, but he didn't need to - the reward for writing is in our ability to express our ideas in a way that moves readers.

I was out one day and came back to a long note from the substitute. You know the kind - a note about every little thing that went wrong and who did what. At the end of the note, the sub had stapled a poem Chase - who was also out that day - sent in with a friend. (I loved it so much I have it memorized.)

Itch, itch, itch, I itch!
Mosquito bites are itchy.
Oh no - chicken pox!

This poem - this haiku - may not have similes and metaphors or vivid verbs and awesome adjectives. In fact, on first glance, it may actually seem pretty plain - language anyone would use. But at the same time, it's a perfect poem: the use of repetition, an explicit simple sentence followed by an exclamation, which could be considered a functional fragment, all capturing that moment when you think you might go crazy with how much bug bites itch - only to find out that it's chicken pox and you're in for a long week!

This is what writers do as they craft language. It's not about knowing a lot of grammar or using flashy figurative language. It's about panache. Each writer has their own style, their own voice, their own way of putting words together. Sometimes authors show huge feelings and actions and ideas with great flair like Julius Lester and Jerry Pinkney's work in *John Henry*. But other authors reveal big moments with simple words and sentences that rip right at your heart like Ellen Levine and Kadir Nelson's work in *Henry's Freedom Box: A True Story from the Underground Railroad*.

It's helpful to marvel over sentences we love and study, with deep focus, how they were crafted. Wondering - *How did the author write this sentence?* Asking - *Is the sentence powerful by itself or is it the way it connects to the rest of the text that makes it powerful? How can I write a sentence like this? What crafting strategies can I learn from studying this sentence?*

Whether you call it "reading like a writer" or "studying mentor texts" with sentence digs, we focus our instructional lens on a showcase sentence - taking it apart to see its different chunks, putting it back together to see how those chunks build meaning together, and practicing the same kind of craft in our own writing. In this intentional exploration, students not only investigate how to use grammar structures to craft sentences, but they'll also learn more about when to do so - as they study other sentences or additional parts of the text.

As you dive into the lessons that follow in this chapter, you'll note a slight change in their introduction sections. Instead of launching this by studying and discussing the sentence, each lesson kicks off with an opportunity to "set the scene." This small but important shift is a reminder that, if we're going to study not only *how* authors craft sentences but also *when* these craft moves are most effective, we need to be in the zone, so to speak. We need to be wrapped in the context of the story to feel the full effect of the sentence's power and to find moments to try these same efforts in our own writing.

You'll also notice a slight change in the number of sentences in a dig. In some of the following sentence digs, you'll see that we're studying a series of brief sentences. This is because authors sometimes pull craft moves across sentences. This lifts the level of the dig beyond students thinking about one sentence at a time to considering how several sentences can work together to create an effect for the reader. Looking at sentences this way, digging into how craft is constructed and carried across sentences, will give young writers another powerful strategy for their toolbox.

SHOWCASE SENTENCES AT A GLANCE

Lesson	Focus	Author's Purpose/ Grammatical Structure	Text	Sentence
W6.1	Simile	Building tension Character reaction	"One Hot Mess" by Carmen Deedy in *Funny Girl: Funniest Stories Ever* by Betsy Bird	Then, in infinitesimal increments – **like molasses seeping from a broken jar along a cold winter floor**, one millimeter at a time – a smile spread across his face.
W6.2	Alliteration	Imagery Character relationships	*Playing the Cards You're Dealt* by Varian Johnson	The boy had even tacked on Love Anthony at the end of the note – **a little sugar to soothe the sting of slipping out** on his parents.
W6.3	Onomatopoeia	Supporting detail to main idea	*Insect Superpowers: 18 Real Bugs That Smash, Zap, Hypnotize, Sting, and Devour!* By Kate Messner, illustrated by Jillian Nickell	When another insect flies too close – **Buzz-Swish-Zap!** – the robber fly darts out and captures it with long, strong, bristly legs that can hold tight to prey.
W6.4	Repeated subjects and verbs	Building tension	*Henry's Freedom Box: A True Story from the Underground Railroad* by Ellen Levine, illustrated by Kadir Nelson	**He couldn't** move. **He couldn't** think. **He couldn't** work.

SENTENCE DIG W6.1: SIMILE: BUILDING TENSION

Text: "One Hot Mess" by Carmen Deedy in *Funny Girl: Funniest. Stories. Ever* edited by Betsy Bird, page 45

Grades: 4-6

Book summary: This book is a collection of short stories about girls written by female writers. These short stories highlight the humor of everyday life found in experiences with family, friends, and by just being ourselves. "One Hot Mess," written by Carmen Deedy, is about the time she and her family moved into a new apartment. Every time the family moves, Carmen's mother deep cleans the apartment. One thing she does to deep clean is to set the bathtub on fire in order to kill all of the germs. But, what if a young Carmen decides to sell tickets to the neighborhood kids to see this spectacle? And what if the bathtub isn't a cast iron tub - able to withstand the fire? What if the bathtub is fiberglass and isn't meant to contain fire? Chaos. Written with the sense of humor and familial love Carmen Deedy has become known for, this short story will resonate with anyone who thought their family was normal... until they realized they weren't.

> **Showcase sentence:** Then, in infinitesimal increments | - **like molasses seeping from a broken jar along a cold winter floor,** | one millimeter at a time - | a smile spread across his face.

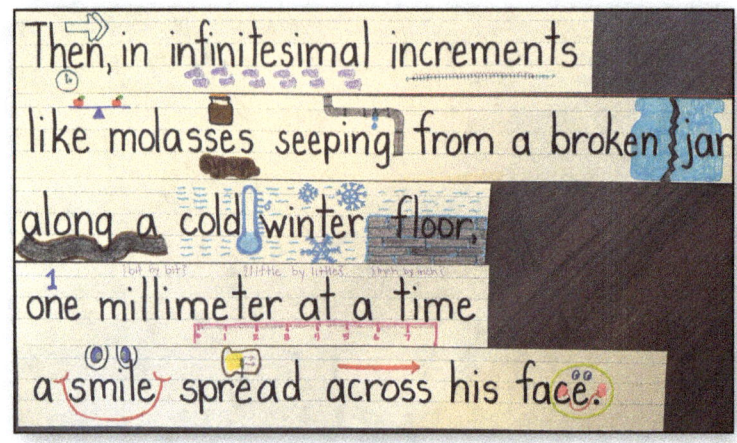

FIGURE 6.1
Annotated sentence dig with sketches to support comprehension

Rationale: Carmen Deedy's work is worth returning to again and again because of the writing gems she has tucked inside her work. I love this sentence - it may be my favorite in the whole book. This sentence works at being slow: it's a long sentence, it has lots of punctuation, the vocabulary is rich with sounds and meaning, and the mental picture it creates is perfect for this spot in the story. Most of all, the simile creates a full comparison. Carmen Deedy doesn't just say - *Then, in infinitesimal increments - like molasses - a smile spread across his face.* No way! In true Deedy storytelling style, she drags that moment out - she makes sure we not only visualize molasses but we feel the slowness of the moment. That slowness creates tension and fully captures the feeling during those few seconds when you have just met someone and realized you said something that seems perfectly normal to your own family but may not be "normal" in society. And you're waiting for that judgment - you're either cool or you're doomed. Meanwhile this sentence also captures the split second drama of hearing something that gives you pause and you have to decide whether or not you're going to lean into the situation or hightail it and run. Although the actual time may only be a couple of seconds, it feels slow - not molasses slow - but slow like molasses seeping from a broken jar along a cold winter floor kind of slow. Drama - this sentence is all about the drama!

Set the scene: Just before this moment, the main character, Carmen, is moving into a new apartment with her family. She has just eaten lunch and is running out the door to catch up with her father, who is going to the old apartment for the last load. When she gets outside, she meets a "shaggy-haired" boy who asks if she is the new neighbor. Now, Carmen wants to make a good impression and smiles and asks him, "You wanna watch my mom set fire to the bathtub?"

Can you imagine - this is the first thing out of her mouth! This boy doesn't know her. She doesn't know him, and she's talking about her mom setting fires. His reaction in that moment demonstrates how startled both of them are and yet a friendship is forged.

TAKE APART

Remember, your chunks are on sentence strips. Move them around to help students focus on one chunk and then another. You'll move them back together later.

NOTE: This sentence dig starts with the simple sentence - the subject and predicate. To highlight this, we'll explore the chunks out of order.

Chunk	Possible Questions to Ask	Possible Answers
Ask the question first, then select the chunk to start. a smile spread across his face.	Every sentence – no matter how elaborate – has the basic parts of a sentence: a subject and a predicate. Which chunk has the simple subject and predicate of this sentence? What is the subject? What is the predicate? What did the smile do? Turn and show your partner *a smile spread across your face.*	 ...a smile spread across his face. A smile... specifically the boy's smile. ...spread across his face. If some students smiled slowly, you might ask them why they did that.

(Continued)

146 SENTENCE DIGS

Chunk	Possible Questions to Ask	Possible Answers
Then, in infinitesimal increments	What are increments? The word infinitesimal comes from the word infinite. You may have heard a form of this word in *Toy Story*: "To infinity and beyond!" Knowing this, what do you think infinitesimal means? (Turn and talk.) Take a moment to think about this, and then turn and talk to your partner: If the smile spreads across his face in infinitesimal increments, is the smile appearing fast or slow? Try to act it out together. Let's read this chunk together – Then, in infinitesimal increments… Why do you think Carmen Deedy chose to use alliteration here? What's the effect?	The amount by which something changes. Some students may say – unending. Infinitesimal means *extremely small*. It refers to the idea that no matter how much you divide something, you'll never reach zero. Give affirmative or corrective feedback as needed. Students should figure out that this means an extremely small amount of change, so their smiles should be spreading across their faces rather slowly. The words are hard to say and it feels like a tongue twister. The effect is you can't read it very fast… it slows the reader down. And she wants us to know this moment – this smile – is spreading slowly. The character is not sure how to react to hearing Carmen's mom sets bathtubs on fire.
– like molasses seeping from a broken jar along a cold winter floor,	Which literary device does the author use in this chunk? How do you know? What two things is this simile comparing?	Students may identify this as a simile because it uses *like* to compare something. It's comparing the way the boy's smile spreads across his face to molasses on a cold winter floor.
one millimeter at a time –	Show me with your fingers, how much is a millimeter? How does this chunk connect to the rest of the sentence?	Students should show a very small amount of space – fingers almost touching. Some students may say that it is showing how slow the molasses is going, which means the boy's smile, too, is spreading only a millimeter at a time. Other students may say that it connects to *infinitesimal increments* because millimeters are very small.

PUT TOGETHER

During this part, the sentence chunks may be mixed up or off to the side. Invite students to manipulate the chunks when putting the sentence back together and/or while rearranging them.

Ask	Possible Answers	Food for Thought
What is the correct order of this sentence?	Then, in infinitesimal increments | – **like molasses seeping from a broken jar along a cold winter floor**, | one millimeter at a time – | a smile spread across his face.	This is a tricky sentence to recreate, as the simple sentence is the last chunk. Typically, students write sentences with the simple sentence first and layer on details in the predicate. Consider underlining or highlighting the simple subject and predicate (in different colors) to help anchor this in students' minds.
There are multiple chunks of this sentence that mean: very slow. Can you remove any of the chunks in a way that still lets the reader know that the boy's smile spread slowly across his face? What's the effect of removing one of the chunks?	~~Then, in infinitesimal increments~~ | – **like molasses seeping from a broken jar along a cold winter floor**, | one millimeter at a time – | a smile spread across his face. Then, in infinitesimal increments | – ~~like molasses seeping from a broken jar along a cold winter floor~~, | one millimeter at a time – | a smile spread across his face. Then, in infinitesimal increments | – like molasses seeping from a broken jar along a cold winter floor, | ~~one millimeter at a time –~~ | a smile spread across his face.	The chunks that mean very slowly can be removed individually from this sentence. The reader still gets the sense that the smile wasn't immediate. One thing students may notice is that when you remove the simile, you remove a strong mental image from the reader's mind. This image is particularly useful when trying to help a reader understand just how slow the boy's smile spread. The chunks "one millimeter at a time" in "infinitesimal increments" also provide a mental image, although not quite as strong and the vocabulary may be less familiar to readers.
Notice how the first part of the sentence is difficult to read – causing the reader to read it slowly. At the end of the sentence, Deedy relies on sibilance – in this case creating a soft hiss, like a release of energy – with *…smile spread across his face*. This is easier for a reader to read, and they may find themselves reading that part more quickly. Why do you think the author did this at this point in the story? What is the effect on the reader?	Some students may infer the slowness of the beginning of this sentence represents the boy thinking about what Carmen just said. Likewise, it can represent Carmen's nervousness as she wonders about the boy's reaction. The slowness builds the tension in the scene. The end of the sentence – when the reader realizes the boy is smiling and everything is going to be okay – releases the tension. It's almost like the reader and the characters are breathing a sigh of relief.	A sentence, like this, can not only reveal a character's reaction but it can create and release tension for the reader as well.

APPLY

During this part, students quickly apply their new knowledge about the sentence to their reading and writing. These are quick efforts and may be followed up with more practice.

Discuss: The author's simile is very specific: *...like molasses seeping from a broken jar along a cold winter floor...* Sketch this image.

[ ]

Discuss with your group: Why do you think Carmen Deedy included so many details about the molasses? What was the overall effect on the reader? If it helps, chunk the simile like we chunk a sentence. Discuss each part.

Writing focus: Crafting the just-right simile for a sentence can not only create a mental picture for the reader but also it allows the writer to add depth to the plot, setting, or character.

> **Showcase sentence:** Then, in infinitesimal increments – **like molasses seeping from a broken jar along a cold winter floor**, one millimeter at a time – a smile spread across his face.

Heavy scaffold: Then with top speeds – like _____ _____
                                                          What?   Does what? participle (-ing verb) phrase

– a fire truck raced past the school.

Example: Then with top speeds – like <u>a cheetah chasing its prey</u> – a fire truck raced past the school.

Light scaffold: Then, _____ – like _____
                                    prepositional phrase – how   simile with a participle phrase

_____, _____ – _____
    prepositional phrase – where/when   noun phrase   subject + predicate

Example: Then, <u>without a moment's hesitation</u> – like <u>a parent rescuing her daughter from being hit by a car</u>, <u>a lightning fast, superhero move</u> – <u>my best friend distracted my dad before he saw me sneak a lizard into the house.</u>

No scaffold: Invite students to emulate the showcase sentence within their own writing.

SENTENCE DIG W6.2: ALLITERATION

Text: *Playing the Cards You're Dealt* by Varian Johnson

Grades: 4-6

Book summary: *Playing the Cards You're Dealt* by Varian Johnson is about a ten year old boy, Anthony "Ant" Johnson, who wants to compete in a cards tournament. His family has a rich tradition of playing the game of spades, and Anthony wants to team with his best friend, Jamal, in the junior tournament. But when Jamal gets grounded, the only other player good enough is the new girl in class - Shirley. This book is about their friendship, as well as growing up with imperfect families.

Showcase sentence: The boy had even tacked on | Love Anthony at the end of the note | - **a little sugar to soothe the sting | of slipping out** on his parents.

Rationale: This book is filled with well-written sentences that deserve some attention. This sentence appears quickly after the one presented earlier in Sentence Dig W4.2. Yet, the use of alliteration in this sentence is too good to pass up. If your students struggle to craft alliteration in a way that smoothly slips details into a scene, then this lesson is a must.

The alliteration in this sentence softens the sentence's tone like the way "Love Anthony" soothes the sting for his parents. In this sentence, …*a little sugar to soothe the sting of slipping out* is actually an appositive phrase telling us more about the motivation behind the note. However, the repeated /s/ sound gives off a soft vibe, a quick vibe, a slipping-out-but-I-don't-want-you-to-be angry kind of vibe. It leaves the reader walking away thinking, *this kid is smooth!*

Setting the Scene: Anthony is in his first year of middle school. He wants to walk to school by himself, and maybe meet his friend Jamal to practice their card game. Anthony's parents like to walk him to school, and they definitely want his mind on school - not cards. One morning, Anthony leaves for school early, hoping he'll be out of the house before his parents are up and dressed. Because he is a responsible son, he leaves a note, so they won't worry.

TAKE APART

Remember, your chunks are on sentence strips. Move them around to help students focus on one chunk and then another. You'll move them back together later.

Chunk	Possible Questions to Ask	Possible Answers
The boy had even tacked on	Who is the subject of this sentence? What is the verb phrase? What does it mean to *tack on*? Why do you think the author used the word *even* in the middle of the verb phrase *...had even tacked on...*	The boy (Ant). ...had even tacked on... Tacked on means to add on. When *even* is used like this, it typically is used to emphasize something that can be surprising. A middle schooler who is sneaking out to leave for school early may not typically take the time to write a note and end it with such a sweet closing.
Love Anthony at the end of the note	How does this chunk connect to the sentence?	This is what Anthony "tacked on." He ended his note with *Love Anthony*.
– a little sugar to soothe the sting	What does this chunk mean? Does it literally mean there is sugar on the note? Anthony is sneaking off to school early in the morning without his parents' permission. They'll likely be upset. Why do you think the author added this on at the end of the sentence?	A little sugar is an idiom often used in the South that means sweetness or love. So in this chunk, it means that "Love Anthony" was a little sweetness to offset the sting or the frustration his parents might feel that he left for school early. He knew they'd be upset – "the sting" – so he wanted to give them a little sweetness, something that might soften the blow.
of slipping out on his parents.	How does this chunk bring meaning to the sentence?	This chunk lets us know that the "sting" is Ant's act of leaving early without his parents. It reminds us of why his parents will likely be upset and why he was sure to sign the note, Love, Anthony.

PUT TOGETHER

During this part, the sentence chunks may be mixed up or off to the side. Invite students to manipulate the chunks when putting the sentence back together and/or while rearranging them.

Ask	Possible Answers	Food for Thought
What is the original order of this sentence?	The boy had even tacked on	Love Anthony at the end of the note	**– a little sugar to soothe the sting**	**of slipping out** on his parents.	The first two chunks form the basic, simple sentence. The last two chunks give us more information about the end of the note and the significance of Love, Anthony.
Can we rearrange this sentence and it still make sense?	A little sugar to soothe the sting	of slipping out on his parents,	the boy ~~even~~ tacked on	Love Anthony at the end of the note.	Likely students will notice that whatever way they rearrange the sentence, it still doesn't feel as satisfying as the original one. If so, discuss this further.

(Continued)

Ask	Possible Answers	Food for Thought
What if we removed the last two chunks of the sentence? What effect does it have on the meaning of the sentence?	The boy had even tacked on | Love Anthony at the end of the note | ~~– a little sugar to soothe the sting~~ | ~~of slipping out on his parents.~~	The sentence still makes sense, but the reader can't tell if the boy is being manipulative or sweet. *A little sugar to soothe the sting of slipping out on his parents* helps the reader understand that Anthony is being intentionally kind even if he's going against his parents' wishes.

APPLY

During this part, students quickly apply their new knowledge about the sentence to their reading and writing. These are quick efforts and may be followed up with more practice.

Discuss: When authors take time to develop a relationship between characters, it is usually important to the story's plot and theme. What does this sentence tell you about the kind of relationship Anthony has with his parents? How is this relationship important in the story so far?

Writing focus: We can use alliteration to give more information in a sentence.

> **Showcase sentence:** The boy had even tacked on Love Anthony at the end of the note – **a little sugar to soothe the sting of slipping out** on his parents.

Heavy scaffold: The boy had even _____ _____ –
                                            Done what?   Where or when?

_____.
    appositive – say more about that

Example: The boy had even <u>made his bed</u> <u>on</u> <u>Monday</u> <u>morning</u> – <u>making his mamma proud.</u>

Light scaffold: _____ had even _____ _____ –
                            Who?   verb   prepositional phrase – where or when?

_____.
    appositive – say more about it (Revise for alliteration)

Example: <u>Ant's Mama</u> had even <u>put her hands</u> <u>on her hips</u> – <u>a warning of wrath and wariness.</u>

No scaffold: Invite students to emulate the showcase sentence within their own writing.

SENTENCE DIG W6.3: ONOMATOPOEIA: SUPPORTING DETAILS

Text: *Insect Superpowers: 18 Real Bugs That Smash, Zap, Hypnotize, Sting, and Devour!* by Kate Messner, illustrated by Jillian Nickell, page 10

Grades: 2-5

Book summary: In *Insect Superpowers: 18 Real Bugs That Smash, Zap, Hypnotize, Sting, and Devour!* Kate Messner and Jillian Nickell capture the essence of a superhero comic book while revealing scientific details about bugs. Bugs - typically a part of our world that most readers try to squash from their minds... and homes - are the superheroes of this text. The author-illustrator team helps us marvel at these small yet mighty creatures as we learn about everything from self-defense mechanisms to secret skills! Even the most entomophobic readers will delight in this action-packed nonfiction book.

Showcase sentence: When another insect flies too close | - **Buzz-Swish-Zap! -** | the robber fly | darts out and captures it | with long, strong, bristly legs | that can hold tight to prey.

Rationale: This sentence has a lot going on. It's a complex sentence starting with the subordinating conjunction *when* followed by onomatopoeia set off by dashes. It has a compound predicate that is extended with a prepositional phrase using three adjectives. The beauty of this sentence is that it's perfectly balanced in a way students will be able to make meaning and replicate in their own writing. The trick will be to stay focused with instruction and not teach everything this sentence offers in one, long, rambling lesson.

Setting the scene: This sentence appears in the paragraph where the author is describing the robber fly's superpower: speed in flight. How fast is this fly? In this paragraph, the robber fly is lying in wait, watching its surroundings, waiting for prey to fly by... and then... BUZZ, SWISH, ZAP! Dinner time!

TAKE APART

Remember, your chunks are on sentence strips. Move them around to help students focus on one chunk and then another. You'll move them back together later.

Chunk	Possible Questions to Ask	Possible Answers
Ask the question first, then pull the chunk. the robber fly	Which chunk tells us who or what this sentence is about? How do you know?	...the robber fly is the subject of the sentence. The first chunk of the sentence is a dependent clause, so it can't have the subject of the sentence. The focus of the sentence is what the robber fly does and when it does it. So we know the robber fly must be the subject.
Ask the question first, then pull the chunk. darts out and captures it	Which chunk in this sentence tells us what the robber fly did? Which part is the predicate? How many verbs are in this predicate? What does the robber fly do in this sentence? What does the author mean ...*darts out*? Where is it darting out from? How do we know?	...darts out and captures it There are two verbs: darts and captures. This is called a compound predicate. The subject does two things. When dart is a verb, it means to move suddenly and quickly. It darts out from its hiding place – a twig or a leaf, which is stated earlier in the paragraph.
When another insect flies too close	What does this chunk tell us? What kind of clause is this chunk – is it an independent clause or a dependent clause? How do you know?	It tells us when the robber fly will dart out. It also tells us what the robber fly captures... another insect. It's a dependent clause. It does not hold a complete thought in order to be a complete sentence. It is a dependent clause because it begins with a subordinating conjunction – *when*. It is a clause because it has a subject and a predicate.
– **Buzz-Swish-Zap!** –	These words represent sounds; this is known as onomatopoeia. In your reading mind, what mental image does this create? Turn and tell your partner.	Students may say it helps them visualize the robber fly going after the insect. Some students may say the buzz is the prey flying by, swish is the robber fly darting out, and zap is the capture. Other students may say the buzz is the robber fly darting out, the swish is the robber fly capturing the prey, and the zap is the robber fly eating its prey.
with long, strong, bristly legs	How does this chunk add meaning to the sentence?	This chunk tells the reader *how* the robber fly captures its prey.
that can hold tight to prey.	How does this chunk add meaning to the sentence? What does the word *that* refer to in the sentence?	This tells us *why* the fly uses its legs. The word *that* refers to legs.

PUT TOGETHER

During this part, the sentence chunks may be mixed up or off to the side. Invite students to manipulate the chunks when putting the sentence back together and/or while rearranging them.

Ask	Possible Answers	Food for Thought
What is the original order of this sentence?	When another insect flies too close | – **Buzz-Swish-Zap!** – | the robber fly | darts out and captures it | with long, strong, bristly legs | that can hold tight to prey.	If students struggle to put this together, have them start with the subject and the verb. Then use questions to help them add on to the sentence with the other chunks: When does the robber fly dart out and capture it? What might we hear when the robber fly gets its prey? How does the robber fly capture it? Why does the robber fly use its legs?
Why do you think the author included sound effects – onomatopoeia?	It helps the reader imagine what is happening. It makes the sentence come alive.	Writers depend on the readers' senses to help them imagine different scenes as they read. Here, the writer uses onomatopoeia to ignite the reader's sense of hearing.
Why do you think the author used dashes to set off the onomatopoeia?	The dashes indicate a pause in the sentence. The dashes signal this happens very quickly.	The use of dashes here sets the onomatopoeia apart from the rest of the sentence. This helps to reduce confusion around it. If it had commas, it may come across as having a semantic role in the main part of the sentence, when in reality, it's an intentional craft move – a sound effect.
What if we removed the onomatopoeia from the sentence? Does it change the meaning? Which version do you like better – with or without the onomatopoeia?	When another insect flies too close | – ~~Buzz-Swish-Zap!~~ – | the robber fly | darts out and captures it | with long, strong, bristly legs | that can hold tight to prey. Answers will vary.	Removing this chunk does not change the meaning of the sentence – but it might be worth exploring how the onomatopoeia engages the reader ever more effectively.
Is there another way to arrange this sentence?	**Buzz-Swish-Zap!** – | When another insect flies too close | the robber fly | darts out and captures it | with long, strong, bristly legs | that can hold tight to prey.	Because of the compound predicate, it's difficult to rearrange this sentence and doing so compromises the fluency of the original.
How could you rewrite this one sentence as two or three separate sentences?	Buzz-Swish-Zap – another insect flies too close. The robber fly darts out and captures it. It uses its long, strong bristly legs that can hold tight to prey. When another insect flies too close – Buzz-Swish-Zap! – the robber fly darts out. It captures it with long, strong bristly legs that can hold tight to prey.	There are several ways to do this. Students may find that dividing this sentence up into two or more sentences is a lot of work that, in the end, causes the sentences to become wordy or lose the energy of the original sentence.

APPLY

During this part, students quickly apply their new knowledge about the sentence to their reading and writing. These are quick efforts and may be followed up with more practice.

Discuss: With a partner, reread your informational writing. Is there a place you can insert onomatopoeia to add a supporting detail and keep your reader engaged?

Writing focus: Using onomatopoeia is not only fun, but it can bring life to your detail sentences. Try writing some complex sentences with onomatopoeia.

> **Showcase sentence:** When another insect flies too close – **Buzz-Swish-Zap!** – the robber fly darts out and captures it with long, strong, bristly legs that can hold tight to prey.

Heavy scaffold: When _____ – _____ – the _____
  What happens?   *onomatopoeia – what does it sound like?*   *Who or what?*

_____ and _____ with _____.
  action   *action*   *What?*

Example: When <u>thunder rumbles</u> – <u>BOOM! BANG! BAM!</u> – the <u>dog</u> <u>shakes</u> and <u>trembles</u> with <u>its whole body</u>.

Light scaffold: _____ – _____
  dependent Clause (subordinate conjunction + subject + predicate)   *onomatopoeia*

_____ _____ _____
  subject (noun)   *compound predicate (verb + and + verb)*   *prepositional phrase – How? Or When?*

that _____.
    How? Or Why?

Example: <u>When I fell off my bike</u> – <u>Whoa! Thump! Ouch!</u> – <u>my best friends</u> <u>ran toward me and screamed for help</u> <u>with their loudest voices</u> that <u>could be heard down the street</u>.

No scaffold: Invite students to emulate the showcase sentence within their own writing.

SENTENCE DIG W6.4: REPEATING SUBJECTS AND VERBS: BUILDING TENSION

Text: *Henry's Freedom Box: A True Story from the Underground Railroad* by Ellen Levine, illustrated by Kadir Nelson, page 17

Grades: 2-4

Book summary: When Henry's family is sold to a new owner, Henry knows he must escape his enslaved situation. With help from the Underground Railroad, Henry packs himself into a crate and then mails himself to freedom. Based on a true story, this narrative captures the love Henry has for his family and the courage it took for him to risk everything to do what was right.

Showcase sentence: He couldn't move. | He couldn't think. | He couldn't work.

Rationale: Because there are times when writers craft language using a series of brief sentences, in this sentence dig, we'll look at three separate sentences that work together. In this example, Ellen Levine and Kadir Nelson use three short sentences to create a repetitive rhythm. They change just the last word to show the depths of Henry's despair. In doing so, they slow the text down and let the reader feel just a hint of Henry's reaction to his family being sold - paralyzing despair. What makes these three sentences even more dramatic is the context of the story. Henry is enslaved; he has no power in this situation. On top of that, as an enslaved person at this time, if he doesn't work the consequences are severe.

Setting the scene: Henry is enslaved but is given permission to marry and have children. He is in love and happy. One night, Henry's wife tells him she fears their master will sell their children. While Henry is working and trying to forget what his wife said about their children being sold, his friend whispers in his ear that Henry's wife and children have just been sold at the slave market.

TAKE APART

Remember, your chunks are on sentence strips. Move them around to help students focus on one chunk and then another. You'll move them back together later.

Chunk	Possible Questions to Ask	Possible Answers
He couldn't move.	What word is the subject of this sentence? Who is *he*? What does the contraction *couldn't* mean? What couldn't he do? Why can't he move? What are you imagining happening at this moment?	He Henry Could not Move Henry is stunned by the news. He stops moving – he goes perfectly still... frozen.

(Continued)

CHAPTER 6 Writing: Crafting Language 157

Chunk	Possible Questions to Ask	Possible Answers
He couldn't think.	What is happening in this sentence? How does this add meaning to this event in the story?	Henry could not think. His mind is racing. Henry is so upset, he is frozen and can't concentrate. It's like this is so traumatic for him he doesn't know what to do because he has no power to save his family.
He couldn't work.	What is happening in this sentence? How does this sentence add meaning to this event in the story?	Henry stops working and can't make himself continue working at that moment. Because Henry is enslaved, if he doesn't work, the consequences are severe. So for him to stop working – to be so devastated that he can't make himself work – tells the reader just how upset Henry is about the situation. It also gives the reader insight into how awful the conditions were for enslaved people.

PUT TOGETHER

During this part, the sentence chunks may be mixed up or off to the side. Invite students to manipulate the chunks when putting the sentence back together and/or while rearranging them.

Ask	Possible Answers	Food for Thought
Let's look at these sentences all together. What do you notice?	He couldn't move. He couldn't think. He couldn't work. Students might notice: The three sentences have the same sentence structure: He couldn't _____ (verb). The three sentences use repetition with the subject and helping verb. The three verbs at the end of the sentences get more and more severe, which demonstrates the depth of his despair.	The use of repetition here helps the writer build tension and drag out the moment. There are times we want to have our readers pause and linger with a character in a pivotal moment in the text. Here, the author uses three short, slow sentences to help us sit alongside Henry, freezing us in time with him.

(Continued)

Ask	Possible Answers	Food for Thought
How can we rearrange the sentences? Does it have the same effect?	He couldn't think. He couldn't work. He couldn't move. He couldn't work. He couldn't move. He couldn't think. He couldn't work. He couldn't think. He couldn't move.	Readers may have different opinions about whether a new arrangement of these sentences is effective. Consider asking students to explain why they like a different order. Ultimately, this is a writer's decision, so guide the conversation into why the author may have chosen the order they did.
How can we combine these sentences into one sentence? Does it have the same effect? Why or why not?	He couldn't move, think, or work. He couldn't move, think, nor work.	The repetitive use of the same subject and helping verb allows for emphasis of the fact Henry *couldn't* do these things... even if he wanted to, he was too distraught. Typically, we wouldn't use the conjunction *and* to combine these verbs. *And* means all together. These actions are separate. He couldn't do any of those things, so the conjunctions *or* and *nor* would be appropriate. Combining the sentences doesn't have the same effect as the three separate sentences. One sentence moves the reader too fast through the emotions. The writer wanted to slow the reader down, so three sentences is better in this case.

APPLY

During this part, students quickly apply their new knowledge about the sentence to their reading and writing. These are quick efforts and may be followed up with more practice.

> **Discuss:** Turn and talk with a partner or small group. Describe Henry's character. How does the writer use this scene to reveal Henry's desire to escape his situation?
>
> **Writing focus:** Writers can add a touch of drama when they slow down a scene with three short sentences. Try revising a later scene in the text by adding three short sentences.
>
> > **Showcase sentence:** He couldn't move. He couldn't think. He couldn't work.

(Continued)

CHAPTER 6 Writing: Crafting Language

Setting the scene: Think about that moment in *Henry's Freedom Box* when James, Henry, and Dr. Smith are trying to find an excuse for Henry to stay home from work. James points to Henry's finger, and Henry pours a bottle of vitriol on his finger. James shouts, NO! (27).

Draw a quick sketch of this scene. Zero in on each of the character's facial reactions.	Think about **one** character in this scene. Write three short sentences that describe his reaction.
	_____ _____ _____ . Character/subject Auxiliary verb Verb _____ _____ _____ . Character/subject Auxiliary verb Verb _____ _____ _____ . Character/subject Auxiliary verb Verb

Share your work with a partner.

    Did each sentence repeat the same character?
    Did each sentence repeat the same verb?
    Is the last word in each sentence different?

Heavy scaffold:

Draw a quick sketch of this scene. Zero in on each of the character's facial reactions.	Think about **one** character in this scene. Write three short sentences that describe his reaction.
	_____ didn't _____ . Character/subject Do what? _____ didn't _____ . Character/subject Do what? _____ didn't _____ . Character/subject Do what?

Example: Henry didn't <u>scream</u>. Henry didn't <u>cry</u>. Henry didn't <u>move his hand</u>.

(Continued)

Light scaffold:

Draw a quick sketch of this scene. Zero in on each of the character's facial reactions.	Think about **one** character in this scene. Write three short sentences that describe his reaction.
	_____ _____ _____. Character/Subject Auxiliary verb Verb _____ _____ _____. Character/Subject Auxiliary verb Verb _____ _____ _____. Character/Subject Auxiliary verb Verb

Example: <u>Dr. Smith</u> <u>didn't</u> <u>protest</u>. <u>Dr. Smith</u> <u>didn't</u> <u>look away</u>. <u>Dr. Smith</u> <u>didn't</u> <u>say a word.</u>

No scaffold: Invite students to emulate the showcase sentence within their own writing.

SECTION 3
Digging into Content Area Learning

> Writing isn't just a skill, it's also a powerful method of teaching content.
> - Hochman and Wexler (2017)

Language comprehension is foundational to learning the curriculum our students will encounter in their content area studies. Reading and writing are instrumental in helping them experience and learn about people, places, things, and ideas when they can't observe them firsthand. When we teach the content areas - whether in a self-contained classroom or if we're departmentalized and specialized - we rely on students' oral language comprehension. Whether they're doing a soil experiment or reading and discussing the structure of different governments, students gain knowledge from listening, speaking, reading, and writing. So it is imperative that we are intentional with how we leverage these skills to help students build knowledge and master the content area curriculum.

Time is short in the school day with a lot of things to do. All too often, in elementary school, some subjects are cut short more than others - usually writing, social studies, or science. Too many times teachers have been asked to integrate reading and writing into social studies and science. But is integrating really the same as teaching? I'm all for integrating subjects but I'm wondering - how often does that take the place of actual instruction? Content area teachers who are departmentalized often claim they are not reading teachers - they're not writing teachers. Nor, they often lament, do they want to be. Yet, how or when do we teach students to read a scientific text with a critical eye or teach students to write a cause and effect essay around important issues such as the Great Depression? I'm not advocating for reading and writing to take over the content area curriculums. What I am advocating is that we help students transfer key literacy skills so they can build knowledge and remember information they learn in these subject areas.

When we think about social studies and science, for example, we need to comprehend and express ideas that answer Who? What? When? Where? Why? and How? And although the connection between these questions may seem obvious to us as adults, once students cross over from reading time to social studies time, we have to make those connections crystal clear.

In addition, in the content areas, students also need to be able to glean the meaning of academic vocabulary in context and use that kind of vocabulary in their content area writing.

We have to use the strategies we learn in reading and writing in an explicit way to help students leverage them throughout the day - especially in their content area coursework. One way we can do this is by zeroing in on the sentence dig routine. We can lean on the reciprocity of reading and writing in a sentence dig not as a way to integrate the subject areas - and check it off as done - but as a powerful tool to teach curriculum.

In this section of the book, we'll explore sentence digs that are rooted in the content areas by grounding our conversations in three specific but universally applicable contexts: vocabulary, important details, and text structure. As in the previous lessons, you'll find some Think Sheets included along the way that give students an opportunity to delve more into the work at hand. Because the content areas you teach and your standards may be different from the examples used in the lessons, you'll want to read this section as a mentor text of sorts, paying close attention to the rationale - why and how I selected each sentence to leverage *content* (curriculum/standards) and *form* (syntax and semantics). Because we'll use the same routine - Take Apart - Put Together - Apply - you'll be able to quickly see how they fit into your content area work, adjust them for use with your own texts and resources if needed, and dig right in!

CHAPTER 7
Vocabulary

> While without grammar very little can be conveyed, without vocabulary nothing can be conveyed.
> - *David Wilkins*

The time we're allotted for our content area instruction is precious indeed. In many elementary classrooms, science and social studies aren't taught daily. Even when they are, the time is often squeezed into an already overpacked schedule, offering limited precious minutes for the work. So as content area teachers, we have to be mindful of how best to use our time. We need to be thinking about how we can build students' knowledge in both receptive and productive ways. It's not enough to simply lecture or tell kids just the essential facts... and yet many teachers have unfortunately been forced in that direction - often out of default.

One way we can use reading and writing as powerful teaching tools within the content areas is to pay attention to academic vocabulary. We know that the more people read, the stronger their vocabulary. But this doesn't happen through osmosis. It's not like we read a book and instantly know a bunch of new vocabulary words. Students need to not only have access and opportunities to read quality texts in science and social studies, they also need to have opportunities to analyze the text and use the new vocabulary in both oral and written expression. Enriching student vocabulary for a test is a minimal goal; enriching their vocabulary so they can process information and convey their understanding about a variety of topics is the primary goal. Without the right words, it's difficult for students to express a full understanding of a standard in social studies or science. In addition, without the right academic words, it's difficult for students to gain a full understanding - to build a strong foundational knowledge base - about the topics we study in these content areas.

Research has shown that memorizing a list of vocabulary words simply isn't going to cut it. However, students remember more when they use academic vocabulary in oral and written expression (Moats and Tolman 2019). The more we give students opportunities to grapple with the vocabulary in context, the more authentically they're thinking about and talking about the content area. There are many ways to accomplish this, and one of those ways is a solid sentence dig routine. In this section, we'll look at the sentence dig routine to not only lean on the reciprocal nature of reading and writing but also to support students' engagement with the rich content science and social studies have to offer.

SENTENCE DIGS

The following sentence digs will dip into ways authors reveal vocabulary meaning in a text. We will still investigate the sentence as readers and writers while also turning the instructional focus to the content area - *What are we learning here? Why is this sentence important to our understanding of the topic? How does this build our knowledge in a way that we can speak, read, and write about it with expertise?* Because not every social studies and science topic can be explored in the brief selection of sample lessons that follow, as you explore them, consider how you might lift these same kinds of sentences from the science and social studies resources your class is reading and how the sentence digs you could build around them might support your students as they grow their understanding of the content vocabulary, while building even stronger success with grammatical structures they encounter every day.

SHOWCASE SENTENCES LESSONS AT A GLANCE

Lesson	Focus	Author's Purpose/ Grammatical Structure	Text	Sentence
CA7.1	Vocabulary	Definition is in an appositive phrase mid-sentence, signaled by dashes.	*Disasters by the Numbers: A Book of Infographics* by Steve Jenkins	**Hail – solid balls of ice that can be as small as a blueberry or as large as a cantaloupe** – sometimes falls during a thunderstorm.
CA7.2	Vocabulary	Definition at the end of the sentence signaled by a dash.	*The Split History of Westward Expansion in the United States: American Indian Perspective* by Nell Musolf	The treaties also said that the tribes would have to move off their land to **reservations – land the government had chosen specifically for them.**
CA7.3	Vocabulary	Use of a synonym.	*Beavers: Radical Rodents and Ecosystem Engineers* by Frances Backhouse	They **gnaw** at the woody mass until they've **chewed** their way up and into the center, where they **carve out** their living quarters.
CA7.4	Vocabulary	Definition is explained by examples.	*If You Lived During the Plimoth Thanksgiving* by Chris Newell, illustrated by Winona Nelson	The boundaries between the different nations, and villages or communities within them, were marked by **natural features such as rivers, ponds, hills, or mountains.**

SENTENCE DIG CA7.1: DEFINITION WITHIN A SENTENCE

Text: *Disasters by the Numbers: A Book of Infographics* by Steve Jenkins, page 25

Grades: 3-6

Book summary: Steve Jenkins does it again with this book that is anything but a disaster. *Disasters by the Numbers: A Book of Infographics* expertly weaves in informative text with a variety of infographics. Jenkins divides the disasters in this book into four sections: Earth, Weather, Life, and Space. Through these lenses he investigates everything from earthquakes to hurricanes to pandemics and even falling satellites. With a robust vocabulary, exact numbers to help the details pop, and infographics to fill in the missing pieces, Jenkins again surrounds us with scientific facts and mathematical statistics that make us all feel wiser.

**Showcase sentence: Hail | - solid balls of ice | that can be as small as a blueberry or as large as a cantaloupe - | sometimes falls during a thunderstorm.

Rationale: Oftentimes, writers will embed definitions within a sentence. It's important to point out to students when it's happening and the different ways writers can do this. In this case, Jenkins chose to use an appositive phrase set off by dashes. An appositive phrase is a phrase that follows a noun to give the reader more information or details about that noun. In this case, the author is defining the noun - hail. It's helpful to note that an appositive phrase can be removed and the sentence will still make sense. Students can learn to use this grammatical structure to clarify definitions in their expository writing. As readers, it's important for students to keep their eye out for these, as it might confuse learners who don't understand why the information is there or what its function is in the sentence.

How does understanding this sentence help the student build knowledge in this content area? Hail is a characteristic of a severe thunderstorm and sometimes occurs before a tornado. It's a common noun in the field of meteorology. If students are studying weather or natural disasters, this is a word they'll need to know and understand. What I love about this particular definition is that the author not only gives a quick definition for hail - balls of ice - but also gives a couple of comparisons to show how big and small hail can be. Because children don't see a lot of hail in real life, having the fruity comparisons makes the definition more accessible to readers.

Ask: Why do you think the author is using dashes in this sentence? *The author is trying to set off this information from the rest of the sentence. The author is trying to clarify information about hail that isn't necessary for the rest of the sentence.*

TAKE APART

Remember, your chunks are on sentence strips. Move them around to help students focus on one chunk and then another. You'll move them back together later.

Chunk	Possible Questions to Ask	Possible Answers
Hail	What is the function of the word hail in this sentence?	It is the subject of the sentence. It's what the sentence is about.
– solid balls of ice	How does this chunk add to our understanding of the subject – hail?	This defines the word hail. Hail is/are solid balls of ice.
that can be as small as a blueberry or as large as a cantaloupe –	What is this chunk talking about? How do you know? Why do you think the author included these comparisons in this chunk?	It's talking about the size of the hail. We know this because the word *that* is referring to solid balls of ice. It helps us visualize the size of hail when it falls. It can be really small like blueberries or it can be really big like cantaloupes. Having these visuals can help us remember the definition of the word hail.
sometimes falls during a thunderstorm.	What is the function of this chunk in the sentence?	This is the predicate of the sentence. It tells us what the hail does – it falls during a thunderstorm.

PUT TOGETHER

During this part, the sentence chunks may be mixed up or off to the side. Invite students to manipulate the chunks when putting the sentence back together and/or while rearranging them.

Ask	Possible Answers	Food for Thought
What is the original order of this sentence?	Hail | – solid balls of ice | that can be as small as a blueberry or as large as a cantaloupe – | sometimes falls during a thunderstorm.	Consider underlining the subject and the predicate in different colors to reinforce that the definition in the appositive phrase gives us extra information about a noun, in this case the subject of the sentence.
What can we take out of the sentence? What is the effect on the sentence?	Hail | – solid balls of ice | ~~that can be as small as a blueberry or as large as a cantaloupe –~~ | sometimes falls during a thunderstorm.	When we take out the comparisons, it removes some of the impact from the sentence. The comparisons not only help us visualize but they also help us to understand that hail can be very dangerous. Imagine balls of solid ice the size of a cantaloupe falling from the sky? YIKES!

(Continued)

Ask	Possible Answers	Food for Thought
	Hail	~~– solid balls of ice	that can be as small as a blueberry or as large as a cantaloupe –~~	sometimes falls during a thunderstorm.	Without the definition, the author is assuming we know what hail is and its size, leaving us with only a partial understanding of the term.
	~~Hail	–~~ Solid balls of ice	that can be as small as a blueberry or as large as a cantaloupe –	sometimes fall during a thunderstorm.	This sentence sounds very dramatic. However, it lacks the scientific word for those ice balls.
How else can you rearrange this sentence? What is the effect of this change?	Solid balls of ice	that can be as small as a blueberry and as large as a cantaloupe –	hail –	sometimes fall during a thunderstorm.	The longer subject followed by the one word – hail – is a little awkward. One might add the phrase *known as* to smooth it out.

APPLY

During this part, students quickly apply their new knowledge about the sentence to their reading and writing. These are quick efforts and may be followed up with more practice.

Discuss: As we read this book, we're studying different kinds of disasters, specifically natural disasters. Why do you think the author included hail in this book? Why do we need to know about it?

Writing focus: Whenever we add a definition to a sentence, no matter the topic, we can use an appositive phrase set off by dashes.

> **Showcase sentence:** Hail – solid balls of ice that can be as small as a blueberry or as large as a cantaloupe – sometimes falls during a thunderstorm.

Heavy scaffold: Tornadoes – _____ – sometimes strike _____.
                              quick definition   *Where? When?*

Example: Tornadoes – <u>funnel shaped clouds that hit the ground</u> – sometimes strike <u>before a thunderstorm.</u>

Light scaffold: _____ – _____ – _____
                              word to define   *definition*   *Does what?*

_____?
        When or where?

Examples: <u>Flash floods</u> – <u>floods that happen very quickly</u> – <u>can wash away bridges over streams or small rivers.</u> <u>The pond's biodiversity</u> – <u>the variety of plant and animal life</u> – <u>thrives through the summer months.</u>

No scaffold: Invite students to emulate the showcase sentence within their own writing.

Thought Partners: _____

Sentence Dig: CA7.1
THINK SHEET FOCUS: WRITING

STRATEGY: Sentence Extension

Write the showcase sentence from the sentence dig in the space below:

[   ]

Part 1 Directions: Work with your partner to extend each sentence by adding a definition for the underlined word.

Example: In a blizzard, visibility can be reduced to less than ¼ mile.

In a blizzard, visibility - **the distance one can see clearly** *- can be reduced to less than ¼ mile.*

1. An earthquake is especially deadly when buildings collapse.

   _____
   _____

2. A tsunami forms when a volcano erupts near the sea.

   _____
   _____

3. In a tornado, people may be injured by flying debris if they do not find shelter before the storm hits.

   _____
   _____

WORD BOX

| **collapse** - fall down; crumble | **tsunami** - a giant wave |

debris - pieces of trash; loose natural material like broken pieces of rocks or tree branches

Part 2 Directions: Reread the showcase sentence. Notice how the author includes comparisons to explain the size of the hail so the reader has a strong image in their mind.

Work with your partner to extend the sentences below by adding a comparison or example to illustrate the underlined word or phrase. Use commas or dashes if needed.

Example: *During a blizzard the temperatures can drop <u>below 10 degrees Fahrenheit</u> in the northern United States -* **which is cold enough to make your eyelashes freeze.**

1. Lightning can damage <u>property</u>.

   _____

   _____

2. During the summer, the temperature can rise to <u>95 degrees Fahrenheit</u> in the southern United States.

   _____

   _____

3. When <u>too many grasshoppers</u> get together, they can eat every plant in their path.

   _____

   _____

Look at your own writing. Find a word you'd like to define or a place where you can add a comparison. Practice extending a new sentence that includes a definition or a comparison with your partner. Then add it to your writing.

SENTENCE DIG CA7.2: DEFINITION AT THE END OF A SENTENCE

Text: *The Split History of Westward Expansion in the United States: American Indian Perspective* by Nell Musolf, page 14

Grades: 3-6

Book summary: Nell Musolf's book, *The Split History of Westward Expansion in the United States: American Indian Perspective*, presents history through two different perspectives. Known as a perspective flip book, one half of the book gives the US government's perspective about Western Expansion in the United States. Then you flip the book over, and the other half of the book tells this period of history from the indigenous people's perspective. By giving a voice to the indigenous people's perspective, readers can explore this part of American history through various lenses, giving them a fuller - truer - understanding of what happened.

Showcase sentence: The treaties also said | that the tribes would have to move off their land to **reservations** | - *land the government had chosen specifically for them*.

Rationale: The word *reservations* is key to gaining a full understanding of the lack of fairness and good faith with which the American government dealt with the indigenous people. The author uses an appositive phrase at the end of the sentence to define reservations. He also leaves the term a bit vague, and it deserves some unpacking. One could read through this sentence thinking that this is a reasonable thing. The government is making the tribes move but they're also giving them free land. (Raise your eyebrow here, dear reader.) Because the author leaves this definition to the end of the sentence, it's like an invitation to explore further.

How does understanding this sentence help the student build knowledge in this content area? In elementary school, many social studies curriculums (and state standards) teach students about the indigenous people of the United States and their cultures. We do this to better understand not only more about these cultures but also to frame our history accordingly. Understanding what a reservation is and how it was forced upon Native Americans helps students realize and grapple with the cruel methods the government used while trying to expand our country's land mass for white settlers.

Ask: Some words have multiple meanings. Reservation is one of those words. When you think of the word reservation - what do you think of? What does it mean to you?
- Saving something for later - like a hotel reservation, the hotel saves your room for you.
- A doubt - My mom expressed reservations about whether or not I should go camping this weekend.
- Land set aside for the occupation of indigenous people.

Today we're going to dig into this sentence to really think about what this word means in the context of Western Expansion.

TAKE APART

Remember, your chunks are on sentence strips. Move them around to help students focus on one chunk and then another. You'll move them back together later.

Chunk	Possible Questions to Ask	Possible Answers
The treaties also said	Who or what is this sentence about? What is a treaty?	The treaties – specifically the treaties between the US government and the Native American tribes A treaty is an agreement – typically between two countries. NOTE: The word treaty assumes that both parties have autonomy in the agreement. As students are ready, you may want to discuss the uneven power dynamic at play in this historical inequality.
that the tribes would have to move off their land to reservations	What does this chunk tell us?	It tells us what the treaties said – that the tribes would have to move off their land.
– land the government had chosen specifically for them.	What does this chunk tell us? How does it connect to the sentence?	This chunk defines *reservations*, which is the last word in the previous chunk.

PUT TOGETHER

During this part, the sentence chunks may be mixed up or off to the side. Invite students to manipulate the chunks when putting the sentence back together and/or while rearranging them.

Ask	Possible Answers	Food for Thought
What is the original order of this sentence?	The treaties also said / that the tribes would have to move off their land to reservations / – land the government had chosen specifically for them.	Authors can use a dash (or a comma) after a noun to add more details about that noun. In this case, the author defined the word *reservations*. When authors use dashes, as readers, we need to notice and pay attention.

(Continued)

Ask	Possible Answers	Food for Thought
When the author uses the word *tribes* what does he mean? What is another word we can use for *tribes*? What effect does that have on the sentence?	Tribes are communities of indigenous people. There can be thousands of people in a tribe. The treaties also said that the *indigenous people* would have to move off their land to reservations – land the government had chosen specifically for them.	Using the phrase *indigenous people* – or even the word *people* instead of tribes – reminds the reader that these were human beings we're talking about. The word tribes helps us understand it wasn't all indigenous people, just the people in the tribes – or communities – that were in the settlers' way.
What if we changed the phrase – *off their land* – to *from their home*? What effect does that have on the sentence?	The treaties also said that the *indigenous people* would have to move *from* their *home* to reservations – land the government had chosen specifically for them.	Replacing the phrase **off their land** with **from their home** would humanize this sentence. Although, indigenous people lived off the land, they had shelters, homes they'd have to leave.
The last part says a reservation is land the government had chosen specifically for them. What do you think this land is like?	The reservations were hundreds of miles away from the home lands. The reservations were not good farming lands and did not have a lot of wildlife. This was land that was not profitable – no one wanted it.	Teachers, this is a good time to refer to a map and note the distance between the home land and the reservations, as well as the type of land that has been specifically chosen in historical instances like this.

APPLY

During this part, students quickly apply their new knowledge about the sentence to their reading and writing. These are quick efforts and may be followed up with more practice.

> **Discuss:** We discussed the multiple meanings of the word *reservations* before we began this work. In the context of this sentence, the word *reservation* refers to the land set aside for people. How can you use the word reservation meaning a doubt people may have in the context of this topic?
>
> **Writing focus:** Writers can slip in a word's definition using an appositive phrase. This phrase (definition) appears right after the vocabulary word and is set off by commas or dashes.
>
> > **Showcase sentence:** The treaties also said that the tribes would have to move off their land to reservations – land the government had chosen specifically for them.
>
> **Heavy scaffold:** Some indigenous people followed the buffalo and lived in tepees – _____.
> Define tepees
>
> *Example: Some indigenous people followed the buffalo and lived in tepees – <u>portable, cone-shaped tents made of buffalo hide and poles.</u>*
>
> **Light scaffold:** _____ _____ on the frontier – _____.
> Who? Subject (noun)   Did what? Verb or verb phrase   Define frontier
>
> *Example: <u>Many settlers</u> <u>built new homes</u> on the frontier – <u>out west where no one lived yet.</u>*
>
> **No scaffold:** Invite students to emulate the showcase sentence within their own writing.

SENTENCE DIG CA7.3: USING SYNONYMS

Text: *Beavers: Radical Rodents and Ecosystem Engineers* by Frances Backhouse, pages 113-114

Grades: 1-6

Book summary: Beavers show up in literature as clever creatures for a reason - they really are. In this book, *Beavers: Radical Rodents and Ecosystem Engineers* by Frances Backhouse, the author teaches readers about this unique animal and its habitat. Readers learn not only of the body adaptations and cunning beavers use when building their shelters, but also of the significant effect their presence - or absence - has on an ecosystem. Beavers are not just an animal in the food chain, they create spaces for ecosystems to grow and thrive. This book is full of interesting facts and photos that will give any reader a new appreciation for this species.

Showcase sentence: They **gnaw** at the woody mass | until they've **chewed** their way up and into the center, | where they **carve out** their living quarters.

Rationale: This is an excellent example of how an author uses a synonym within a sentence. For writers, synonyms are ways to diversify our word choice. For readers, synonyms provide vocabulary and comprehension support in a subtle, yet powerful way.

How does understanding this sentence help the student build knowledge in this content area? Students often study animal adaptations for their science curriculum. Understanding how animals use their bodies to survive - build their shelters, find their food, and protect themselves from predators - helps students to better understand how ecosystems work. In this sentence, students study how a beaver uses its teeth in different ways to build and design their homes.

Ask: This sentence describes how beavers build their homes. Which body part do the beavers use to build their home? (Teeth)

- They use their teeth to cut through wood and build their homes. (Consider having students point to their two front teeth and remind them that the beavers use their two front teeth to bite through the wood.)
- As we study this sentence, we'll notice that the author uses different verbs to tell us how the beaver is using its teeth. We'll determine how those words are related.

TAKE APART

Remember, your chunks are on sentence strips. Move them around to help students focus on one chunk and then another. You'll move them back together later.

Chunk	Possible Questions to Ask	Possible Answers
They **gnaw** at the woody mass	Who or what is this chunk (independent clause) about? How do you know?	It's about beavers. We know this because the author uses the pronoun *they* and the topic of the text is beavers.
	What are the beavers doing in this chunk?	They **gnaw**. This is a verb. It means to repeatedly bite in order to wear or tear away or cut off something – typically with your front teeth but not always.
	What is an example of something we might gnaw?	Answers will vary but think about biting something to pull or break it apart: carrots, celery, apples, pork ribs *a woody mass*
	Which words in the chunk tell us what the beavers are gnawing?	A woody mass is a large amount of wood that has no shape – it's a big pile of wood.
until they've **chewed** their way up and into the center,	What does this chunk tell us about the first one? How do you know?	This chunk tells us how long the beavers gnaw on the woody mass. The word "until" means up to a certain point (in time or place).
	When do the beavers stop chewing?	When they reached the center of the woody mass.
	Which word in this chunk is a synonym for the verb *gnawed*?	Chewed: If you don't know the meaning of gnaw, chew is a synonym that means close to the same thing.
where they **carve out** their living quarters.	What are the beavers doing in this chunk?	They're *carving out* their living quarters.
	How are they doing this? Which body part are they using?	They're carving with their teeth.
	What does the phrase "carve out" mean?	It means to take something from a bigger whole. In this case, take wood out of the center of the mass so they can live in the dam.

PUT TOGETHER

During this part, the sentence chunks may be mixed up or off to the side. Invite students to manipulate the chunks when putting the sentence back together and/or while rearranging them.

Ask	Possible Answers	Food for Thought
What is the original order of this sentence?	They **gnaw** at the woody mass	until they've **chewed** their way up and into the center,	where they **carve out** their living quarters.	Consider highlighting the three verbs: gnaw, chewed, carve out. Note the subject (they = beavers) stays the same throughout the sentence but the verbs change.

(Continued)

Ask	Possible Answers	Food for Thought
How are the verbs – gnaw, chewed, and carve out – connected?	They are things the beavers are doing. They all have similar meanings.	In the context of this sentence, the verbs all have similar meanings. They're synonyms for how the beavers use their teeth to create living space in the dam.
Which other words or phrases can we replace with synonyms?	Woody mass = pile of wood Center = middle Living quarters = home	Remind students that this is a scientific text, so the author may have chosen words that sounded more academic like living quarters instead of home. As readers, we can use synonyms to clarify meaning.
Is there any way to rearrange and/or remove something from the sentence and it will still make sense?	Until they've **chewed** their way up and into the center, | where they **carve out** their living quarters, | they **gnaw** at the woody mass. They **gnaw** at the woody mass | until they've **chewed** their way up and into the center, | ~~where they carve out their living quarters.~~ They **gnaw** at the woody mass | ~~until they've chewed their way up and into the center,~~ | where they **carve out** their living quarters.	It's important to note that the chunk *where they carve out their living quarters* tells us more about the center of the woody mass. That's where the living quarters are – in the center. You can remove the last part of this sentence and it still makes sense. Consider asking: Why do you think the author included this chunk? If you remove this middle chunk, the sentence is complete and gives the reader the sense that the beaver's home is in the woody mass (pile). However, it's not as clear as the original sentence.

APPLY

During this part, students quickly apply their new knowledge about the sentence to their reading and writing. These are quick efforts and may be followed up with more practice.

Discuss: Compare how beavers use their teeth to another animal you are studying or know well. What verbs best describe how each animal uses their teeth?

Writing focus: The author uses an independent clause and two dependent clauses to create this complex sentence. The author does this by keeping the subject of each clause the same and changes the verb phrases.

> **Showcase sentence:** They **gnaw** at the woody mass until they've **chewed** their way up and into the center, where they **carve out** their living quarters.

Heavy scaffold: _____ _____, until they've
   animal (plural)   *verb phrase*

_____, where they _____.
   verb phrase   *verb phrase*

Example: <u>Chameleons</u> <u>turn colors</u>, until they've <u>camouflaged themselves into the environment</u>, where they <u>hide from predators</u>.

Light scaffold: _____ _____ _____, _____ they
   plural noun *verb* *prepositional phrase* *subordinating conjunction*

_____, _____ they _____.
   verb phrase   *subordinating conjunction*   *verb phrase*

Example: <u>Eagles</u> <u>hunt</u> <u>high in the sky</u>, <u>until</u> they <u>stoop through the air</u>, <u>as</u> they <u>dive toward their prey</u>.

No scaffold: Invite students to emulate the showcase sentence within their own writing.

SENTENCE DIG CA7.4: DEFINITION BY EXAMPLE

Text: *If You Lived During the Plimoth Thanksgiving* by Chris Newell, illustrated by Winona Nelson, page 35

Grades: 2-5

Book summary: Using a question and answer format, Chris Newell takes readers back to the time of early settlement when the Pilgrims landed at Plimoth. With questions that probe perspectives of all the people in the area, Newell gives readers a fresh look at this moment in history.

Showcase sentence: The boundaries | between the different nations, | and villages or communities within them, | were marked by **natural features** | **such as** rivers, ponds, hills, or mountains.

Rationale: One way writers help unpack academic vocabulary is to use examples. However, authors don't always use the words *for example*, sometimes they'll use the phrase *such as*. Being aware of this phrase and the examples that follow it can help students comprehend longer sentences that may be filled with a lot of information.

How does understanding this sentence help the student build knowledge in this content area? As students begin studying how our country developed, it is difficult for young children to imagine our land without roads and signs and maps to tell us where things begin and where they end. Much of history and physical science relies on students understanding natural features and how humans interact with them. This sentence introduces students to the idea that natural features formed natural boundaries. This is particularly interesting because it sets up the indigenous people's frame of reference - the land provided for them, including boundaries for their nations and villages. This is a cultural difference between the Europeans and the indigenous North Americans. Europeans were ready to mark their boundaries and create their own nations and villages with man-made (permanent) structures, however the indigenous people often looked to the boundaries already provided by nature.

Ask: What is this sentence trying to teach us? *This sentence is trying to teach us about how the indigenous people determined boundaries for their nations and their villages or communities.*

As we dig into this sentence, think about why natural features make good boundaries.

TAKE APART

Remember, your chunks are on sentence strips. Move them around to help students focus on one chunk and then another. You'll move them back together later.

Chunk	Possible Questions to Ask	Possible Answers
The boundaries	What are boundaries?	The word *boundary* has different meanings in different contexts. In the context of this sentence and of this text, a boundary is something that sets the limit of an area – for example a line on a map.
Ask the question before talking about this chunk. between the different nations,	Which chunk tells us *which* boundaries the text is talking about? What does the word nations mean in this sentence? What is the author referring to? What do these first two chunks mean when we read them together: *The boundaries between the nations,*	between the different nations The author is referring to the Native American nations – or large groups known also as tribes – and the general area in which they lived. This means the author is talking about the boundaries that separate the nations. It's how groups of people know where their living space ends and another's living space begins.
and villages or communities within them,	How does this chunk connect to the previous one?	This means that the nations have smaller villages of people or communities of people that also have boundaries. It's like the United States has boundaries between other nations – Mexico and Canada. The United States also has boundaries between its 50 states – smaller chunks of land than the whole nation.
were marked by **natural features**	What does the author mean by the phrase *were marked*? What are natural features? What in the sentence helps you to understand this phrase?	Identified, denoted, designated, pointed out In this context, you could also accept: created, made Natural features are land characteristics that are formed naturally or by nature. People didn't put them there. The next chunk gives us this clue.
such as rivers, ponds, hills, or mountains	What does this chunk do for the reader? Which words does the author use to connect this chunk to the previous one? What do those words signal to the reader?	It gives examples of natural features. *Such as* – this phrase signals to the reader that the author is going to list some examples.

SENTENCE DIGS

PUT TOGETHER

During this part, the sentence chunks may be mixed up or off to the side. Invite students to manipulate the chunks when putting the sentence back together and/or while rearranging them.

Ask	Possible Answers	Food for Thought
What is the original order of this sentence?	The boundaries | between the different nations, | and villages or communities within them, | were marked by **natural features** | **such as** rivers, ponds, hills, or mountains.	This sentence has a lot going on and the simple subject is not next to the verb phrase. This can cause some confusion when reordering the sentence. Consider underlining the subject *the boundaries* in blue and the simple predicate *were marked* in red to help students identify the core pieces of this sentence.
Which two chunks do we have to have to make a complete sentence?	The boundaries | ~~between the different nations, | and villages or communities within them,~~ | were marked by **natural features** | ~~**such as** rivers, ponds, hills, or mountains.~~	The simple sentence within this longer one is: The boundaries were marked by natural features. Although this may seem obvious to a strong reader, the additional wording that separates and surrounds the simple subject and the simple predicate can be confusing to striving readers.
With a partner, decide which of the other chunks you would add back in if you were the author. Be prepared to explain your thinking.	The boundaries | between the different nations, ~~| and villages or communities within them,~~ | were marked by **natural features** | ~~**such as** rivers, ponds, hills, or mountains.~~	Students may want to add in *between the different nations* because it clarifies **where** or **which** ones the author is talking about.
	The boundaries | between the different nations, | and villages or communities within them, | were marked by **natural features** | ~~**such as** rivers, ponds, hills, or mountains.~~	Students may also want to include *and villages or communities within them* to communicate that the natural features were not just used for boundaries between nations but also between villages and communities. Again answering the questions *where* or *which ones?*
	The boundaries | between the different nations, | and villages or communities within them, | were marked by **natural features** | **such as** rivers, ponds, hills, or mountains.	Students may want to include *such as rivers, ponds, hills, or mountains* because it answers the question of what natural features are by giving examples. NOTE: One way writers extend their sentences is by answering the questions: who, what, when, where, why, how, and which ones?

APPLY

During this part, students quickly apply their new knowledge about the sentence to their reading and writing. These are quick efforts and may be followed up with more practice.

> **Discuss:** Looking at a current map of our country, which states have natural features as boundaries? Why do you think those natural features make good boundaries?
>
> **Writing focus:** Authors can support readers with vocabulary by including examples. When you write sentences with academic vocabulary, you can include examples using the words *such as* or *for example* to clarify the meaning for your reader.
>
> Hint: When writing these sentences, consider which vocabulary word you want to include in your sentence, first. Then write the sentence.
>
> > **Showcase sentence:** The boundaries between the different nations, and villages or communities within them, were marked by **natural features such as** rivers, ponds, hills, or mountains.
>
> **Heavy scaffold:** When the Pilgrims arrived in Plymouth, they established their colony with man-made structures, such as _____ , _____ ,
>   example of a structure (what?)   example of a structure (what?)
>
> and _____ .
>   example of a structure (what?)
>
> *Example:* When the Pilgrims arrived in Plymouth, they established their colony with man-made structures, such as <u>a church</u>, <u>a town hall</u>, and <u>a large fence</u>.
>
> **Light scaffold:** The _____ _____ _____ , such as _____
>   noun   verb   vocabulary   word examples
>
> *Example:* The <u>Mayflower</u> <u>carried</u> <u>cargo</u>, such as <u>tools for farming, household items, and light weapons.</u>
>
> **No scaffold:** Invite students to emulate the showcase sentence within their own writing.

CHAPTER 8
Important Details

> Paper is to write things down that we need to remember.
> Our brains are used to think.
> - Albert Einstein

Writing in the content areas is often limited to note taking. The purpose of note taking is to write things down to help us remember. Although the actual act of writing things down helps to lighten the cognitive load of the working memory in the brain - thereby helping people remember things - many student habits around note taking do not help them process information - to learn it, analyze it, and express new ideas. Students, if they revisit the notes at all, may just memorize the information. In a perfect world, students and teachers are reading and writing in the content areas as a means of learning - processing information to think and talk about it. Thinking - not just memorizing - to build strong knowledge bases, draw conclusions, and develop individual viewpoints.

I'm not saying note taking is wrong or doesn't have a place in the content areas. Writing things down and thinking are integral parts of being a reader and a writer in the content areas. As readers, we determine what kind of notes to take, which details are important to the main idea, and which details are simply for entertainment. We may even create graphic organizers or note-catchers to support our students in determining what to write down. As readers we have to think about the big ideas the writer is presenting on a topic and then determine what and how we'll write about it. We're constantly sifting through details in the text to make decisions about what to think more deeply about and how to support our thinking about the text. So as readers, whether we're reading closely to take notes to memorize for a test or we're taking notes in preparation for a class conversation, we need to be able to decipher when and how authors reveal important details.

As informational writers - content area writers - we have a similar charge to determine which details we'll include for the reader. How will we develop an idea with enough information to help the reader think deeply about a topic but not so much detail that we overwhelm and bore them? Which details need their own sentences or paragraphs, and which ones can be tucked into a sentence with something else? As writers we think deeply about the topic and then write - picking and choosing the most important details to express our ideas whether we're creating an informational book or a persuasive essay.

SENTENCE DIGS

What makes reading and writing in the content areas even more interesting is that many times students are working with limited background knowledge. A lot of the vocabulary and information is new to them and is presented in an academic context. The purpose of reading and writing in the content areas is to process and learn information by building knowledge, processing that knowledge, and moving that knowledge to long-term memory (hopefully). Leaning on the reciprocity of reading and writing can be quite useful for this work. For example, learning how appositives are feeding a reader more information about the subject of the sentence or understanding how a conjunction can help a reader determine relationships between clauses can boost a reader's understanding of the explicit and implicit ideas the author is trying to convey. Authors reveal bias and perspectives through tone and the smallest of details. As readers, we want to lean on what we know about syntax and semantics to develop our understanding of the text and topic. Likewise, learning how to leverage appositives to tuck more information into a sentence or how to use participles to express multiple actions happening at once or using conjunctions to better express relationships between people, places, events, and ideas are all ways students can own the knowledge they are trying to champion. In this way, making time for a biweekly or weekly sentence dig with a content area text can provide explicit instruction and practice for students to decompose difficult sentences encountered in text and to write sentences with language features that can hold their new, big ideas.

The following sample sentence digs will dip into ways authors reveal details about their topic. While investigating this work as a reader and writer, some questions will also turn to the content focus - what are we learning here? Why is this sentence or this writing more important to our topic? How does this build our knowledge in a way that we can speak, read, and write about it with expertise? Because not every social studies and science topic can be explored in this chapter, if you cannot readily use any of these lessons that follow, you'll still glean a solid understanding of how to find these kind of sentences in the books your class is reading and how to query your students to build understanding about the ways grammatical structures can help us layer details within a sentence.

SHOWCASE SENTENCES LESSONS AT A GLANCE

Lesson	Focus	Author's Purpose/ Grammatical Structure	Text	Sentence
CA8.1	Metaphor	Two simple sentences combined with a semicolon	*Why Longfellow Lied: The Truth About Paul Revere's Ride* by Jeff Lantos	Revere was the arrow; Warren was the bow.
CA8.2	Adding details	Appositive	*Beavers: Radical Rodents and Ecosystem Engineers* by Frances Backhouse	These small creatures, **some so tiny that you need a microscope to see them,** are at the center of the beaver-pond food web.
CA8.3	Supporting the reader to identify a person and a place	Appositive	*The Split History of Westward Expansion in the United States: American Indian Perspective* by Nell Musolf	In 1607, Chief Wahunsenacawh, **known to the settlers as Chief Powhatan**, supplied food to the hungry settlers in the colony of Jamestown, in what is now Virginia.
CA8.4	Using numbers to add details	Using numbers	*The Split History of Westward Expansion in the United States: American Indian Perspective* by Nell Musolf	During the next **three months**, the chief and his band led the army on a **1,400 mile (2,253 kilometer)** chase into what is now Montana, fighting **four major battles** along the way despite being **outnumbered 10 to one**.
CA8.5	Modifying a noun by describing actions	Participle phrase	*Disasters by the Numbers* by Steve Jenkins	Pressure builds up until the plates suddenly move **releasing energy and shaking the ground.**

SENTENCE DIG CA8.1: USING A SEMICOLON: METAPHORS

Text: *Why Longfellow Lied: The Truth About Paul Revere's Midnight Ride* by Jeff Lantos, page 71

Grades: 4-6

Book summary: Jeff Lantos takes an opportunity for readers to pull back the curtain and see what's happening behind the scenes of the famous poem, "The Midnight Ride of Paul Revere" by Henry Wadsworth Longfellow. Stanza by stanza, chapter by chapter, Lantos takes readers back in time to the secretive and often cunning events that led to that famous ride. With information that will seem new to most readers, Lantos reveals a web of characters and circumstances that brings the sense of urgency and danger that permeated this time period. Readers - young and old - will be captivated by this fast-paced and informative book that will effectively bring "The Midnight Ride of Paul Revere" to another generation of Americans.

Showcase sentence: Revere was the arrow; | Warren was the bow.

Rationale: This is a great sentence for study for two reasons. First, it effectively models how to use a semicolon in place of a coordinating conjunction to join two independent clauses. In non-grammar-speak - it's a cool way to join sentences. Also, it's a metaphor that cements Warren's role in the mind of the reader. Lantos didn't have to convince us Warren was important. With this metaphor, we understand that Warren is essential to this midnight ride. The sentence is concise but packs a lot of punch.

How does understanding this sentence help the student build knowledge in this content area? People in history are important. It's important that we know who did what and when. This is the essence of understanding how events unfold the way they do and why people act the way they do. Most students - and adults who have studied American history - know about Paul Revere. Longfellow made his midnight ride sound courageous, dangerous, and successful. It was a pivotal moment in history, as without it, the Revolutionary War might not have happened. But Revere didn't work alone.

Ask:

- This sentence is an example of a metaphor. What is a metaphor? (A comparison that does not use *like* or *as*/a phrase that is symbolic.)
- What image does this sentence bring to mind? (A bow and arrow.)
- Let's act out how a bow and arrow work together. (Model and let students imitate pulling a bow and launching an arrow at a target.)
- As we unpack this sentence, keep this image (symbol/metaphor) in mind.

TAKE APART

Remember, your chunks are on sentence strips. Move them around to help students focus on one chunk and then another. You'll move them back together later.

Chunk	Possible Questions to Ask	Possible Answers
Revere was the arrow;	Who or what is this chunk about?	Paul Revere.
	What do we know about Paul Revere?	He was a Patriot during the Revolutionary War era. He was part of the Sons of Liberty and often rode for the Committee of Correspondence to deliver messages.
	What do you think the author means when he says "Revere was the arrow?"	He means that – like an arrow – Revere will launch or race toward a target. The target in this case is Lexington and Concord.
	If Revere is "the arrow," can he just take off any time he wants?	No, he has to wait to be launched. The bow is the force that moves the arrow. So Revere is waiting for someone to tell him when and where to go.
Warren was the bow.	Who or what is this chunk about?	Joseph Warren
	What do we know about Joseph Warren?	Warren was a doctor and a Revolutionary War leader in Boston where Revere lived. Warren had spies all over the city who reported back to him as his patients.
	According to the metaphor, what is Warren's relationship to Revere?	Warren is the bow – he is the force behind the arrow. So in real life, Warren would tell Revere when and where to ride and what message to deliver.

PUT TOGETHER

During this part, the sentence chunks may be mixed up or off to the side. Invite students to manipulate the chunks when putting the sentence back together and/or while rearranging them.

Ask	Possible Answers	Food for Thought
What is the original order of this sentence?	Revere was the arrow; | Warren was the bow.	You might note that there are two independent clauses – two sentences joined by the semicolon. If needed, consider identifying the subject of both clauses and the predicate of both clauses.
How can this sentence be rearranged and still make sense?	Warren was the bow; | Revere was the arrow.	We often say – bow and arrow not arrow and bow. This arrangement follows the order for bow and arrow.

(Continued)

Ask	Possible Answers	Food for Thought
Why do you think the author chose to put Revere first in the sentence?	Students may come up with a number of reasons. Some ideas are: • Readers are more familiar with Revere, so the author started the sentence with Revere. • The book is about the *behind* the scenes action of the poem, and the bow is physically *behind* the arrow.	When you look at this sentence in context on page 71, you'll notice this is actually a transition sentence at the beginning of a chapter that introduces Warren. So it makes sense to put his name last in this sentence, as it leads into the next paragraph that talks about Warren, not Revere.
What if we took out the semicolon? How can we combine these sentences? What effect does it have on the sentence?	Examples that emphasize Warren's role over Revere's: • Revere was the arrow *but* Warren was the bow. • Revere was the arrow, *however*, Warren was the bow. • *Although* Revere was the arrow, Warren was the bow. • Revere was the arrow, *yet* Warren was the bow. Examples that show equal emphasis: • Revere was the arrow, *and* Warren was the bow. • Revere was the arrow *because* Warren was the bow. • Revere was the arrow *for* Warren was the bow.	Using conjunctions like: *but*, *however*, *although*, and *yet* seem to place more emphasis on Warren's role than Revere's. By using the semicolon, the author keeps both roles of equal importance. Conjunctions like *and*, *because*, and *for* seem to show an equal relationship between the two men's roles. *Because* and *for* create a cause/effect relationship.
Why do you think the author decided to use a semicolon and no conjunction to join these clauses?	Answers may vary: • The author liked the way it sounded – like two distinct jobs. • The author couldn't decide on which conjunction to use. • The author wants to emphasize the subjects' different yet equally important roles.	By using a semicolon, the author gives equal weight to the men involved and their jobs. He seems to be saying they work together – one without the other is ineffective. Just like a bow and an arrow are ineffective without each other.

APPLY

During this part, students quickly apply their new knowledge about the sentence to their reading and writing. These are quick efforts and may be followed up with more practice.

Discuss: What other people or groups of people in the Revolutionary War era fit this metaphor?

Writing focus: Writers use metaphors to give readers a mental image for comparison. In this case, we not only get a mental image but we understand how the two images work together to show the relationship between the two people (or things) being compared. Try this with some other examples.

> **Showcase sentence:** Revere is the arrow; Warren is the bow.

Heavy scaffold: _____ (Who? What? or Where?) is the match; _____ (Who? What? or Where?) is the fire.

Example: <u>Boston</u> is the match; <u>Lexington/Concord</u> is the fire.

Heavy scaffold 2: Washington is the _____ (thing (noun)); King George is the _____ (thing (noun)).

Example: Washington is the <u>lion tamer</u>; King George is the <u>lion</u>.

Light scaffold: _____ (person/place/thing) is _____ (comparison/noun); _____ (person/place/thing) is _____ (comparison/noun).

Example: The <u>moonlight</u> is <u>death</u>; the <u>shadows</u> are <u>life</u>.

No scaffold: Invite students to emulate the showcase sentence within their own writing.

Thought Partners:_____

Sentence Dig CA8.1
THINK SHEET: WRITING FOCUS

STRATEGY: Sentence Combining

Writers can combine clauses in different ways to help the reader understand information. Writers can combine sentences with:

- A coordinating conjunction (for, and, nor, but, or, yet, so)
- A subordinating conjunction (although, when, because, since, after, before, while)
- A semicolon (as shown in the showcase sentence)

Write the showcase sentence from the sentence dig in the space below:

[   ]

Directions:

Think, Talk, Write: With a partner, discuss multiple ways you can combine the groups of sentences. Then write your two favorite ideas on the lines below.

Example: George Washington is the President of the Continental Congress.
Thomas Jefferson wrote the Declaration of Independence.

Combination #1:

George Washington is the President of the Continental Congress; Thomas Jefferson wrote the Declaration of Independence.

Combination #2:

George Washington is the President of the Continental Congress, while Thomas Jefferson wrote the Declaration of Independence.

Talk with a partner about how to combine these sentences:

*Paul Revere was captured by British soldiers.
Samuel Prescott evaded capture and warned Lexington and Concord.*

Write your two favorite combinations:

1. _____

_____

_____

_____

2. _____

_____

_____

_____

Talk with a partner about how to combine these sentences:

*John Hancock and Samuel Adams chose to hide from the British in Concord.
Joseph Warren chose to stay behind in Boston.*

Write your two favorite combinations:

1. _____

_____

_____

_____

2. _____

_____

_____

_____

SENTENCE DIG CA8.2: APPOSITIVE PHRASE: NAMING KEY CHARACTERISTICS

Text: *Beavers: Radical Rodents and Ecosystem Engineers* by Frances Backhouse, page 173

Grades: 3-5

Book summary: Beavers show up in literature as clever creatures for a reason - they really are. In this book, *Beavers: Radical Rodents and Ecosystem Engineers* by Frances Backhouse, the author teaches readers about this unique animal and its habitat. Readers learn not only of the body adaptations and cunning beavers use when building their shelters, but also of the significant effect their presence - or absence - has on an ecosystem. Beavers are not just an animal in the food chain, they create spaces for ecosystems to grow and thrive. This book is full of interesting facts and photos that will give any reader a new appreciation for this species.

Showcase sentence: These small creatures, | **some so tiny that you need a microscope to see them,** | are at the center of the beaver-pond food web.

Rationale: This sentence is one way scientists can use an appositive to add information about the subject of their sentence. When writers include an appositive, often set off by commas or dashes, they're including important information about the subject that enriches the readers' understanding of the sentence but it's not necessary for the sentence. This is a helpful tool for students to have in their back pocket as readers and writers. As a reader, students will know how to connect the information and categorize the information they're learning. As a writer, it's a tool to use to give extra information to provide clarity and to prevent overuse of simple sentences.

How does understanding this sentence help the student build knowledge in this content area? This particular sentence is helping the reader understand the scope and scale of a beaver ecosystem and the food web that is created there. This ecosystem supports plenty of plant and animal life that one can see but it also supports life that we can't see easily. Understanding this concept helps the learner to grasp the significance a beaver has on an area. This idea is generalizable to other ecosystems and food webs and the role an individual animal may have on them.

Ask: What is a food web? Explain this concept to your partner. *Possible answers: A food web is how energy is passed through an ecosystem. A food web has producers, consumers, and decomposers. A food web has predators and prey. It's how the plant and animal life feed off each other.*

As we analyze this sentence, keep in mind that we're talking about a food web. Depending on your group, you may want to take a moment before you get started to clarify what a food web is and discuss how it is different from a spider web, which students may be thinking of initially.

TAKE APART

Remember, your chunks are on sentence strips. Move them around to help students focus on one chunk and then another. You'll move them back together later.

Chunk	Possible Questions to Ask	Possible Answers
These small creatures,	Who or what is this sentence about?	Small creatures
	Why does the author start the sentence with the word *These*? Why doesn't the author just start the sentence with *small creatures*?	*These* is a demonstrative pronoun that is referring to plankton and insects from the previous sentence. It's not just any kind of small creatures, it's "these" small creatures – plankton and insects.
some so tiny that you need a microscope to see them,	What does the author want us to know about the small creatures?	They're very small. You can see some of them without a microscope.
	What is a microscope?	It's a tool that helps people see things that you cannot see with just your eye. It magnifies an object that is small enough to fit on a slide, so a person can see it.
	Does the author have a microscope there? Why does the author mention the microscope?	This is the author's way of saying how teeny-tiny plankton and some insects are. You can't see them. You would need a microscope to see them. But, if you're in the wild, you just have to know they are there even though you can't see them.
are at the center of the beaver-pond food web.	How does this chunk connect to the rest of the sentence?	This tells us where the small creatures are – they're at the center of the beaver-pond food web.
	What does the author mean "at the center?"	In this case, it means these small creatures are heavily involved in the food chain. They're not the physical center but a lot of the other animals prey on them. They're *essential* to the food web.
	Why did the author hyphenate the words beaver and pond?	The author wanted to make clear that beaver is describing the kind of pond. It's a pond where beavers live. Not all ponds have beavers.

PUT TOGETHER

During this part, the sentence chunks may be mixed up or off to the side. Invite students to manipulate the chunks when putting the sentence back together and/or while rearranging them.

Ask	Possible Answers	Food for Thought
Looking at these chunks, which two chunks are the subject and predicate of the sentence?	These small creatures (subject)... are at the center of the beaver-pond food web (predicate).	It's helpful for students to see this sentence in its most basic form. Understanding the basic sentence helps students determine how the other phrases add on to the central meaning of the sentence.
How do you know that these chunks represent the subject and predicate?	*These small creatures* tell what the sentence is about. The subject is the who or what of the sentence. The chunk *are at the center of the beaver-pond food web* is the predicate because it begins with the verb *are*.	It's helpful for students to articulate why something is the subject and/or predicate of the sentence, especially when the verb reflects a state of being like the verb *are*.
Where should we put the chunk that is left to show the sentence as the author wrote it?	It goes between the subject and predicate.	The appositive always goes after the noun about which it is giving more information.
Is there a different phrase we can use to replace the second chunk?	...plankton and insects, ...many of which live in the water, ...so small they're hard to see...	Accept any answer that tells more about the "small creatures" and makes sense in the sentence.

APPLY

During this part, students quickly apply their new knowledge about the sentence to their reading and writing. These are quick efforts and may be followed up with more practice.

Discuss: What other plants and animals are part of the beaver-pond food web? With a partner (or small group) use the text to help you create a food web diagram.

Writing focus: Writers use appositive phrases to tell more about a noun in the sentence. The phrase comes after the noun and is often set off by commas or dashes.

> **Showcase sentence:** These small creatures, **some so tiny that you need a microscope to see them,** are at the center of the beaver-pond food web.

Heavy scaffold: Beavers, _____ (something specific about beavers) _____, are a keystone species.

Example: Beavers, animals that create wetlands, are a keystone species.

Light scaffold: Beavers, _____ (appositive) _____, _____ (verb phrase) _____.

Example: Beavers, known for being busy, check their dams for leaks at night.

No scaffold: Invite students to emulate the showcase sentence within their own writing.

Thought Partners:_____

Sentence Dig CA8.2
THINK SHEET: WRITING FOCUS

STRATEGY: Sentence Expansion

Write the showcase sentence from the sentence dig in the space below:

```
┌─────────────────────────────────────────────────────┐
│                                                     │
│                                                     │
└─────────────────────────────────────────────────────┘
```

Directions:
Read these simple sentences about ecosystems below.
Expand them by adding more information in the form of an appositive phrase.

Example: *Wetlands are home to many plants and animals.*

Wetlands, including swamps and ponds, are home to many plants and animals.

1. Swamps are home to many animals like fish and alligators.

   Swamps, _____, are home to many animals like fish and alligators.

2. Beavers create habitats when they build their dams and change the landscape.

   Beavers, _____, create habitats when they build their dams and change the landscape.

   Beavers create habitats, _____, when they build their dams and change the landscape.

3. Beavers know how to do many things.

   Beavers, _____, know how to do many things.

SENTENCE DIG CA8.3: APPOSITIVE PHRASE: RENAMING THE SUBJECT

Text: *The Split History of Westward Expansion in the United States: American Indian Perspective* by Nell Musolf, page 8

Grades: 3-6

Book summary: The Split History series is unique as it takes different time periods in American History and presents two different perspectives. The first part of the book features one perspective, and then after flipping the book over, the same events are told from a second point of view. In *The Split History of Western Expansion*, Nell Musolf relates the perspective most of us have learned in school as how America was settled and then expanded to include lands west of the Mississippi River leading to the United States' vast size and power. In this book, Musolf also presents the perspective of the indigenous people whose lives were uprooted and cultures were repressed due to these same events, giving readers a clearer picture of how the glory of Western Expansion came at a price.

Showcase sentence: In 1607, | Chief Wahunsenacawh, | **known to the settlers as Chief Powhatan,** | supplied food to the hungry settlers | in the colony of Jamestown, | in what is now Virginia.

NOTE: To pronounce Chief Wahunsenacawh correctly, consider visiting the website Life Along the River at americanindian.si.edu. They have a page of audio files that can help.

Rationale: This is a juicy sentence that has a lot going on. One of the reasons I love this sentence is there are layers of details that answer basic sentence questions like Who? What? When? and Where? It also has an appositive that it tells the reader another name for Chief Wahunsenacawh - one our history books have used.

How does understanding this sentence help the student build knowledge in this content area? This sentence helps the students build knowledge in a couple of ways. First, in history, names are important. It's important for students to know who Chief Wahunsenacawh is and why he is important to our country's history. It also gives us a model for how we can relay information about a person within an appositive by using the phrase *known as* or *known for*.

Ask: How many people is this sentence about? How do you know? The answer is one - Chief Wahunsenacawh is the same person as Chief Powhatan. However, there may be confusion among your students if they're still grappling with appositive phrases. Still others may think this sentence is about a bunch of people - the settlers - which would indicate confusion with identifying the subject of a sentence. One way to figure this out is to ask the questions – How many people is this sentence about? How do you know? And then ask the class for a thumbs up or thumbs down to show whether or not they agree. If students disagree, ask them to talk about their thinking, and again ask the class to agree or disagree. Then begin the sentence dig, keeping this initial conversation in mind. You'll want to artfully circle back to this to provide clarity.

TAKE APART

Remember, your chunks are on sentence strips. Move them around to help students focus on one chunk and then another. You'll move them back together later.

Chunk	Possible Questions to Ask	Possible Answers
In 1607,	What does this chunk tell the reader about the event in the sentence?	It tells us when this happened. This happened in 1607. This happened 13 years before the Pilgrims settled in Plymouth.
Chief Wahunsenacawh,	Who or what is the subject of our sentence?	Chief Wahunsenacawh is the subject of our sentence. He is the chief of the Powhatan tribe.
known to the settlers as Chief Powhatan,	What is the function of this chunk? How does it add meaning to the sentence? How do you know?	This chunk tells us a more familiar name for the chief – Chief Powhatan. Chief Powhatan *is* the same person as Chief Wahunsenacawh. We know this because of the phrase *known to the settlers as*. This means the settlers called him a different name than his given one.
supplied food to the hungry settlers	What did Chief Wahunsenacawh do?	He supplied food to the hungry settlers.
in the colony of Jamestown,	We already noted that this happened before the Pilgrims came to Plymouth and the first Thanksgiving. So, which chunk tells us which settlers Chief Wahunsenacawh helped in 1607?	The settlers in the colony of Jamestown. This chunk not only tells us where the event happened, it specifically identifies the settlers by their geographic region. This is important to a reader to differentiate between the settlers from the Mayflower and these. It also helps students to see a pattern in "settlers'" behavior and needs. They're very unprepared and many of them relied on the indigenous people to help them.
in what is now Virginia.	How does this last chunk add meaning to the sentence?	It tells us where Jamestown is on our map today. "What is now…" means "today." There was not a colony or state called Virginia in 1607.

PUT TOGETHER

During this part, the sentence chunks may be mixed up or off to the side. Invite students to manipulate the chunks when putting the sentence back together and/or while rearranging them.

Ask	Possible Answers	Food for Thought
This is a long sentence, so let's circle back to our original question. How many people is this sentence about? Which chunk (or chunks) tells us this?	This sentence is about one person: Chief Wahunsenacawh, | known to the settlers as Chief Powhatan,	Both of these chunks answer the question – who is this sentence about. Chief Wahunsenacawh *is* Chief Powhatan.
Which of these chunks functions as the subject of the sentence and which chunk functions as the appositive phrase?	Chief Wahunsenacawh functions as the subject of the sentence. ...known to the settlers as Chief Powhatan, is an appositive phrase.	Remind students that the subject of the sentence cannot be removed from the sentence, but an appositive phrase can. The writer is just letting us know that the chief had more than one name.
Now that we know the subject of the sentence, what is the original order of the complete sentence?	In 1607, | Chief Wahunsenacawh, | known to the settlers as Chief Powhatan, | supplied food to the hungry settlers | in the colony of Jamestown, | in what is now Virginia.	If students are having trouble organizing this sentence, consider asking them sentence building questions: When did this happen? What did Chief Wahunsenacawh do? Which ones – which settlers? Where?
Is there a way to rearrange this sentence and it still makes sense? What effect does the new order have on the reader?	Answers will vary. Here are some possibilities: In 1607, | known to the settlers as Chief Powhatan, | Chief Wahunsenacawh | supplied food to the hungry settlers | in the colony of Jamestown, | in what is now Virginia. In 1607, | in the colony of Jamestown, | in what is now Virginia. | Chief Wahunsenacawh, | known to the settlers as Chief Powhatan, | supplied food to the hungry settlers.	NOTE: Due to the length of this sentence, it may be helpful to give students smaller strips with these chunks written on it to manipulate with their partners or in a small group. Here the appositive comes before the noun it embellishes. This is still a functional sentence. The order of this sentence now gives emphasis to the name Chief Powhatan rather than Chief Wahunsenacawh. The author may put Chief Wahunsenacawh first in the sentence to honor his given name rather than the one the settlers could remember. It's no coincidence that Chief Powhatan is the leader of the Powhatan tribe. In this arrangement the chunk *in the colony of Jamestown* now tells us more about where this happens rather than emphasizing which settlers the chief was helping. It is a nuance to the writing that may not seem significant to the reader. The important thing to glean is that settlers were hungry and needed help in the beginning – whether in Jamestown or Plymouth.

(Continued)

Ask	Possible Answers	Food for Thought
Is there any information we can remove from the sentence? What effect does this have on the meaning of the sentence? NOTE: There are a lot of different ways to remove information from this sentence. A few examples are explained.	~~In 1607,~~ | Chief Wahunsenacawh, | ~~known to the settlers as Chief Powhatan,~~ | supplied food to the hungry settlers | ~~in the colony of Jamestown,~~ | ~~in what is now Virginia.~~	You can remove any and all of the chunks until you get down to the basic sentence: Chief Wahunsenacawh | supplied food to the hungry settlers.
	~~In 1607,~~ | Chief Wahunsenacawh, | known to the settlers as Chief Powhatan, | supplied food to the hungry settlers | in the colony of Jamestown, | in what is now Virginia.	Removing the date does not change the meaning of the sentence. However, it does leave readers wondering when this happened. In history, dates are important to help us understand relationships between people, places, and events.
	In 1607, | Chief Wahunsenacawh, | ~~known to the settlers as Chief Powhatan,~~ | supplied food to the hungry settlers | in the colony of Jamestown, | in what is now Virginia.	You can remove the appositive phrase *known to the settlers as Chief Powhatan*. This phrase helps to connect the name of the chief most people have learned in American history to his real name. In a time when we are trying to be more culturally competent and responsive, it's important for students of history to know people's given names. Without the appositive, readers may not realize that Chief Wahunsenacawh *is* Chief Powhatan.
	In 1607, | Chief Wahunsenacawh, | known to the settlers as Chief Powhatan, | supplied food to the hungry settlers | ~~in the colony of Jamestown,~~ | in what is now Virginia.	Removing *in the colony of Jamestown* without removing *in what is now Virginia* creates ambiguity. It's not clear where this happened, as the state of Virginia is a large place. In addition, there is no connection between Virginia and this event without mentioning Jamestown unless the reader was well versed in the life of Chief Wahunsenacawh and where he lived.
The author uses the preposition *in* three times within this one sentence. Is there another way we can introduce the date using a different preposition or conjunction?	*During the winter of 1607, ...* *Because 1607 was a difficult year for the settlers, ...* *By the end of 1607, ...*	When writers reread and revise, they often notice when they use a word too many times. Sometimes it works with a sentence and there is no change. Other times, it's helpful to change the wording to reduce repetitiveness.

APPLY

During this part, students quickly apply their new knowledge about the sentence to their reading and writing. These are quick efforts and may be followed up with more practice.

Discuss:

- How can you rewrite this sentence so that the subject is *the settlers*?
- What does this sentence tell you about Chief Wahunsenacawh's character – the kind of person he is?
- How do we know these hungry settlers are not the same people as the Pilgrims? What does this say about the preparedness of the European settlers?

Writing focus: Using an appositive phrase allows the writer to include more information about the noun it follows. In the content areas, this is a way for students to connect information they are learning about people, places, things, events, and ideas.

> **Showcase sentence:** In 1607, Chief Wahunsenacawh, known to the settlers as Chief Powhatan, supplied food to the hungry settlers in the colony of Jamestown, in what is now Virginia.

Heavy scaffold: In 1607, Captain James Smith, who was known for _____ (What?), established a "no work, no food" rule in Jamestown.

Example: In 1607, Captain James Smith, who was known for <u>being an explorer and a soldier</u>, established a "no work, no food" rule in Jamestown.

Light scaffold: _____ (When?), _____ (person (name)), who was known for (or as) _____ (more about that person), _____ (Did what?) _____ (Where?).

Example: <u>Before getting off the Mayflower</u>, the Pilgrims, who were known as <u>religious outcasts</u>, <u>created and signed the Mayflower Compact on the ship</u>.

No scaffold: Invite students to emulate the showcase sentence within their own writing.

SENTENCE DIG CA8.4: USING NUMBERS: DURATION, DISTANCE, AMOUNT, AND RATIOS

Text: *The Split History of Westward Expansion in the United States: American Indian Perspective* by Nell Musolf, page 10

Grades: 3-6

Book summary: The Split History series is unique as it takes different time periods in American History and presents two different perspectives. The first part of the book features one perspective, and then after flipping the book over, the same events are told from a second point of view. In *The Split History of Western Expansion*, Nell Musolf relates the perspective most of us have learned in school as how America was settled and then expanded to include lands west of the Mississippi River leading to the United States' vast size and power. In this book, Musolf also presents the perspective of the indigenous people whose lives were uprooted and cultures were repressed due to these same events, giving readers a clearer picture of how the glory of Western Expansion came at a price.

Showcase sentence: During the next **three months,** | the chief and his band | led the army | on a **1,400 mile (2,253 kilometer)** chase | into what is now Montana, | fighting **four major battles** along the way | despite being **outnumbered 10 to one.**

Rationale: This delicious sentence is full of numbers! Numbers that set a time period, the distance travelled, the number of battles and a ratio! It's a mathematician's dream sentence set in a historical context. But one person's dream is another person's nightmare. This is why it's an important sentence to dig into. Historians often use numbers to describe when, where, why and how events take place. Numbers can deliver drama to drive home the significance of a situation. In other words, numbers are as important to a writer of history as they are to a mathematician. As readers, we need to be able to unpack the meaning of numbers and interpret them within the context they are used. Once students dig into this sentence, they'll have a new respect for this small yet fierce band.

How does understanding this sentence help the student build knowledge in this content area? This sentence helps to build knowledge around the relationship between the US government and the indigenous people. This situation grew from the US government stealing millions of acres from these people. A small band of warriors retaliated. In the US army's chase to find the warriors, the whole tribe set off for Canada. This sentence, these numbers, helps the reader understand the relentless and ruthless manner in which the US government treated Native Americans.

Ask: There are a lot of numbers in this sentence. Why do you think the author included so many?

Consider highlighting all the numbers, since they are represented with digits and words.

Student answers will vary but may include: *The author included numbers to answer the questions when, how long, and how many.*

TAKE APART

Remember, your chunks are on sentence strips. Move them around to help students focus on one chunk and then another. You'll move them back together later.

Chunk	Possible Questions to Ask	Possible Answers
During the next three months,	What does this chunk tell us about the rest of the sentence?	It tells us how long the action of this sentence lasts.
the chief and his band	What is the function of this chunk of text in the sentence?	This is the subject of the sentence. The sentence is about the chief [Chief Joseph] and his band. It is a compound subject because there is more than one named subject using the conjunction *and*.
	What does the word *band* mean in this sentence?	In this case, the author is not referring to a musical band but rather a small group of people with a similar purpose or interest. In this case the Nez Percé warriors and their families were the band.
led the army on a 1,400 mile (2,253 kilometer) chase	How does this chunk connect to the subject of the sentence?	It tells us what the chief and his band did – they led the army on a chase.
	Which army is this sentence referring to and how do you know?	It's referring to the US Army because earlier in the text, the author refers to a conflict between the US government and the Nez Percé people.
	What does the phrase *1400 mile chase* mean?	It means that the army chased after the chief and his band across 1400 miles! It was a long way. *You might note that it is customary to convert miles into kilometers when writing. This is because most countries – most readers in the world – use kilometers instead of miles to measure distance.*
into what is now Montana,	Where did they lead the army? How do you know?	This chunk lets us know where the chase ended – in Montana. But, it started in Oregon. We know this because in the text it tells us that is where the crisis started and the chase led into Montana. If you have a map handy, you can show students that the chase crossed land in what is now Oregon, Idaho, and Montana. Without cars and likely not enough horses, that is a very long way.

(Continued)

Chunk	Possible Questions to Ask	Possible Answers
fighting four major battles along the way	What does this chunk tell us?	That the army and the band of Nez Percé met up and fought four times – four major battles. The Nez Percé escaped at least three times.
	What does the phrase *along the way* mean?	*Along the way* means while traveling... so while the chief and his band were traveling to Canada, they were being chased by the US army and had to stop and fight them four times.
despite being outnumbered 10 to one.	What does this chunk mean?	Despite means without being affected. Being outnumbered means the other side (the army) had more people. The ratio 10 to 1 means there were 10 US soldiers for every one Nez Percé.
	What is the effect this chunk has on the sentence?	It makes the numbers even more impressive because the Nez Percé had so few people compared to the army.

PUT TOGETHER

During this part, the sentence chunks may be mixed up or off to the side. Invite students to manipulate the chunks when putting the sentence back together and/or while rearranging them.

Ask	Possible Answers	Food for Thought
What is the original order of this sentence?	During the next three months, | the chief and his band | led the army | on a 1,400 mile (2,253 kilometer) chase | into what is now Montana, | fighting four major battles along the way | despite being outnumbered 10 to one.	If students have a difficult time putting this back together, use sentence-building questions to help guide them: When did this happen? *During the next three months.* Who did what? *The chief and his band | led the army on a 1400 mile (2,253 kilometer) chase.* Where? *Into what is now Montana.* What else happened? *Fighting four major battles along the way.* How? *Despite being outnumbered 10 to one.*
If we took out the numbers from the sentence, what is the effect?	During the next ~~three~~ months, | the chief and his band | led the army | on a ~~1,400 mile (2,253 kilometer)~~ chase | into what is now Montana, | fighting ~~four~~ major battles along the way | despite being outnumbered ~~10 to one~~.	Students may notice that the sentence still makes sense but it doesn't have a lot of specific information. You don't really know how far they traveled or how many battles they fought or by how much the band was outnumbered. At first, numbers may intimidate a reader, but they often provide clarity in the sentence. This is why it is helpful to slow down your reading when you come across a lot of numbers and think about what those numbers are telling you. As a writer we want to think about using numbers to provide clear and important details. In all of the content areas – social studies, science, and math – numbers can give specific information that will build the readers' knowledge and understanding of the text.

APPLY

During this part, students quickly apply their new knowledge about the sentence to their reading and writing. These are quick efforts and may be followed up with more practice.

Discuss: Work with your partner. Create a visual representation of this sentence.

During the next **three** months, the chief and his band led the army on a **1,400 mile (2,253 kilometer)** chase into what is now Montana, fighting **four** major battles along the way despite being outnumbered **10 to one**.

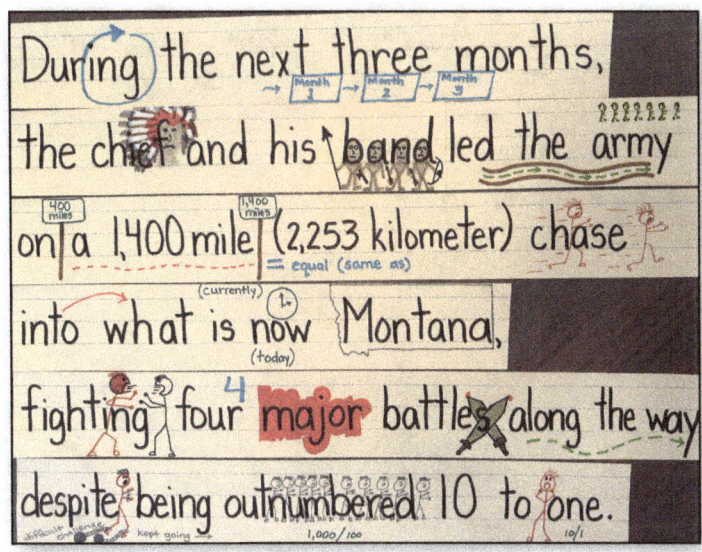

FIGURE 8.1
Annotated sentence dig with sketches to support comprehension

Writing focus: Writers use numbers to reveal important details when writing about people, places, things, events, and ideas.

> **Showcase sentence:** During the next three months, the chief and his band led the army on a 1,400 mile (2,253 kilometer) chase into what is now Montana, fighting four major battles along the way despite being outnumbered 10 to one.

NOTE: The showcase sentence is quite complex with using numbers in four different ways. The scaffolds below support students to use numbers in their sentences to reveal time, distance, and frequency.

(Continued)

Heavy scaffold: During the next _____ months, the coach and their players
                                              Number

_____ _____ playing _____ along the way.
  Did what   How far   How many

Example: During the next <u>two</u> months, the coach and their players <u>traveled</u> <u>300 miles</u> playing <u>seven</u> games along the way.

Light scaffold: _____ , _____ _____
                   Time compound   Subject   Verb – did what

_____ _____ _____ .
  How far   What else happened   How many

Example: <u>Within the next three years</u>, <u>Maggie and her friends</u> <u>will visit colleges</u> <u>over 500 miles from home</u> <u>while studying for</u> <u>six classes</u>.

No scaffold: Invite students to emulate the showcase sentence within their own writing.

SENTENCE DIG CA8.5: PARTICIPLE PHRASES: MODIFYING A NOUN BY DESCRIBING ACTIONS

Text: *Disasters by the Numbers: A Book of Infographics* by Steve Jenkins, page 8

Grades: 3-6

Book summary: Steve Jenkins does it again with this book that is anything but a disaster. *Disasters by the Numbers: A Book of Infographics* expertly weaves in informative text with a variety of infographics. Jenkins divides the disasters in this book into four sections: Earth, Weather, Life, and Space. Through these lenses he investigates everything from earthquakes to hurricanes to pandemics and even falling satellites. With a robust vocabulary, exact numbers to help the details pop, and infographics to fill in the missing pieces, Jenkins again surrounds us with scientific facts and mathematical statistics that make us all feel wiser.

Showcase sentence: Pressure builds up | until the plates suddenly move | **releasing energy and shaking the ground.**

Rationale: Writers often add important details about a noun in the sentence with a participle phrase. This can be confusing because the participle looks like a verb but it's really describing a noun. Without getting lost in the complications of English grammar, students can use this sentence dig to study how to effectively interpret and compose participle phrases revealing important details.

How does understanding this sentence help the student build knowledge in this content area? This particular sentence is a process sentence - it's explaining how an earthquake happens. This will help students build knowledge about how energy is stored and released in the ground. This basic understanding is foundational not only for understanding earthquakes but for other geographic phenomena like tsunamis and volcanic eruptions.

Ask: The sentence in the text that comes before our showcase sentence is: "As they slide past each other, the plates can get stuck, sometimes for centuries." How long is a century? *100 years*. So the text is telling us that the plates can move past each other and get stuck for hundreds of years. This next sentence is going to tell us what happens while the plates are stuck until an earthquake happens.

TAKE APART

Remember, your chunks are on sentence strips. Move them around to help students focus on one chunk and then another. You'll move them back together later.

Chunk	Possible Questions to Ask	Possible Answers
Pressure builds up	What is this sentence about?	Pressure.
	What is pressure?	Pressure is force – in this case the amount of force between the two plates trying to move. Energy is the amount of work it takes to apply the force. The plates are using energy to try to get unstuck; the pressure is the amount of force it takes to get unstuck.
	What does it mean that the pressure builds up?	It's being stored or adding up. Energy doesn't just disappear. If it has nowhere to go it stays in one place and gets more intense... it builds up like dirt on a car.
until the plates suddenly move	How does this chunk add meaning to the sentence?	Until means up to a point in time – so this chunk means the pressure kept building until the plates moved – were no longer stuck.
releasing energy and shaking the ground.	How does this chunk connect to the sentence? What is it telling us?	This chunk tells us more about what the plates are doing when they suddenly move. The plates not only move but they release energy that shakes the ground.

PUT TOGETHER

During this part, the sentence chunks may be mixed up or off to the side. Invite students to manipulate the chunks when putting the sentence back together and/or while rearranging them.

Ask	Possible Answers	Food for Thought
What is the original order of this sentence?	Pressure builds up | until the plates suddenly move | releasing energy and shaking the ground.	The subject of this sentence – *pressure* – may still feel a bit abstract for some of your students. If needed, guide them to put this sentence together using the questions: *What is this sentence about?* *What is happening to the subject?* *How long does the pressure build?* *What happens when the plates move?*
Can you rearrange the sentence and it still makes sense?	Until the plates suddenly move | releasing energy and shaking the ground, | pressure builds up.	The only way to rearrange this sentence is to move the simple sentence *pressure builds up* to the end. The chunk *releasing energy and shaking the ground* needs to stay near the noun it describes – *plates*.
How can we write this sentence as two separate sentences? What effect does it have on the reader?	Pressure builds up. The plates suddenly move, releasing energy and shaking the ground. Pressure builds up until the plates suddenly move. Then the plates release energy and shake the ground.	This can be written in two different sentences, however it feels clunky. It makes the events feel like separate things. However, it's all happening at the same time. The pressure builds until the exact moment the plates move and at that exact moment energy is released and the ground shakes. By keeping these chunks all together, the reader gets the sense that all of this happens at the same time.

APPLY

During this part, students quickly apply their new knowledge about the sentence to their reading and writing. These are quick efforts and may be followed up with more practice.

Discuss: Based on this bit of text discussed today, if tectonic plates are always in motion, why do we not have earthquakes every day?

Writing focus: Writers can use participle phrases to modify a noun by describing action.

> **Showcase sentence:** Pressure builds up until the plates suddenly move **releasing energy and shaking the ground.**

Heavy scaffold: During an earthquake the ground moves, _____ ing
                                                            participle

_____ and _____ ing _____.
noun/prepositional phrase   *participle*   *noun/prepositional phrase*

Example: During an earthquake the ground moves, <u>rumbling under roadways</u> and <u>rocking tall buildings</u>.

Light scaffold: During _____, _____ _____ _____ ing
                            event   *noun/subject*   *Does what? (verb)*   *participle*

_____ and _____ ing _____.
noun/prepositional phrase   *participle*   *noun/prepositional phrase*

Example: During a <u>snowstorm</u>, <u>the wind</u> <u>whips through the air freezing water</u> <u>on roadways</u> and <u>pushing snow against buildings</u>.

No scaffold: Invite students to emulate the showcase sentence within their own writing.

CHAPTER 9
Sentence Structure

A sentence should contain no unnecessary words, a paragraph no unnecessary sentences, for the same reason that a drawing should have no unnecessary lines and a machine no unnecessary parts.
- Strunk and White (2000)

Writing in the content areas serves two purposes. First, students can write to process the information they are learning. This might include summaries, graphic organizers, or responses to a constructive response question. Writing in this way helps to move information from students' working memory to long-term memory. Students can also write to synthesize information from across texts by producing various texts like lecture notes, essays, multimodal informational pieces, or even podcast scripts. Now that we are beyond the onset of technology, the opportunities for writing - and writing well - have exploded. What sets apart well-written essays, award-winning podcasts, and viral tik-toks from others is arguably... the structure.

If we think of all texts - multimodal and print - there is a structure and organization to them that allows the reader or viewer to experience the text in a way that resonates with them. My son used to have a YouTube channel where he produced videos of himself playing a video game. He spent hours planning the games from what time he would play to record, who else would be playing, to game moves and strategies he planned to use. Then, he worked for hours on editing the video using a structure that took the viewer on an experience through the game - unfolding the the action bit by bit with a change in scenery, developing tone with background music and/or background colors, zooming in or out of the scene - every crafting move he made reflected the overall structure of the video he was making. The videos were only five to ten minutes long, but he made sure there were no unnecessary clips, no unnecessary commentary, no unnecessary music... everything he did had a function - a role to play. He planned and organized the experience and material first, then he created his videos.

I mention this because our students live in a multimodal world, and this book zeros in on the context of one sentence at a time. Yet, from each sentence we can learn about text structure. We can think about the experience the author is setting up for us as readers and, in turn, as writers, we can develop the experience we want to establish for our readers. In many of today's informational texts, writers are mixing text structure. Sometimes each chapter has a different structure, sometimes different paragraphs have different structures, and often, sentences within a paragraph may have different structures. With that, just teaching "text structure" as a standard is quite difficult when using more complex texts. For example, *Plasticus Maritimus: An Invasive Species* by Ana Pêgo, Bernado P. Carvalho, and Isabel Martins and translated by Jane Springer (2020), starts off with a narrative structure introducing the marine biologist (Pêgo) and her preoccupation with plastics. Then the text moves into a problem solution format, where the authors present the problems caused by plastic in the ocean with a persuasive slant - convincing the reader that plastic in the ocean is a worthy fight. The text also leverages cause and effect, chronological, and comparative text structures.

Text structures are the backbone of any well-written text. As readers and writers, we have to be flexible with our knowledge about text structures. As readers, we need to be able to seamlessly move from one text structure to the next within a text, while synthesizing the information to understand the author's message. As writers, we need to be able to leverage text structures to express our ideas clearly and highlight our central ideas while also informing and/or entertaining the reader.

Text structure is complex because the concept is not as rigid as it might have been twenty years ago. Students need to understand the different types of text structures in order to comprehend texts they are reading (or viewing or listening to); likewise, writers need to lean on text structure to clearly communicate their ideas. One way to study text structure is at the sentence level. Not all sentences will have "key words" to flag a certain kind of structure, so it's important that we teach children to dig in and discover what the structure organically reveals about the meaning.

In the following sample sentence digs, you and your learners will explore the various ways authors can reveal text structure at the sentence level. Naturally, your inquisitive conversations will eventually turn to the content focus as you move to ask - what are we learning here and why is this showcase sentence or its writing move important to the topic at hand? As you do, you'll consider how its structure builds on your knowledge in a way that you can speak, read, and write about it with expertise. Since this group of sample lessons isn't an exhaustive one, use this collection as a model for these kinds of sentences in the content area books your class is reading. You may also want to provide your students with different sentences that showcase other structures that they may struggle with in their own reading or writing. Use these digs as a starting place for looking at the way grammatical structures within content area sentences can help readers create meaning from the text.

SHOWCASE SENTENCES LESSONS AT A GLANCE

Lesson	Focus	Author's Purpose/ Grammatical Structure	Text	Sentence
CA9.1	Cause/effect	Conjunction *since*	*Bright Dreams: The Brilliant Ideas of Nikola Tesla* by Tracy Dockray	Nikola and Westinghouse were chosen to illuminate the Chicago's World Fair **since their AC cost much less** than Edison's DC.
CA9.2	Compare/ contrast	Subordinating conjunction *Even though*	*Bright Dreams: The Brilliant Ideas of Nikola Tesla* by Tracy Dockray	**Even though Nikola faced rejection and hardship**, he didn't stop.
CA9.3	Cause/effect	Complex sentence with conjunction *because*	*Plasticus Maritimus: An Invasive Species* by Ana Pêgo, Bernado P. Carvalho, Isabel Minhós Martins	For the planet to be healthy, the ocean's phytoplankton must be healthy, **because they begin the nutrient cycle** that feeds an enormous number of living beings on earth.
CA9.4	Sequential order	Verb phrases	*Why Longfellow Lied: The Truth About Paul Revere's Ride* by Jeff Lantos	Four hundred of these patriots **mustered**, **marched** to the fort, **scaled** the walls, **subdued** the six British soldiers inside, and **made off** with all the gunpowder.

SENTENCE DIG CA9.1: CAUSE AND EFFECT

Text: *Bright Dreams: The Brilliant Ideas of Nikola Tesla* by Tracy Dockray, page 21

Grades: 3-5

Book summary: *Bright Dreams: The Brilliant Ideas of Nikola Tesla* by Tracy Dockray is a nonfiction narrative that tells the biography of famous scientist, Nikola Tesla. This picture book uses the entire page spread to tell Nikola's life story through pictures and words while incorporating sidebars in the margins to explain the science embedded in his story. This lovely mix of text structure helps students practice reading dexterity by moving from the narrative to the informational text while synthesizing the information as they read. Living in a world with AI and self-driving cars, this is a timely biography that will inform, entertain, and inspire.

Showcase sentence: Nikola and Westinghouse were chosen | to illuminate the Chicago's World Fair | **since their AC cost much less** | than Edison's DC.

Rationale: This is a complex sentence that uses the conjunction *since* to indicate a cause and effect relationship. Unlike the conjunction *because* - which mainly serves to indicate a cause/effect structure - the word *since* has multiple meanings. In this case it acts as a conjunction and signals a cause/effect relationship. In addition, there are several pronouns and abbreviations in the sentence, conventions that young readers often ignore. This sentence gives us an opportunity to explicitly discuss those words and their meanings and the importance of tuning into them when they appear.

How does understanding this sentence help the student build knowledge in this content area? When students study electricity or inventors, they inevitably learn about Thomas Edison. When students think about Tesla, they think of an electric car. This sentence not only reminds us that Edison and Tesla were both electrical engineers at the same time, but they were also fierce competitors. This sentence explains the edge Tesla had over Edison to light up the Chicago's World Fair. It also requires students to remember what they read about AC (alternating current) and DC (direct current) earlier in the text.

Ask: In this sentence, the author uses abbreviations that they expect the reader to know. In the context of electricity, what does AC and DC mean? *AC refers to alternating current and DC refers to direct current; they both indicate how electricity is flowing through a current.*

NOTE: Consider putting a sticky note with the words *alternating current* and *direct current* under the abbreviations to support students through the sentence dig.

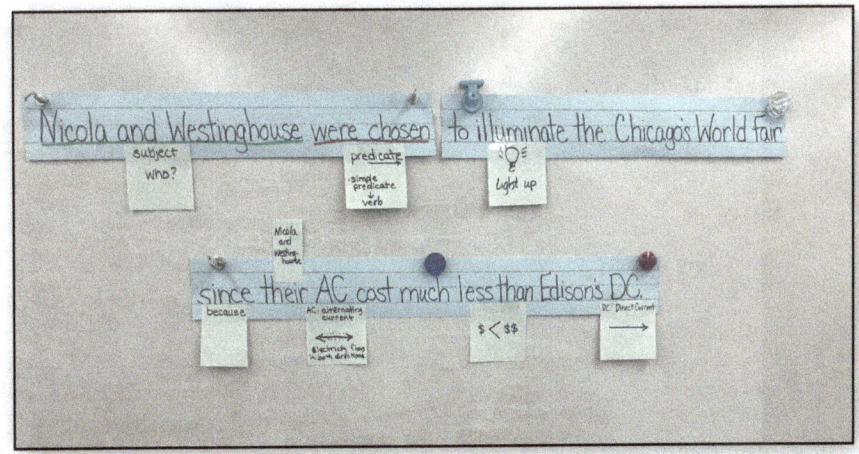

FIGURE 9.1
Annotated sentence dig with sketches to support comprehension

TAKE APART

Remember, your chunks are on sentence strips. Move them around to help students focus on one chunk and then another. You'll move them back together later.

Chunk	Possible Questions to Ask	Possible Answers
Nikola and Westinghouse were chosen	How many people is this chunk referring to? How do you know?	Two, Nikola and Westinghouse. Nikola is the first name of Nikola Tesla and Westinghouse is the last name of George Westinghouse.
	What happened to Nikola and Westinghouse?	They *were chosen*. *Were chosen* is the verb phrase. *Were* is an auxiliary (helping) verb that indicates the past tense for the main verb chosen.
	Which words here indicate the subject of the sentence? Which words indicate the simple predicate of the sentence?	Nikola and Westinghouse are the subject of the sentence; *were chosen* is the simple predicate.
to illuminate the Chicago's World Fair	How does this chunk connect to the rest of the sentence?	It tells us what Niola and Westinghouse would do.
	What does *illuminate* mean? How do you know?	Illuminate means to light up. Students may figure this out using context clues (the book is about inventing with electricity and AC refers to the current light bulbs use) or picture clues from the text.

(Continued)

SENTENCE DIGS

Chunk	Possible Questions to Ask	Possible Answers
since their AC cost much less	What does the word *since* mean in this chunk? What is a synonym for *since*?	*Since* means *for the reason that...* or a synonym for *since* is *because*. The word *since* is going to tell us *why* something happened... the cause.
	Who is *their* referring to?	*Their* refers to Nikola and Westinghouse.
	What does it mean to *cost much less*?	It means it won't take as much money to pay for it – it will use less electricity.
than Edison's DC.	How does this chunk add meaning to the sentence?	This chunk compares the cost of Tesla's AC to Edison's DC. It helps us understand that the Chicago's World Fair committee was considering two choices – AC or DC and they went with AC.

PUT TOGETHER

During this part, the sentence chunks may be mixed up or off to the side. Invite students to manipulate the chunks when putting the sentence back together and/or while rearranging them.

Ask	Possible Answers	Food for Thought
What is the original order of this sentence?	Nikola and Westinghouse were chosen | to illuminate the Chicago's World Fair | since their AC cost much less | than Edison's DC.	Consider highlighting the word *since* and remind students that this is a complex sentence. If helpful, underline the subject (*their AC*) and predicate (*cost much less than Edison's DC*) in the dependent clause.
What type of sentence structure is used here? (sequential; compare/contrast; cause/effect; explanatory; problem/solution; description; etc.) How do you know?	This is a cause and effect sentence. The word *since* is a clue. The sentence is saying *why* (cause) Nikola and Westinghouse were chosen (effect).	The overall sentence structure is cause and effect. The independent clause: *Nikola and Westinghouse were chosen to illuminate the Chicago's World Fair* is the effect. The cause (or reason why they were chosen) is the dependent clause: *their AC cost much less than Edison's DC*.
	Some students may say: compare and contrast because of the dependent clause: *their AC cost much less than Edison's DC*.	Students are not wrong if they noticed that the dependent clause uses a comparative structure, which is why it is important to explicitly state that this is a complex sentence first. When considering sentence structure, we consider the whole sentence, not just one clause.

(Continued)

Ask	Possible Answers	Food for Thought
Is there another conjunction you can use instead of *since*? Does that affect the sentence structure? If so, how?	Nikola and Westinghouse were chosen | to illuminate the Chicago's World Fair | **for** their AC cost much less | than Edison's DC.	The conjunction *for* can be used in this sentence as a synonym for *since*. It does not change the cause/effect structure.
	Nikola and Westinghouse were chosen | to illuminate the Chicago's World Fair | **provided that** their AC cost much less | than Edison's DC.	The subordinating conjunction *provided* can be used here as well. It sets up a condition or a "cause." It does not change the structure of the sentence.
Can we rearrange this sentence so that it still makes sense?	Since their AC cost much less | than Edison's DC, | Nikola and Westinghouse were chosen | to illuminate the Chicago's World Fair.	Students can put the dependent clause first and the sentence will still make sense.
	To illuminate the Chicago's World Fair, Nikola and Westinghouse were chosen | since their AC cost much less | than Edison's DC.	Students can start the sentence with the verb phrase *to illuminate the Chicago's World Fair*, followed by the rest of the sentence.
Why do you think the author chose to write the sentence leading with Nikola and Westinghouse's names?	• The book is about Nikola, not the Chicago's World Fair. • The author wants to emphasize that Nikola and Westinghouse were picked over Edison for this event.	Since this is a biography of Nikola Tesla, it makes sense that the author would want to emphasize Nikola's accomplishments. Starting the sentence with his name alongside Westinghouse accomplishes this.

APPLY

During this part, students quickly apply their new knowledge about the sentence to their reading and writing. These are quick efforts and may be followed up with more practice.

Discuss: Aside from earning money for illuminating the Chicago's World Fair, why is this a significant event in Tesla's life?

Writing focus: Writing a sentence with cause/effect structure.

> **Showcase sentence:** Nikola and Westinghouse were chosen to illuminate the Chicago's World Fair, since their AC cost much less than Edison's DC.

Heavy scaffold: _____ and _____ were chosen to _____

since they _____.

Example: <u>Raphael</u> and <u>Natalie</u> were chosen to <u>be back up dancers for Taylor Swift</u> since they <u>learn dances faster than Jonathon and Maria.</u>

Light scaffold: _____ and _____ were _____ to _____
                     subject/noun   subject/noun   adjective   verb/verb phrase

since _____.
      dependent clause to show the cause – explain why

Example: <u>Wilbur</u> and <u>Orville Wright</u> were <u>eager</u> to <u>fly their invention</u> since <u>they designed and built the first "heavier than air" plane.</u>

No scaffold: Invite students to emulate the showcase sentence within their own writing.

SENTENCE DIG CA9.2: COMPARE AND CONTRAST

Text: *Bright Dreams: The Brilliant Ideas of Nikola Tesla* by Tracy Dockray, page 25

Grades: 3–5

Book summary: We return to the book, *Bright Dreams: The Brilliant Ideas of Nikola Tesla* by Tracy Dockray about the famous scientist, Nikola Tesla. This picture book is structured as traditional page spreads that tell Tesla's life story through pictures and words while including additional sidebars in the margins to explain the science embedded in his story. This lovely mix of text structure helps students practice reading dexterity by moving from the narrative to the informational features, synthesizing the information as they read. The writing also provides a wide use of sentence structures, like the one you'll study in this sentence dig. Living in a world with AI and self-driving cars, this is a timely biography that will inform, entertain, and inspire.

Showcase sentence: Even though Nikola faced rejection and hardship, | he didn't stop.

Rationale: This sentence uses the subordinating conjunction *even though* to set up contrasting ideas. Moreover, this sentence beautifully states one of the themes of Tesla's life story.

How does understanding this sentence help the student build knowledge in this content area? Tesla's perseverance helps us understand how he was able to invent many things in the 20th century that still have a great effect on us today in the 21st century. This particular sentence summarizes his character and work ethic and taps into the trait of perseverance. Perseverance is a theme that threads through human history. From inventors of electricity like Nikola Tesla to astronauts like Sally Ride, humans have to overcome obstacles. Understanding when and how giants of industry overcome obstacles not only builds our knowledge about the content but can also inspire us to persevere as well.

Ask: Why do you think the author saved this sentence for the end of this book? *This is a summary-sentence of Nikola's life. He did have many obstacles but he still kept inventing things.*

TAKE APART

Remember, your chunks are on sentence strips. Move them around to help students focus on one chunk and then another. You'll move them back together later.

Chunk	Possible Questions to Ask	Possible Answers
Even though Nikola faced rejection and hardship,	Who is the subject of this sentence?	Nikola [Tesla]
	What is the function of the word *faced* in this sentence?	In this sentence, *faced* is a past tense verb.
	What does the word *faced* mean in this sentence?	It means to confront, deal with, or accept something unpleasant.
	What does rejection mean? What is an example?	Rejection is when someone's ideas are dismissed or not accepted. For example, Edison rejected (didn't accept) Tesla's ideas around AC.
	What is an example of hardship?	Hardship is severe suffering. An example would be not having enough money to buy food.
	Why do you think the author starts this chunk with *even though*?	The author is letting us know that they are going to present contrasting ideas – two ideas that are opposite each other.
he didn't stop.	Who is *he* referring to in this chunk?	The pronoun *he* refers to Nikola Tesla.
	How does this chunk connect to the rest of the sentence?	This is the contrasting idea. Most people would stop trying with a lot of rejection or hardship and use those things as excuses. But Nikola did not. Nikola didn't stop.
	What didn't Nikola stop?	He didn't stop trying. He didn't stop inventing. He didn't stop dreaming and thinking.

PUT TOGETHER

During this part, the sentence chunks may be mixed up or off to the side. Invite students to manipulate the chunks when putting the sentence back together and/or while rearranging them.

Ask	Possible Answers	Food for Thought
What is the original order of this sentence? What kind of sentence is this? How do you know?	Even though Nikola faced rejection and hardship, | he didn't stop.	This is a complex sentence. The first part *even though Nikola faced rejection and hardship...* is dependent as it doesn't express a complete thought yet. The conjunction *even though* indicates there is more to the sentence after the clause. It also refers to all the hardships and rejection over the course of time.
Is there another way to arrange this sentence?	He didn't stop | even though Nikola faced rejection and hardship.	You can start this sentence with the independent clause, and it will still make sense.

(Continued)

Ask	Possible Answers	Food for Thought
What if we changed the conjunction? Does it change the meaning of the sentence? If so, how?	*When* Nicola faced rejection and hardship, | he didn't stop.	The conjunction *when* changes the sentence to mean the rejection and hardship were happening at the same time as when he didn't stop. Meaning, Tesla worked through the hard times.
	After Nicola faced rejection and hardship, | he didn't stop.	The conjunction *after* changes the sentence to mean that Nicola faced rejection and hardship first, then he didn't stop working.
	Unless Nicola faced rejection and hardship, | he didn't stop.	The conjunction *unless* changes the sentence to mean that Nikola would stop working if he faced rejection and hardship.

APPLY

During this part, students quickly apply their new knowledge about the sentence to their reading and writing. These are quick efforts and may be followed up with more practice.

Discuss: What characteristics make Nikola Tesla a worthy person for us to study?

Writing focus: One reason authors are particular about the subordinating conjunctions they use is because the conjunction sets up the structure of the sentence. The conjunction *even though* sets the writer up to write a sentence embedding some contrast. Try it out.

> **Showcase sentence:** Even though Nikola faced rejection and hardship, he didn't stop.

Heavy scaffold: Even though Nikola believed in AC, _____.
dependent clause that shows a contrast

Example: Even though Nikola believed in AC, <u>Edison's DC was more popular.</u>

Light scaffold: Even though _____, _____.
subject + verbdependent clause that shows a contrast

Example: Even though <u>Wilbur and Orville Wright worked together to design and build the first plane, only one of them could take the first flight.</u>

No scaffold: Invite students to emulate the showcase sentence within their own writing.

SENTENCE DIG CA9.3: CAUSE AND EFFECT

Text: *Plasticus Maritimus: An Invasive Species* by Ana Pêgo, Bernado P. Carvalho, Isabel Minhós Martins, page 37

Grades: 3-5

Book summary: *Plasticus Maritimus: An Invasive Species* by Ana Pêgo, Bernado P. Carvalho, Isabel Minhós Martins is based on Ana Pêgo's life work as a marine biologist and her fight against what she calls an invasive species Plasticus Maritimus, aka plastic. With engaging text and illustrations, the narrator invites readers in to explore this species and its effect on not only our lakes, rivers, and oceans but on living things as well. This informational text is rich with facts and uses a variety of text structures to help the reader grasp the extent of this issue.

> **Showcase sentence:** For the planet to be healthy, | the ocean's phytoplankton must be healthy, | **because they begin the nutrient cycle** | that feeds an enormous number | of living beings on earth.

Rationale: This sentence itself is cause and effect, and it sets off a short paragraph that uses this same structure. It's also a key sentence to the entire text itself, when supporting one of the main ideas of the text: plastic is an invasive species that affects our life on earth.

How does understanding this sentence help the student build knowledge in this content area? Everyone knows we should recycle plastic and not throw it in the ocean. But most children - people - may not know how plastic gets into the ocean and once it does how it affects human life. This one sentence starts to build that understanding with a microscopic creature which nibbles and consumes the plastic, a whole nutrient cycle - consisting of living and nonliving things - is affected. Human beings are part of that nutrient cycle.

Ask: Are there any words in this sentence that we need to define before we start thinking about the different parts?

Consider drawing a quick sketch or adding a synonym to the chunks to support students during the language dig. Some words students may want defined include:

- Phytoplankton - microscopic marine (water/ocean) algae
- Nutrient cycle - the process by which matter and energy are exchanged between living organisms and the nonliving parts of an environment
- Living beings - includes any living thing including humans

TAKE APART

Remember, your chunks are on sentence strips. Move them around to help students focus on one chunk and then another. You'll move them back together later.

Chunk	Possible Questions to Ask	Possible Answers
For the planet to be healthy,	Which planet is the author referring to?	Earth For Earth to be healthy.
	Why do you think the author started this sentence this way?	To remind the reader that this sentence is about the whole planet, and we all want our planet to remain healthy because we need it to live.
the ocean's phytoplankton must be healthy,	This chunk is an independent clause – a whole sentence. What is the subject of this sentence?	This sentence is about phytoplankton.
	In what condition is the phytoplankton?	Healthy – the phytoplankton must be healthy
	Based on these two chunks (first and second) put together, what might happen if the phytoplankton isn't healthy?	The planet won't be healthy.
because they begin the nutrient cycle	What does the word *because* signal to the reader?	The writer is going to tell us why the phytoplankton must be healthy in order to have a healthy planet. The word *because* tells us this is a cause and effect sentence.
	Who or what does the pronoun *they* refer to?	*They* refers to the phytoplankton that is the subject of the independent clause.
	What does it mean that the phytoplankton *begin* the nutrient cycle?	They start the cycle.
that feeds an enormous number	What does the word *that* refer to?	*That* is a relative pronoun which refers to the nutrient cycle. The nutrient cycle feeds an enormous number.
of living beings on earth.	How does this chunk add meaning to the sentence?	This chunk completes the thought from the previous chunk – answering the reader's question – *feeds an enormous number of what?*

PUT TOGETHER

During this part, the sentence chunks may be mixed up or off to the side. Invite students to manipulate the chunks when putting the sentence back together and/or while rearranging them.

224 SENTENCE DIGS

Ask	Possible Answers	Food for Thought
What is the original order of this sentence?	For the planet to be healthy, | the ocean's phytoplankton must be healthy, | because they begin the nutrient cycle | that feeds an enormous number | of living beings on earth.	If students struggle to put this together, ask them to identify the independent clause of this sentence. Remind them, an independent clause can stand alone. *…the ocean's phytoplankton must be healthy* Then ask students sentence-building questions to help them recompose the original text: Why? *Because they begin the nutrient cycle.* What does the nutrient cycle do? *That feeds an enormous number of living things.*
What type of sentence structure is used here? How do you know?	Cause and effect; the sentence uses the word *because*.	If students struggle with this question, try rephrasing the question: Let's figure out the text structure based on this sentence. Could it be problem/solution? Why or why not? *No, because there is no problem to solve in the sentence.* Could it be chronological or sequential? *No, because there is not a series of things happening or events occurring.* Could it be cause and effect? *Yes. The author uses the word "because" which always indicates a cause/effect structure.*
According to this sentence, what causes the planet to be healthy? How do you know?	Healthy plankton causes the planet to be healthy because it starts the nutrient cycle. If the plankton is unhealthy, everything that eats it or gleans energy from it will also become unhealthy.	This may be difficult for students to articulate, since it's not explicitly written in the sentence. However, digging into the sentence should reveal this relationship that the planet will become unhealthy if the phytoplankton is unhealthy.
Can this be broken down into two sentences?	For the planet to be healthy, | the ocean's phytoplankton must be healthy. ~~Because~~ they begin the nutrient cycle | that feeds an enormous number | of living beings on earth.	This is a complex sentence. *If* can easily create two sentences by removing the subordinate conjunction.
Can we remove or rearrange chunks in this sentence to make it clearer or easier to read?	Because they begin the nutrient cycle | that feeds an enormous number | of living things, the ocean's phytoplankton must be healthy | for the planet to be healthy.	You can rearrange the sentence by putting the dependent clause first.

(Continued)

Ask	Possible Answers	Food for Thought
	For the planet to be healthy,	the ocean's phytoplankton must be healthy,	because they begin the nutrient cycle	~~that feeds an enormous number~~	~~of living things.~~	You can remove the relative clause telling more about the nutrient cycle. The sentence still makes sense.
	~~For the planet to be healthy,~~	the ocean's phytoplankton must be healthy,	because they begin the nutrient cycle	that feeds an enormous number	of living things.	One could take away the opening phrase and the sentence will still hold its own. However, the sentence loses its sense of urgency.

APPLY

During this part, students quickly apply their new knowledge about the sentence to their reading and writing. These are quick efforts and may be followed up with more practice.

Discuss: Explain why phytoplankton are important to the health of our planet.

Writing focus: Create a cause and effect sentence by using the word *because*.

> **Showcase sentence:** For the planet to be healthy, the ocean's phytoplankton must be healthy, because they begin the nutrient cycle that feeds an enormous number of living beings on earth.

Heavy scaffold: For a food chain to be healthy, the producer must be _____
adjective (adj. phrase)

because _____.
Reason – why? dependent clause: subject + predicate

Example: For a food chain to be healthy, the producer must be <u>healthy</u> because <u>consumers eat the producers</u>.

Light scaffold: For _____ to be _____, _____ must be _____
noun   adj., adv., or verb phrase   subject (noun)   adj., adv., or verb phrase

because _____.
Reason – why? dependent clause: subject + predicate

Example: For <u>my school</u> to be <u>healthy</u>, <u>the sinks</u> must be <u>working</u> because <u>they provide a place for us to wash our hands</u>.

No scaffold: Invite students to emulate the showcase sentence within their own writing.

SENTENCE DIG CA9.4: SEQUENTIAL ORDER

Text: *Why Longfellow Lied: The Truth About Paul Revere's Ride* by Jeff Lantos

Grades: 3-6

Book summary: Jeff Lantos takes an opportunity for readers to pull back the curtain and see what's happening behind the scenes of this famous poem, "The Midnight Ride of Paul Revere" by Henry Wadsworth Longfellow. Stanza by stanza, chapter by chapter, Lantos takes readers back in time to the secretive and often cunning events that led to that famous ride. With information that will seem new to most readers, Lantos reveals a web of characters and circumstances that brings the sense of urgency and danger that permeated this time period. Readers - young and old - will be captivated at this fast-paced and informative book that will effectively bring "The Midnight Ride of Paul Revere" to another generation of Americans.

Showcase sentence: Four hundred of these patriots **mustered**, | **marched** to the fort, | **scaled** the walls, | **subdued** the six British soldiers inside, | and **made off** with all the gunpowder.

Rationale: We return to this text to study a beautifully written sentence with a sequential structure. The verbs are positioned in the order they occur. Students will quickly realize that they cannot change the order of this sentence. When students want to combine sentences, one way is to layer the verbs like this sentence does. This adds complexity to the sentence because the writer needs to make sure the subject agrees with each verb and the reader needs to remember the subject is doing all of these things... in order. What seems like an easy sentence to read or write can actually be quite complex for young students.

How does understanding this sentence help the student build knowledge in this content area? This sentence will add to student knowledge about the beginning of the Revolutionary War. Nothing about that night was easy. It took planning, cunning, and a lot of courage to prepare for the beginning of that war... including getting supplies.

Ask:

- Who is this sentence about? What makes you think this?

    Students should be able to pick out "patriots" as the subject.

- Dig a little deeper - who are the patriots? If the patriots are on the side of the colonies, then who are the soldiers in the sentence and how do you know?

    Students should be able to determine that the soldiers are the British soldiers, as it says in the sentence. It will be helpful for the students to be clear on who the two groups of people are in the sentence before starting the dig.

TAKE APART

Remember, your chunks are on sentence strips. Move them around to help students focus on one chunk and then another. You'll move them back together later.

Chunk	Possible Questions to Ask	Possible Answers
Four hundred of these patriots mustered,	How many patriots went on this mission?	Four hundred: Note that this is a lot of people. Keep this in mind as you unpack all the things they did. Also note: they are the subject of the sentence.
	What does *mustered* mean?	Mustered is past tense because this happened long ago. It means to assemble troops and prepare for battle.
marched to the fort,	What does this chunk tell us?	The four hundred patriots marched – walked to the fort.
	Who is doing this? How do you know?	Four hundred patriots – they are the subject of the sentence.
	Whose fort did they march to? How do you know?	It is a British fort because we know the patriots are fighting or preparing to fight the British. Plus we already noted that the British soldiers are referred to in this sentence – it's their fort.
scaled the walls,	What does this chunk mean?	Scaled the walls means to climb over the walls.
	Who is climbing over the walls?	Four hundred patriots.
subdued the six British soldiers inside,	What does the word subdued mean?	Subdue means to bring someone under control (or to quieten) by force.
	How many British soldiers did they subdue?	The patriots subdued six British soldiers.
	What does the word *inside* refer to? Inside what?	Inside the fort.
and made off with all the gunpowder.	What does this chunk mean?	The patriots took all of the gunpowder.
	What does the term "made off" mean?	Students may say – to take. It really means to leave quickly – escape. So the patriots left quickly with all of the gunpowder.
	Who has made off with the gunpowder?	The four hundred patriots.

PUT TOGETHER

During this part, the sentence chunks may be mixed up or off to the side. Invite students to manipulate the chunks when putting the sentence back together and/or while rearranging them.

Ask	Possible Answers	Food for Thought
What is the original order of this sentence?	Four hundred of these patriots mustered, | marched to the fort, | scaled the walls, | subdued the six British soldiers inside, | and made off with all the gunpowder.	If students struggle putting this back together, ask them questions like: What did they do next?
How can we say this sentence in our own words?	Answers will vary. Example: The American colonists got their guns and went to the fort. They climbed the walls and secured the soldiers. Then they took the gunpowder and left.	Listen for the synonyms students use for the verbs to ensure they understand the meaning of the sentence. If students struggle, you may ask, what did the patriots do first? Second? Next?
When we used our own words, we replaced the verbs with synonyms. Why do you think the author used the verbs muster, marched, scaled, subdued, and made-off?	These are words that reflect things that soldiers do.	Writers often select verbs or vocabulary that describe their subject. Using academic vocabulary in this sentence makes a huge difference in the quality of the writing.
How many things did the patriots do in this sentence? How do you know?	They did five things: mustered, marched, scaled, subdued, and made off. We know this because these are the verbs of the sentence.	If students are unsure, go back and ask chunk by chunk – what did they do here? Then highlight or label the verb. After, list the five things they did by naming the verbs. This is important because some students will not connect each verb back to the subject. The subject is doing all of these things because this is one long sentence.
Can we rearrange this sentence? If so, how?	This sentence cannot be rearranged.	Students may try to rearrange the sentence, but each time, ask them does the order make sense? Would a patriot march to the fort, then muster, then scale the walls…? Note that the verbs are in sequential order. They happen in this order and cannot be rearranged. Whenever a writer uses verbs in this way, they often use a sequential structure to help their readers envision the sentence.

(Continued)

Ask	Possible Answers	Food for Thought
How can we break this down into more than one sentence?	Answers will vary. Here are a couple of examples: Four hundred of these patriots mustered *and* marched to the fort. *They* scaled the walls *and* subdued the six British soldiers inside. *Finally, they* made off with all the gunpowder. Four hundred of these patriots mustered, and they marched to the fort. After they scaled the walls, the four hundred patriots subdued the six British soldiers inside and made off with all of the gunpowder.	Note the sentence structures students use. They could use simple sentences, or simple sentences with compound predicates. They could use compound sentences or complex sentences. Also note that they'll end up forming a mini-paragraph or at least two sentences together. Have them check that they used a sequential sentence/text structure – keeping the actions in order.

APPLY

During this part, students quickly apply their new knowledge about the sentence to their reading and writing. These are quick efforts and may be followed up with more practice.

Discuss: In this dig, we discussed the importance of using sequential order to describe this scene. The author told us what happened step by step. What are some other topics or scenes where it would be important to use this kind of text structure?

Writing focus: Try writing a sentence using verbs in sequential order. Try to answer the questions: What? Where? How? and When? after the verbs.

> **Showcase sentence:** Four hundred of these patriots mustered, marched to the fort, scaled the walls, subdued the six British soldiers inside, and made off with all the gunpowder.

Heavy scaffold: The protesters at the Boston Tea Party _____ (verb), _____ (verb +), and _____ (verb +).

Example: The protestors at the Boston Tea Party <u>gathered</u>, <u>stormed down to the pier</u>, and <u>dumped the crates of cargo on the ships</u>.

Light scaffold: _____ (subject) at the Battles of Lexington and Concord _____ (verb), _____ (verb +), _____ (verb +), _____ (verb +), and _____ (verb +).

Example: <u>The British soldiers</u> at the Battles of Lexington and Concord <u>thought they were superior soldiers</u>, <u>found the colonial militia ready to fight</u>, <u>fought in their standard formation</u>, <u>did not respond well to the patriots' fighting style</u>, and <u>retreated back to their fort.</u>

No scaffold: Invite students to emulate the showcase sentence within their own writing.

Conclusion

As lovers of language, our work is all about inviting others into the secret: language is worth savoring, understanding, and leveraging. And sentence digs are the perfect instructional strategy to help our young readers and writers unlock this secret.

That's because sentence digs are about empowerment. Empowering readers to crack open the meaning of a complex text. Empowering writers to write sentences that can hold the big thoughts they're trying to convey. Empowering students to build their knowledge and extend their thinking about any content area. This unique method of instruction, where we steep students in conversations around beautiful, effective language, empowers them to build on the ideas of others – whether they're digging into a sentence as a class, discussing its effect on their understanding as a small group, or playfully trying it out in their writing with a partner.

This book is meant to empower you too – to make instructional decisions for your students, expertly curating the sentences you'll celebrate and priming the conversations your students need. I trust that most of you will dabble in the lessons presented in this book, before quickly moving toward building your own sentence digs. And that's the ultimate goal – to empower you with a structure for teaching syntax and semantics in the context of your students' reading and writing experiences. This isn't *the* curriculum, or even *a* curriculum. Sentence digs are an instructional practice designed to give your students access to the knowledge and skills needed to grapple with any complex topics, texts, and assignments they might encounter.

My hope is that every reader and writer, speaker and listener, student and teacher feels confident in their ability to understand and use language in a way that helps them to connect with sentences, words, each other, and the world.

There is room for everyone.

Start digging!

APPENDIX A
Showcase Sentences at a Glance

SECTION 1: DIGGING INTO READING COMPREHENSION: SHOWCASE SENTENCES

Lesson	Focus	Literary Element/ Text Feature	Text	Sentence
R1.1	Multiple meaning words	Setting	*One Hen* by Katie Smith Milway, illustrated by Eugenie Fernandes	On market day he walks among **stalls** of fruits, vegetables, meats, kente cloths, and calabash bowls.
R1.2	Connotation	Character development	*Restart* by Gordon Korman	I'm not back on the team yet, but no one said I couldn't play a **friendly** game of catch as we make our way to community service. The **"friendly"** part is just for us.
R1.3	Definition within the sentence	Process/sequence	*When Lunch Fights Back: Wickedly Clever Animal Defenses* by Rebecca L. Johnson	They may **alternate** eyes, shooting first from one and then the other.
R1.4	Context clues	Problem/solution text structure	*Biodiversity: Eco Facts* by Izzi Howell	It's important to encourage **sustainable** fishing, in which people can catch enough to support themselves, and fish populations are protected for the future.
R2.1	Participle phrases to add movement and details	Plot (climax)/ theme	"The Save" by Joseph Bruchac, found in *The Hero Next Door* edited by Olugbemisola Rhuday-Perkovich.	And that somehow Oren found himself **flying – like a big cat – right over the table**, knocking his grandfather to the floor as a shard of sharp metal spun over their heads.
R2.2	Relative pronoun to develop character	Characterization	"The Friend Who Changed My Life" by Pam Munoz Ryan (found on Commonlit.org)	Indignant and humiliated, I refused to talk to Theresa, **who didn't seem to have any inhibitions about being chatty**.

(Continued)

Lesson	Focus	Literary Element/ Text Feature	Text	Sentence
R2.3	Introductory phrase with a coordinating conjunction	Problem/solution text structure within a nonfiction narrative	*Nefertiti The Spidernaut: The Jumping Spider Who Learned to Hunt in Space* by Darcy Pattison	**But in the microgravity of the International Space Station,** she hung almost weightless in mid-air, just as the scientists had predicted.
R2.4	Complex sentence structure – subordinating conjunction	Cause/effect text structure	*When Lunch Fights Back: Wickedly Clever Animal Defense Mechanisms* by Rebecca L. Johnson	**When seabirds whose feathers are contaminated with fulmar chick vomit land on the ocean's surface,** they may not be able to take off again.
R3.1	Literal vs nonliteral language comparisons	Mood	*Juana & Lucas* by Juana Medina	My **day** is going downhill faster **than** an *elefante* on a skateboard, and there is still more **than** half a day of school left.
R3.2	Simile	Plot/event	*Jovita Wore Pants: The Story of a Mexican Freedom Fighter* by Aida Salazar	Jovita, her sisters, and Abuela **were scattered like pollen** across Mexico, forced to live with different relatives so they could be safe.
R3.3	Metaphor	Author's perspective	*What if There Were No Bees? A Book About the Grassland Ecosystem* by Suzanne Slade and Carol Schwartz	But bees do **the work of giants**.
R3.4	Repetition for emphasis	Character development	*The Boy Who Drew Birds: A Story of John James Audubon* by Jacqueline Davies and Melissa Sweet	**Every** shelf, **every** tabletop, **every** spare inch of floor, was covered with nests **and** eggs **and** tree branches **and** pebbles **and** lichen **and** feathers **and** stuffed birds: redwings **and** grackles, kingfishers, **and** woodpeckers.
R3.5	Simile	Event/character development	*Beauty and the Beak: How Science, Technology, and a 3D-Printed Beak Rescued a Bald Eagle* by Deborah Lee Rose, Jane Veltkamp, et al.	She clenched her talons tightly around it and swam to the shore, **using her wings like oars to row.**

SECTION 2: DIGGING INTO WRITING: SHOWCASE SENTENCES

Lesson	Focus	Author's Purpose/ Grammatical Structure	Text	Sentence
W4.1	Layering clauses and phrases to expand a sentence	Writing small	"One Hot Mess" by Carmen Deedy in *Funny Girl: Funniest Stories Ever* edited by Betsy Bird	But all eyes watched **as** she struck the match and tossed it **in** a perfect flaming arc **into** the bathtub.
W4.2	Verb choice	Mood Character reactions	*Playing the Cards You're Dealt* by Varian Johnson	Before Ant **even touched** the knob to the back door, his mom **appeared** in the kitchen with hands on her hips, lips **pursed,** and eyeballs **zeroed** in on him.
W4.3	Word choice with subordinating conjunctions, prepositions, and verb phrases	Creating mental images	*Next Time You See a Spiderweb* by Emily Morgan	**When** an insect flies **into** or walks **over** this kind of web, it **becomes entangled** in the silk threads, making it easy for the spider to **catch** the insect.
W4.4	Novel word choice; conjunction choice Academic vocabulary	Character development	*Whoosh! Lonnie Johnson's SUPER-SOAKING Stream of Inventions* by Chris Barton and Don Tate	They **flowed whether** Lonnie was working with hundreds of people at NASA **or** up late tinkering with his own inventions in – finally! – his own workshop.
W5.1	Prepositional phrases	Characterization	*Mexikid: A Graphic Memoir* by Pedro Martín	He ran a mule train **between the two warring sides** to make sure all the people had food to eat.
W5.2	Appositive phrase	Theme	*Ruth Bader Ginsburg: The Case of R.B.G. vs Inequality* by Jonah Winter, illustrated by Stacy Innerst	She did so because she wanted people – **especially young women** – to see at least one woman on the Supreme Court.
W5.3	Compound predicate	Theme	*Let 'Er Buck: George Fletcher the People's Champion* by Vaunda Micheaux Nelson, illustrated by Gordon C. James	In the warm glow of the setting sun, spirited spectators **lifted George onto their shoulders and paraded around the arena.**
W5.4	Comparison	Main idea Author's Perspective	*The Magnificent Migration: On Safari with Africa's Last Great Herds* by Sy Montgomery, photos by Roger and Logan Wood	And **though lions may seem more glamorous**, it's wildebeests who drive the ecology and evolution of the largest savanna ecosystem in the world.

(Continued)

Appendix A: Showcase Sentences at a Glance

Lesson	Focus	Author's Purpose/ Grammatical Structure	Text	Sentence
W6.1	Simile	Building tension Character reaction	"One Hot Mess" by Carmen Deedy in *Funny Girl: Funniest Stories Ever* by Betsy Bird	Then, in infinitesimal increments – **like molasses seeping from a broken jar along a cold winter floor**, one millimeter at a time – a smile spread across his face.
W6.2	Alliteration	Imagery Character relationships	*Playing the Cards You're Dealt* by Varian Johnson	The boy had even tacked on Love Anthony at the end of the note – **a little sugar to soothe the sting of slipping out** on his parents.
W6.3	Onomatopoeia	Supporting detail to main idea	*Insect Superpowers: 18 Real Bugs That Smash, Zap, Hypnotize, Sting, and Devour!* by Kate Messner, illustrated by Jillian Nickell	When another insect flies too close – **Buzz-Swish-Zap!** – the robber fly darts out and captures it with long, strong, bristly legs that can hold tight to prey.
W6.4	Repeated subjects and verbs	Building tension	*Henry's Freedom Box: A True Story from the Underground Railroad* by Ellen Levine, illustrated by Kadir Nelson	**He couldn't** move. **He couldn't** think. **He couldn't** work.

SECTION 3: DIGGING INTO CONTENT LEARNING: SHOWCASE SENTENCES

Lesson	Focus	Author's Purpose/ Grammatical Structure	Text	Sentence
CA7.1	Vocabulary	Definition is in an appositive phrase mid-sentence, signaled by dashes	*Disasters by the Numbers: A Book of Infographics* by Steve Jenkins	**Hail – solid balls of ice that can be as small as a blueberry or as large as a cantaloupe –** sometimes falls during a thunderstorm.
CA7.2	Vocabulary	Definition at the end of the sentence signaled by a dash	*The Split History of Westward Expansion in the United States: American Indian Perspective* by Nell Musolf	The treaties also said that the tribes would have to move off their land to **reservations – land the government had chosen specifically for them.**
CA7.3	Vocabulary	Use of a synonym	*Beavers: Radical Rodents and Ecosystem Engineers* by Frances Backhouse	They **gnaw** at the woody mass until they've **chewed** their way up and into the center, where they **carve out** their living quarters.
CA7.4	Vocabulary	Definition is explained by examples	*If You Lived During the Plimoth Thanksgiving* by Chris Newell, illustrated by Winona Nelson	The boundaries between the different nations, and villages or communities within them, were marked by **natural features such as rivers, ponds, hills, or mountains.**
CA8.1	Metaphor	Two simple sentences combined with a semicolon	*Why Longfellow Lied: The True Story About Paul Revere's Ride* by Jeff Lantos	Revere was the arrow; Warren was the bow.
CA8.2	Adding details	Appositive	*Beavers: Radical Rodents and Ecosystem Engineers* by Frances Backhouse	These small creatures, **some so tiny that you need a microscope to see them,** are at the center of the beaver-pond food web.
CA8.3	Supporting the reader to identify a person and a place	Appositive	*The Split History of Westward Expansion in the United States: American Indian Perspective* by Nell Musolf	In 1607, Chief Wahunsenacawh, **known to the settlers as Chief Powhatan**, supplied food to the hungry settlers in the colony of Jamestown, in what is now Virginia.

(Continued)

Lesson	Focus	Author's Purpose/ Grammatical Structure	Text	Sentence
CA8.4	Using numbers to add details	Using numbers	*The Split History of Westward Expansion in the United States: American Indian Perspective* by Nell Musolf	During the next **three months**, the chief and his band led the army on a **1,400 mile (2,253 kilometer)** chase into what is now Montana, fighting **four major battles** along the way despite being **outnumbered 10 to one.**
CA8.5	Modifying a noun by describing actions	Participle phrase	*Disasters by the Numbers* by Steve Jenkins	Pressure builds up until the plates suddenly move **releasing energy and shaking the ground.**
CA9.1	Cause/effect	Conjunction *since*	*Bright Dreams: The Brilliant Ideas of Nikola Tesla* by Tracy Dockray	Nikola and Westinghouse were chosen to illuminate the Chicago's World Fair **since their AC cost much less** than Edison's DC.
CA9.2	Compare/contrast	Subordinating conjunction *even though*	*Bright Dreams: The Brilliant Ideas of Nikola Tesla* by Tracy Dockray	**Even though Nikola faced rejection and hardship**, he didn't stop.
CA9.3	Cause/effect	Complex sentence with conjunction *because*	*Plasticus Maritimus: An Invasive Species* by Ana Pêgo, Bernado P. Carvalho, Isabel Minhós Martins	For the planet to be healthy, the ocean's phytoplankton must be healthy, **because they begin the nutrient cycle** that feeds an enormous number of living beings on earth.
CA9.4	Sequential order	Verb phrases	*Why Longfellow Lied: The Truth About Paul Revere's Ride* by Jeff Lantos	Four hundred of these patriots **mustered**, **marched** to the fort, **scaled** the walls, **subdued** the six British soldiers inside, and **made off** with all the gunpowder.

APPENDIX B
Questions to Ask During Planning

QUESTIONS ABOUT THE WHOLE SENTENCE

Who or what is this sentence about?

What is happening in this sentence?

How does this sentence connect back to the text/main idea/theme/character/setting?

What words in the sentence are unfamiliar to you?

How can we say this sentence in our own words?

What is the subject? What is the predicate?

How many subjects and predicates are in the sentence?

What kind of sentence is this?

QUESTIONS TO TAKE APART

What does this chunk mean?

How does this connect to other chunk(s) or the text as a whole?

Who or what is this part about?

How does this part bring meaning to the sentence?

What kind of phrase/clause is this? How does it add meaning to the sentence?

Who or what does this phrase/word refer to in the sentence? How do you know?

QUESTIONS TO PUT TOGETHER

What is the original order of this sentence?

How can we rearrange the sentence and it still makes sense?

What can we omit from the sentence? Does this change the meaning of the sentence?

What if we changed the conjunction to _____? How does it change the meaning of the sentence?

What if we changed the verb to _____? How does this change the meaning of the sentence?

What if we added an appositive phrase? What information would we include?

QUESTIONS TO APPLY OUR LEARNING BACK TO READING AND/OR WRITING

How does this sentence reveal the theme/main idea/author's perspective?

How does this sentence support the theme/main idea/author's perspective?

How does this sentence develop the character/setting/plot?

What parts of the sentence can you emulate in your writing?

Where in your writing can you write a similarly structured sentence?

What are some ways you can use this author's craft move in your work?

QUESTIONS ABOUT WORDS WITHIN THE SENTENCE

What does _____ mean in this sentence?

What is a synonym for _____?

What if we changed _____ to _____? How does that change the meaning of the chunk/sentence?

Who or what does this pronoun refer to? How do you know?

GENERATING STUDENT QUESTIONS

What questions do you have about this chunk/sentence?

What questions can we ask about a sentence or chunk?

If our learning goal is _____, what questions should we be asking about our showcase sentence?

APPENDIX C
Blank Sentence Digs Planning Template

BEFORE THE SENTENCE DIG

Title/Author:
Summary of the text or section:
Showcase sentence:
Why did you choose this sentence? What's complex about it?
How does understanding this sentence help the reader? How does it connect back to the text?
What can writers learn from this sentence?
Instructional focus:
Extension:

Showcase sentence in chunks:

THE SENTENCE DIG

Show students the entire sentence and begin the discussion:

Take Apart

Chunk	Questions	Anticipated Student Responses

Put Together

Ask	Anticipated Student Responses	Food for Thought

AFTER THE SENTENCE DIG
Apply

Discuss:

Writing focus:

APPENDIX D
Annotated Sentence Digs Planning Template

Planning a sentence dig can be as simple or as complex as you want it to be. If you are writing up some sentence digs to share with your grade-level team, you'll want to give your team enough notes to ensure consistency across the grade level. If you're planning these for just your class, you can jot down your thinking in ways that will best help you internalize the sentence dig you plan to do.

The next couple of pages include an annotated planning template using the blank planning template found in Appendix C. This is how I plan a sentence dig. Since I'm typically planning for a team, I tend to be more thorough. This may be just the kind of planning you do too. If this seems overwhelming, decide on which parts will need more of your attention, and use the template to support you. Ideally, this is just a starting place until you find your own rhythm.

BEFORE THE SENTENCE DIG

This section is to help you think deeply about the sentence you will showcase. If you are planning with other teachers on your team, this will help orient your teammates to the work.

Title/Author: Jot down the title of the text and the author.
Summary of the text or section: It's important that the sentence is kept in context. Consider jotting a quick summary of the text or part of the text from which the sentence was chosen. Include the page number for easy reference. This may seem unnecessary, but when I circle back to a sentence dig in another school year, I'm always thankful I did this.
Showcase sentence: Write the sentence students will study.
Why did you choose this sentence? What's complex about it? Sentences worthy of study typically have layers of complexity. It's good to think through several layers to determine what you'll focus on in the lesson.

Appendix D: Annotated Sentence Digs Planning Template

How does understanding this sentence help the reader? How does it connect back to the text?

The key to keeping the sentence in context – even when we pull it out of the text to study it – is to keep putting it back into the text. Naming how this sentence will support the reader and how the sentence connects back to the text will keep your conversations from going down rabbit holes and focus on the ultimate task: developing strong reading comprehension.

What can writers learn from this sentence?

Naming all the things writers can learn from this can help us determine how we'll ask students to apply this work to their compositions.

Instructional focus:

What will be the focus of the sentence dig instruction?

Extension:

What other aspects of syntax and semantics will be highlighted with this sentence? Consider the role/meaning of other chunks in the sentence. Consider how this sentence adds to a literary element of the text and/or to the text structure.

Showcase sentence in chunks:

Divide the sentence using | to indicate the chunks you'll study. Many sentences can be chunked in different ways depending on your focus and your students' needs. Consider using grammatical structures to chunk the sentence – for example, keep phrases intact, divide clauses by subject/predicate if necessary. There may be times you'll want one word in a chunk, but be careful about having too many chunks.

Remember, each chunk is on its own sentence strip.

THE SENTENCE DIG

Show students the entire sentence and begin the discussion:

Aside from starting the lesson, the purpose here is to set the intent for the dig. You might start off with an inquiry question or you might name why you chose this sentence to study. Either way, it's important to set this intention, establish your questioning in a way that will invite students into this goal, and design an application and a Think Sheet, if needed, to ground students' learning around this intention.

Take Apart

This is the part of the lesson where you'll be moving the chunks from the full sentence, so students can study it both in isolation and think about its meaning within the context of the sentence.

Chunk	Questions	Anticipated Student Responses
List the chunk – word/phrase/clause – that you'll focus on in the order you want to use in the lesson. You do not *have to* start at the beginning of the sentence every time. Sometimes teachers will start with "who or what is this sentence about?" and that chunk may not be the beginning of the sentence.	List questions you plan to pose in this column. Remember your lesson focus, your students' needs, and any unusual complexities this sentence may hold. Some questions you might ask can be found in Appendix B.	If you're sharing this lesson plan, it's important to fill out this column so everyone using the plan is on the same page. This is also a good spot to think through any if/then scenarios… if students respond one way… the next question may be… Or if students respond another way, I may add on to their understanding by…

Put Together

During this phase of the lesson, the sentence chunks are likely out of order and/or may be scattered across your whiteboard… at least mine are! Encourage students to put the sentence back together in the original order first. Then give them opportunities to reorder the sentence, considering different ways the author might have written this sentence.

Ask	Anticipated Student Responses	Food for Thought
List questions or discussion starters that encourage students to engage in some word play. Opportunities should include: • Reordering • Deleting • Adding On • Breaking into two or more sentences • Combining with another sentence. *Keep your time in mind. If a sentence lends itself to many possibilities, you might consider having students dive deeper in a Think Sheet activity.*	If you're sharing this lesson plan, it's important to fill out this column so everyone using the plan is on the same page. Consider misconceptions students may have and how to redirect them. Consider different ways students may arrange the sentence and/or separate the sentence.	This column is important if you are sharing the plan with others. This can be an explanation for why a different sentence arrangement works and/or information a teacher may want to give students as they work through this section of the lesson. Also, this is where you can jot information you may need to relay to students to help them understand why the rearrangements work (or don't) beyond whether it sounds right or makes sense. You can also slip in some grand grammar nuggets here.

AFTER THE SENTENCE DIG
Apply

In this section of the lesson, we wrap up the teacher-guided discussion and move students toward partnerships. The goal here is to give students an opportunity to process the information they gleaned from the large group discussion and apply it toward writing about reading or toward their own writing.

Discuss:

This is the wrap up. Bring the discussion back to the original focus of the lesson and any extension activities. This typically includes an open-ended question about the showcase sentence that puts it back into the context of the full text.

Writing focus:

Students have an opportunity to use this sentence structure to write about reading or to apply what they've learned to their own writing. Consider providing some sentence frames for students who need support with this process.

PROFESSIONAL BIBLIOGRAPHY

Anderson, Jeff, and Whitney La Rocca. 2017. *Patterns of Power: Inviting Young Writers into the Conventions of Language, Grades 1-5*. Portland, ME: Stenhouse Publishers.

Anderson, Jeff, and Whitney La Rocca. 2024. *Patterns of Revision: Inviting 5th Graders into Conversations That Elevate Writing*. London: Routledge.

Anderson, Nancy L., and Connie Briggs. 2011. "Reciprocity Between Reading and Writing: Strategic Processing as Common Ground." *The Reading Teacher*, 64 (7): 474-558. https://doi.org/10.1598/rt.64.7.12.

Fillmore, Charles, and Lily Wong Fillmore. 2013. *What Does Text Complexity Mean for English Learners and Language Minority Students?* Understanding Language. Stanford University School of Education.

Hennessy, Nancy L. 2021. *The Reading Comprehension Blueprint: Helping Students Make Meaning from Text*. Paul H. Brookes Publishing.

Hochman, Judith C., and Natalie Wexler. 2017. *The Writing Revolution: A Guide to Advancing Thinking Through Writing in All Subjects and Grades*. Jossey-Bass.

"Juicy Sentence Guidance." n.d. https://achievethecore.org/content/upload/Juicy%20Sentence%20Guidance.pdf.

Junior Cycle for Teachers. n.d. *Classroom Talk: What the Research Tells Us*. www.jct.ie/perch/resources/english/classroomtalk-whattheresearchsays.pdf.

Killgallon, Don, and Jenny Killgallon. 2014. *Paragraphs for Elementary School: A Sentence-Composing Approach*. Heinemann.

Moats, Louisa C., and Carol A. Tolman. 2019. *LETRS: Language Essentials for Teachers Reading and Spelling. Volume Two. Units 5-8*. Sopris West Educational Services.

Provost, Gary. 2019. *100 Ways to Improve Your Writing (Updated): Proven Professional Techniques for Writing with Style and Power*. Penguin Publishing Group.

Scarborough, Hollis S. 2011. "Connecting Early Language and Literacy to Later Reading (Dis)abilities: Evidence, Theory and Practice," in S. Neuman and D. Dickinson (eds.), *Handbook for Research in Early Literacy*, pp. 97-110. Guilford Press.

Scott, Cheryl, and Catherine Balthazar. 2013. "The Role of Complex Sentence Knowledge in Reading and Writing Difficulties." *PubMed*, 39 (3): 18-30.

Sedita, Joan. 2023. *The Writing Rope: A Framework for Explicit Writing Instruction in All Subjects*. Brookes Publishing.

Strunk, William, Jr., and E.B. White. 2000. *The Elements of Style*. Pearson.

CHILDREN'S LITERATURE BIBLIOGRAPHY

Applegate, Katherine. 2022. *Odder*. Feiwel and Friends.

Backhouse, Frances. 2021. *Beavers*. Orca Book Publishers.

Barton, Chris, and Don Tate. 2016. *WHOOSH! Lonnie Johnson's SUPER-SOAKING Stream of Inventions*. Charlesbridge.

Bird, Betsy. 2018. *Funny Girl: Funniest. Stories. Ever.* Puffin Books.

CommonLit. n.d. "The Friend Who Changed My Life by Pam Muñoz Ryan." www.commonlit.org/en/texts/the-friend-who-changed-my-life.

Davies, Jacqueline, and Melissa Sweet. 2004. *The Boy Who Drew Birds: A Story of John James Audubon*. Houghton Mifflin.

Deedy, Carmen Agra. 2012. *The Library Dragon*. National Geographic Books.

Dockray, Tracy. 2021. *Bright Dreams*. Raintree.

Friedrich, Elizabeth, and Michael Garland. 1999. *Leah's Pony*. Boyds Mills Press.

Goodall, Jane. 2002. *My Life with the Chimpanzees*. Aladdin Paperbacks.

Howell, Izzi. 2020. *Biodiversity: Eco Facts*. Crabtree Publishing.

Jenkins, Steve. 2021. *Disasters by the Numbers*. Clarion Books.

Johnson, Rebecca L. 2020. *When Lunch Fights Back: Wickedly Clever Animal Defense Mechanisms*. Millbrook Press.

Johnson, Varian. 2021. *Playing the Cards You're Dealt*. Scholastic.

Korman, Gordon. 2017. *Restart*. Scholastic.

Lantos, Jeff. 2021. *Why Longfellow Lied: The Truth About Paul Revere's Midnight Ride*. Charlesbridge.

Lester, Julius, and Jerry Pinkney. 1999. *John Henry*. Puffin Books.

Levine, Ellen, and Kadir Nelson. 2019. *Henry's Freedom Box: A True Story from the Underground Railroad*. Findaway World.

Martín, P. 2023. *Mexikid: A Graphic Memoir*. Penguin.

Medina, Juana. 2016. *Juana & Lucas. #1*. Candlewick Press.

Messner, Kate, and Jillian Nickell. 2019. *Insect Superpowers: 18 Real Bugs That Smash, Zap, Hypnotize, Sting, and Devour!* Chronicle Books.

Milway, Katie Smith, and Eugenie Fernandes. 2020. *One Hen: How One Small Loan Made a Big Difference*. Kids Can Press.

Montgomery, Sy, Roger Wood, and Logan Wood. 2019. *The Magnificent Migration: On Safari with Africa's Last Great Herds*. Houghton Mifflin Harcourt.

Morgan, Emily. 2015. *Next Time You See a Spiderweb*. Next Time You See.

Musolf, Nell, and Malcolm J. Rohrbough. 2013. *The Split History of Westward Expansion in the United States. American Indian Perspective. Settlers' Perspective.* Compass Point Books.

Nelson, Vaunda, and Gordon C. James. 2019. *Let 'Er Buck! George Fletcher, the People's Champion.* Carolrhoda Books.

Newell, Chris. 2021. *If You Lived During the Plimoth Thanksgiving.* Scholastic.

Pattison, Darcy. 2017. *Nefertiti, the Spidernaut.* Triangle Interactive.

Pêgo, Ana, Bernado P. Carvalho, and Isabel Minhós Martins. 2020. *Plasticus Maritimus: An Invasive Species.* Greystone Kids.

Reynolds, Aaron, and Peter Brown. 2014. *Creepy Carrots.* Scholastic.

Rhuday-Perkovich, Olugbemisola. 2021. *The Hero Next Door: A We Need Diverse Books Anthology.* Yearling.

Rose, Deborah Lee, Jane Veltkamp, Glen Hush, Michele Barker, US Fish and Wildlife Service, and Cornell University. 2019. *Beauty and the Beak: How Science, Technology, and a 3D-Printed Beak Rescued a Bald Eagle.* Persnickety Press.

Rowling, J.K. 1997. *Harry Potter and the Sorcerer's Stone.* Vol. 1. New York, NY: Scholastic Inc.

Salazar, Aida. 2023. *Jovita Wore Pants.* Scholastic.

Slade, Suzanne, and Carol Schwartz. 2011. *What If There Were No Bees? A Book About the Grassland Ecosystem.* Picture Window Books.

Winter, J. 2017. *Ruth Bader Ginsburg.* Abrams.

Zamorsky, Tania. 2009. *Classic Starts: Peter Pan.* Sterling Children's Books.

INDEX

alliteration 149-151
Anderson, Jeff 2
annotated planning template 245-248
apply, sentence dig routine 8
appositive phrases 88, 122, 165; naming key characteristics 192-196; renaming subject 197-201; themes 122-126
Audubon, John James 78-81

Backhouse, Frances (*Beavers: Radical Rodents and Ecosystem Engineers*) 174-177, 192-196
Balthazar, Catherine 10
Barton, Chris (*WHOOSH! Lonnie Johnson's SUPER-SOAKING Stream of Inventions*) 1, 6, 105-111
Beauty and the Beak: How Science, Technology, and a 3D-Printed Beak Rescued a Bald Eagle (Rose, Veltkamp et al.) 82-85
Beavers: Radical Rodents and Ecosystem Engineers (Backhouse): appositive phrases 192-196; using synonyms 174-177
Biodiversity: Eco Facts (Howell) 32-38
Bird, Betsy (*Funny Girl: Funniest. Stories. Ever*) 91, 144
blank planning template 241-243
The Boy Who Drew Birds: A Story of John James Audubon (Davies) 78-81
Bright Dreams: The Brilliant Ideas of Nikola Tesla (Dockray): cause and effect 214-218; compare and contrast 219-221
Brown, Peter 16
Bruchac, Joseph ("The Save") 42-46

Carvalho, Bernado P. (*Plastics Maritimus: An Invasive Species*) 212, 222-225
cause and effect 55-61, 214-218, 222-225

character development: just-right conjunctions 105-111; prepositional phrases 116-121; relative pronouns 47-50
character reaction 96-99
clauses and phrases 91-95
Commonlit.org 41
compare and contrast 219-221
complex sentences 10; establishing cause and effect 55-61, 222-225; main idea 133-139
compound predicates 127-132
conjunctions: coordinating 51-54; correlative 105, 111; just-right 105-111; subordinate 60, 104, 138
connotation 23-26
content areas 161-162; important details 183-210; sentence structure 211-230; vocabulary 163-181
context clues 32-38
coordinating conjunctions 51-54
correlative conjunctions 105, 111
Creepy Carrots (Reynolds) 16

Davies, Jacqueline (*The Boy Who Drew Birds: A Story of John James Audubon*) 78-81
Deedy, Carmen ("One Hot Mess") 91-95, 144-148
definition: at end of sentence 170-173; by example 178-181; within sentence 27-31, 165-169
DiCamillo, Kate 4
Disasters by the Numbers: A Book of Infographics (Jenkins): definition within sentence 165-169; modifying a noun 207-210
discourse comprehension 40

253

Dockray, Tracy (*Bright Dreams: The Brilliant Ideas of Nikola Tesla*) 214-218, 219-221
Doctorow, E.L. 113

Einstein, Albert 183
Elster, Charles Harrington 15
empowerment 231

Fernandes, Eugenie 19
Field, Rachel ('Some People') 63
figurative language 63-85; lessons at a glance 65; literal vs. non-literal phrases 66-70; metaphor 75-77; repetition for emphasis 78-81; simile 71-74, 82-85; think sheets 70
Fillmore, Charles and Lily 5
frequency and timing of sentence digs 8
"The Friend Who Changed My Life"(Muñoz Ryan) 47-50
Funny Girl: Funniest. Stories. Ever (Bird) 91, 144

Ginsburg, Ruth Bader 122-126

haiku, student 141-142
Hennessy, Nancy 16-17, 64
Henry's Freedom Box: A True Story from the Underground Railroad (Levine) 156-160
The Hero Next Door (Rhuday-Perkovich) 42
Hochman, Judith 2, 161
Howell, Izzy (*Biodiversity: Eco Facts*) 32-38

If You Lived During the Plimoth Thanksgiving (Newell) 178-181
important details, content areas 183-210; appositive phrases 192-196, 197-201; lessons at a glance 185; participle phrases 207-210; semicolons and metaphors 186-191; think sheets 190-191, 196; using numbers 202-206
important details, reading 39-61; complex sentences 55-61; coordinating conjunctions 51-54; lessons at a glance 41; participle phrases 42-46; relative pronouns 47-50; think sheets 60-61

important details, writing 113-139; appositive phrases 122-126; complex sentences 133-139; compound predicates 127-132; lessons at a glance 115; prepositional phrases 116-121; think sheets 121, 126, 131-132, 138-139
infer, learning to 64
infinitives 121
Innerst, Stacy 122
Insect Superpowers: 18 Real Bugs That Smash, Zap, Hypnotize, Sting, and Devour! (Messner) 152-155
introductory phrases 51-54

James, Gordon C. 113, 127
Jenkins, Steve (*Disasters by the Numbers: A Book of Infographics*) 165-169, 207-210
Johnson, Rebecca (*When Lunch Fights Back: Wickedly Clever Animal Defenses*) 27-31, 55-61
Johnson, Varian (*Playing the Cards You're Dealt*) 96-99, 149-151
Jovita Dreamed of Wearing Pants! The Story of a Mexican Freedom Fighter (Salazar) 71-74
Juana & Lucas (Medina) 66-70

Killgallon, Don and Jenny 114
Korman, Gordon (*Restart*) 17-18

La Rocca, Whitney 2
language, crafting 141-160; alliteration 149-151; lessons at a glance 143; onomatopoeia 152-155; repeating subjects and verbs 156-160; simile 144-148
Lantos, Jeff (*Why Longfellow Lied: The Truth About Paul Revere's Ride*) 186-191, 226-230
Let 'Er Buck: George Fletcher the People's Champion (Nelson) 113-114, 127-132
Levine, Ellen (*Henry's Freedom Box: A True Story from the Underground Railroad*) 156-160
literal vs. non-literal phrases 66-70

Longfellow, Henry Wadsworth ("The Midnight Ride of Paul Revere") 186, 226

The Magnificent Migration: On Safari with Africa's Last Great Herds (Montgomery) 133-139
main idea: complex sentences 133-139; supporting details to 152-155
Martin, Pedro (*Mexikid: A Graphic Memoir*) 116-121
Martins, Isabel Minhós (*Plasticus Maritimus: An Invasive Species*) 212, 222-225
Medina, Juana (*Juana & Lucas*) 66-70
Mendoza, Molly 71
mental images, creating 100-104
mentor sentences 1-4
Messner, Kate (*Insect Superpowers: 18 Real Bugs That Smash, Zap, Hypnotize, Sting, and Devour!*) 152-155
metaphors 75-77, 186-191
Mexikid: A Graphic Memoir (Martin) 116-121
"The Midnight Ride of Paul Revere" (Longfellow) 186, 226
Milway, Katie Smith (*One Hen*) 19-22
Moats, Louisa C. 40, 163
Montgomery, Sy (*The Magnificent Migration: On Safari with Africa's Last Great Herds*) 133-139
Morgan, Emily (*Next Time You See a Spider Web*) 100-104
multimodal texts 211-212
multiple meaning words 19-22, 170
Muñoz Ryan, Pam ("The Friend Who Changed My Life") 47-50
Musolf, Neil (*The Split History of Westward Expansion in the United States: American Indian Perspective*) 170-173, 197-201, 202-206

Nefertiti The Spidernaut (Pattison) 39, 51-54
Nelson, Kadir 156
Nelson, Vaunda Micheaux (*Let 'Er Buck: George Fletcher the People's Champion*) 113-114, 127-132
Nelson, Winona 178
Newell, Chris (*If You Lived During the Plimoth Thanksgiving*) 178-181
Next Time You See a Spider Web (Morgan) 100-104
Nickell, Jillian 152
non-literal vs literal phrases 66-70
note taking 183
nouns, modifying 207-210
numbers, using 202-206

One Hen (Milway) 19-22
"One Hot Mess" (Deedy): clauses and phrases 91-95; simile 144-148
onomatopoeia 152-155

paragraphs 114
Paragraphs for Elementary School (Killgallon and Killgallon) 114
participle phrases: adding movement and details 42-46; modifying a noun 207-210
Patterns of Power (Anderson and La Rocca) 2
Pattison, Darcy (*Nefertiti The Spidernaut*) 39, 51-54
Pêgo, Ana (*Plasticus Maritimus: An Invasive Species*) 212, 222-225
phrases and clauses 91-95
planning: annotated template 245-248; blank template 241-243; questions to ask 239-240
Plasticus Maritimus: An Invasive Species (Pêgo, Carvalho and Martins) 212, 222-225
Playing the Cards You're Dealt (Johnson): alliteration 149-151; verb choice 96-99
prepositional phrases: character development 116-121; prepositions to start 121
Provost, Gary 87
put together, sentence dig routine 7-8

questions to ask during planning 239-240

reading comprehension 13-14; figurative language 63-85; important details 39-61; word meanings 15-38
The Reading Comprehension Blueprint (Hennessy) 16-17, 64
Reading Rope 2-3, 3, 15, 40
relative pronouns 47-50
renaming subject 197-201
repetition: for emphasis 78-81; of subjects and verbs 156-160
Restart (Korman) 17-18
Reynolds, Aaron (*Creepy Carrots*) 16
Rhuday-Perkovich, Olugbemisola (*The Hero Next Door*) 42
Rose, Deborah Lee (*Beauty and the Beak: How Science, Technology, and a 3D-Printed Beak Rescued a Bald Eagle*) 82-85
Ruth Bader Ginsburg: The Case of R.B.G. vs Inequality (Winter) 122-126

Salazar, Aida (*Jovita Dreamed of Wearing Pants! The Story of a Mexican Freedom Fighter*) 71-74
"The Save" (Bruchac) 42-46
Scarborough, Hollis S. 2-3, 3, 15, 40
Schwartz, Carol 75
Scott, Cheryl 10
Sedita, Joan 2, 3, 4
semantics 3, 4, 5
semicolons, using 186-191
sentence dig routine 5-8; apply 8; effectiveness 10-11; frequency and timing 8; put together 7-8; take apart 7
sentence structure 211-230; cause and effect 214-218, 222-225; compare and contrast 219-221; lessons at a glance 213; sequential order 226-230
sequential order 226-230
showcase sentences at a glance 233-238

similes 42, 71-74, 82-85; building tension 144-148
Slade, Suzanne (*What If There Were No Bees? A Book About the Grassland Ecosystem*) 75-77
'Some People' (Field) 63
The Split History of Westward Expansion in the United States: American Indian Perspective (Musolf): appositive phrases 197-201; definition at end of sentence 170-173; using numbers 202-206
Springer, Jane 212
Stoppard, Tom 89
Strunk, William, Jr. 211
subordinate conjunctions 60, 104, 138
supporting details 152-155
Sweet, Melissa 78
synonyms, using 174-177
syntax 3, 4, 5, 89-90

take apart, sentence dig routine 7
Tate, Don 1, 6, 105
template, planning: annotated 245-248; blank 241-243
tension, building 144-148, 156-160
Tesla, Nikola 214-218, 219-221
themes 122-126, 127-132
think sheets 8-9; reading focus 27; sentence combining 60-61, 131-132, 138-139, 190-191; sentence expansion 196; sentence extension 121, 126, 168-169; sketch 104; sketch and revise 110-111; write and sketch 70
timing and frequency of sentence digs 8
Tolman, Carol A. 40, 163

Valdovinos, Jovita 71-74
Veltkamp, Jane (*Beauty and the Beak: How Science, Technology, and a 3D-Printed Beak Rescued a Bald Eagle*) 82-85
verb choice: character reaction 96-99; creating mental images 100-104

verbs, repeating subjects and 156–160
vocabulary 163–181; definition at end of sentence 170–173; definition by example 178–181; definition within sentence 165–169; lessons at a glance 164; think sheets 168–169; using synonyms 174–177

Wexler, Natalie 2, 161
What If There Were No Bees? A Book About the Grassland Ecosystem (Slade) 75–77
When Lunch Fights Back: Wickedly Clever Animal Defenses (Johnson): complex sentences 55–61; definition within sentence 27–31
White, E.B. 141, 211
WHOOSH! Lonnie Johnson's SUPER-SOAKING Stream of Inventions (Barton) 1, 6, 105–111
Why Longfellow Lied: The Truth About Paul Revere's Ride (Lantos): sequential order 226–230; using a semicolon and metaphors 186–191
wildebeests 133–139

Wilkins, David 163
Winter, Jonah (*Ruth Bader Ginsburg: The Case of R.B.G. vs Inequality*) 122–126
Wood, Roger and Logan 133
Wooden, John 39
word choice 89–111; clauses and phrases 91–95; just-right conjunction 105–111; lessons at a glance 90; think sheets 104, 110–111; verb choice 96–99, 100–104
word meanings 15–38; connotation 23–26; context clues 32–38; definition within sentence 27–31; lessons at a glance 18; multiple meaning words 19–22; preparing sentence dig discussions 18; think sheets 27
writing, craft of 87–88; crafting language 141–160; important details 113–139; word choice 89–111
writing, principles for teaching 2
The Writing Revolution (Hochman and Wexler) 2
Writing Rope 2, 3, 4
writing small 91–95

For Product Safety Concerns and Information please contact our EU representative GPSR@taylorandfrancis.com
Taylor & Francis Verlag GmbH, Kaufingerstraße 24, 80331 München, Germany

www.ingramcontent.com/pod-product-compliance
Lightning Source LLC
Chambersburg PA
CBHW080119020526
44112CB00037B/2780